The Body in Tolkien's
Legendarium

The Body in Tolkien's Legendarium
Essays on Middle-earth Corporeality

Edited by CHRISTOPHER VACCARO

McFarland & Company, Inc., Publishers
Jefferson, North Carolina, and London

LIBRARY OF CONGRESS CATALOGUING-IN-PUBLICATION DATA

The body in Tolkien's legendarium : essays on middle-earth corporeality / edited by Christopher Vaccaro.
    p.   cm.
Includes bibliographical references and index.

ISBN 978-0-7864-7478-3
softcover : acid free paper ∞

1. Tolkien, J.R.R. (John Ronald Reuel), 1892–1973. 2. Fantasy fiction, English — History and criticism. 3. Middle Earth (Imaginary place) 4. Human body in literature. 5. Reality in literature. I. Vaccaro, Christopher, editor of compilation.
PR6039.O32Z568 2013
823'.91209 — dc23   2013024716

BRITISH LIBRARY CATALOGUING DATA ARE AVAILABLE

© 2013 Christopher Vaccaro. All rights reserved

No part of this book may be reproduced or transmitted in any form or by any means, electronic or mechanical, including photocopying or recording, or by any information storage and retrieval system, without permission in writing from the publisher.

Cover illustration © 2013 iStockphoto

Manufactured in the United States of America

McFarland & Company, Inc., Publishers
  Box 611, Jefferson, North Carolina 28640
  www.mcfarlandpub.com

Table of Contents

Abbreviations vii

Introduction
CHRISTOPHER VACCARO 1

Part I. The Transformation of the Body

The Body in Question: The Unhealed Wounds of Frodo Baggins
VERLYN FLIEGER 12

Incorporeality and Transformation in *The Lord of the Rings*
YVETTE KISOR 20

Frodo's Body: Liminality and the Experience of War
ANNA SMOL 39

Part II. The Body and the Spirit

The *Hröa* and *Fëa* of Middle-earth: Health, Ecology and the War
MATTHEW DICKERSON 64

The Ugly Elf: Orc Bodies, Perversion, and Redemption in *The Silmarillion* and *The Lord of the Rings*
JOLANTA N. KOMORNICKA 83

Part III. The Discursive Body

Light (noun, 1) or Light (adjective, 14b)? Female Bodies and Femininities in *The Lord of the Rings*
ROBIN ANNE REID 98

A Body of Myth: Representing Sauron in *The Lord of the Rings*
GERGELY NAGY 119

Part IV. The Body and the Source Material

Emblematic Bodies: Tolkien and the Depiction of Female
Physical Presence
    JAMES T. WILLIAMSON   134

Extending the Reach of the Invisible Hand: A Gift Looks for
Gain in the Gifting Economy of Middle-earth
    JENNIFER CULVER   157

Tolkien's Whimsical Mode: Physicalities in *The Hobbit*
    CHRISTOPHER VACCARO   170

About the Contributors   187

Index   189

Abbreviations

All citations from *The Lord of the Rings* will be by book and chapter and page number as they are located in the editions listed below.

FR   *The Fellowship of the Ring.* London: George Allen & Unwin, 1954; Boston: Houghton Mifflin, 1954. 2d ed., Boston: Houghton Mifflin, 1987.

Hobbit   *The Hobbit.* London: George Allen & Unwin, 1937. Boston: Houghton Mifflin, 1938. *The Annotated Hobbit*, 2d ed., rev., ed. Douglas A. Anderson. 2d ed. Boston: Houghton Mifflin, 2002.

Letters   Carpenter, Humphrey, ed. *The Letters of J.R.R. Tolkien.* Boston: Houghton Mifflin, 2000.

RK   *The Return of the King.* London: George Allen & Unwin, 1955; Boston: Houghton Mifflin, 1956. 2d ed., Boston: Houghton Mifflin, 1987.

Sil   *The Silmarillion*, ed. Christopher Tolkien. Boston: Houghton Mifflin, 1977.

TT   *The Two Towers.* London: George Allen & Unwin, 1954; Boston: Houghton Mifflin, 1955. 2d ed., Boston: Houghton Mifflin, 1987.

Introduction

CHRISTOPHER VACCARO

It is a fallen world, and there is no consonance between our bodies, minds, and souls.[1]

How many white wizards fit on the head of a pin? Does the same divine music present at the moment of Arda's creation also resonate within the limbs of Pippin and Sam Gamgee, the Sung Word ensconced in flesh? Did the sculptors of the Argonath strive for physical realism or (as is more likely) did they attempt to convey Isildur's and Anarion's virtues through a culturally recognized and highly symbolic palette of facial and bodily features? Is Frodo's tortured shirtless back a site upon which the orcs of Cirith Ungol inscribe Sauron's temporary power and marred morality? All of these enquiries are meant to steer thoughts toward this one question: Do bodies matter in Middle-earth? To the contributors of *The Body in Tolkien's Legendarium*, the answer is an unqualified "Yes."

Tolkien's emphasis on the spirit (*fëa*) seemed to demand from him a continuous downplaying or sublimation of the physical (*hröa*). As much as he wrote of the beauty of Arda, he often upstaged this creation through his continuous emphasis on the spirit. This is made more apparent by his linking of the material world of Arda to Morgoth.[2] Yet the more closely one examines the text, the more apparent it is that Tolkien found something very wholesome about a simple Shire life full of physical enjoyments (decent hearty food, thirst-quenching drink, leisure, laughter, and play) and no structured religion to speak of. And while Arda may be referred to as Morgoth's Ring, Middle-earth is never completely abandoned by the author or the deities he created, and incarnated spirits evince an appreciation for the physicality in which they are housed. Conceptually the body is an entryway into Tolkien's complex and sometimes contradictory opinions on the state of the postlapsarian world.[3]

The critical collections on Tolkien's texts published recently have made considerable gains in reaching beyond formal, source-specific interpretations, and many of the essays within *Tolkien the Medievalist, J.R.R. Tolkien and His Literary Resonances, Tolkien's Modern Middle Ages,* and *Tolkien's Legendarium: Essays on "The History of Middle-earth,"* and the *Tolkien Studies* journal provide significant contextual frameworks for an analysis of corporeality though none provide scholarship dedicated to the subject.[4] In fact, until now no collection has made a direct case for the body's prominent place in Tolkien scholarship. From this focused interpretive trajectory, scholars may find their interpretations of the Legendarium centered upon a bevy of relevant issues (birth, decay, resurrection, physical discipline, pain, suffering, torture, sickness, hunger, shape-shifting, and more broadly metamorphoses), central binaries (fertility/celibacy, purity/pollution, transparency/translucence, spirituality/materiality, absence/presence, and mortality/immortality), and hitherto untreated subjects (iconography, bodies within the source material, dance, nutrition, and even exercise).

Essays touching upon subjects of race, gender, and sexuality naturally direct the critical conversation towards the body; in fact, these subjects served as a catalyst for its most recent theoretical attention. *The Body in Tolkien's Legendarium* thrusts Tolkien and Middle Earth Studies into a theoretical terrain most recently navigated by contemporary feminist and queer scholarship but initially mapped out in the seminal texts of the patristic and medieval church fathers well known by Tolkien who was, of course, a medieval scholar and a devout Catholic: this terrain being a reflection on human corporeality. The ascetic discourses of the early church prioritized physical discipline and renunciation. One finds in the early English dialogues between the body and soul, the hagiographic and medical texts, and in the Latin and vernacular penitentials a view of the body as both obstacle and aid to salvation. This is a very familiar concept for most: indulgence leads to suffering, renunciation provides salvific effects. During the days of the early Christian church, the human body was seen as a smaller version of the vast cosmic one.[5] Cast in such a light, human bodies were thought to possess the same heat and spirit found in celestial objects.[6]

Many patristic and medieval church fathers subscribed to the widely held belief that there existed beings of two distinct creations: beings of the first were angelic creatures of the pre-fallen state and stood completely outside of the sexual economy. Beings of the second creation were more grounded in the body and manifested the postlapsarian characteristic of sexually differentiation. Augustine was largely responsible for redirecting this line of thought arguing that through the eschatological and messianic event of Christ's birth the Word became incarnate thereby reestablishing the union between humankind and God. It was Augustine also who believed that ascetic control over the body rendered the body transparent to the soul — an interesting notion considering Tolkien's use of transparency and translucency.[7] In a complicated relationship to this discourse of renunciation is the belief in the transubstantiation of the Eucharist and the concept of the body of Christ. The *corpus Christi* was understood not only as pertaining to Christ's actual body, but as the Church and its members as well as the converted and blessed communion host.[8] Tolkien appears to have placed these aspects within his mythological framework in his attention to the resurrection of the body politic in the Reunited Kingdom of Arnor and the revivifying powers of Galadriel's lembas.[9] Biblical, apocryphal, poetic and homiletic texts likewise kindled Tolkien's imagination when it came to the subject. *Genesis* and the gospels supplied literally and symbolically fertile material regarding the distinctions between pre- and fallen as well as mortal and divine bodies. Early English religious poetry and prose was rife with images of martyrs and *miles Christi* and of Christ's body itself shining like a glass filled with light.[10]

Discussions on the issue of physicality continued through to the twentieth century and the nascence of contemporary literary theory. Dramatically changing the theoretical landscape regarding the subject was the work of Michel Foucault.[11] In his three-volume *The History of Sexuality*, he argues that sexuality is not conceptualized today as it was during the Greek and Roman Empires, Medieval Europe, or Victorian England; sex has a history. Categories such as heterosexuality and homosexuality are historically determined, and cultural articulations of ideology, power, and knowledge keep meaning in constant flux. The body, too, has a hermeneutic history and is constituted through and has a direct effect upon the cultural discourses around which it exists. More recently, Judith Butler and Eve Kosofsky Sedgwick have drawn from feminist and queer theoretical perspectives in order to argue in very different ways that the body has no meaning outside of cultural discourse. Butler's *Bodies That Matter: On the Discursive Limits of "Sex"* dismantles the *a priori* notion that the body comes to us naturally sexed, gendered, and heterosexualized.[12]

Building from these theoretical foundations, Tolkien scholars have begun to examine the body in Middle-earth in relation to sex, gender, desire, and power. Jane Chance explores the inarticulation of the body in her *The Mythology of Power*.[13] Where Shelob incarnates an appetite for food and an instinct for survival, Saruman reveals an inarticulate rage, and Gollum sings his "primitive, body-directed song" and reveals his own preoccupation with food.[14] Anna Smol's attention to the continuum of tactile intimacy between men makes permeable the culturally determined boundaries coding some friendships as heterosexual and others as homosexual.[15] Gergely Nagy investigates how meaning is made possible and subjectivities are constituted in the novel through discourses of power, and he pays quite a bit of attention to bodily concerns. Similar to Chance, Nagy finds that Gollum's "bodily-determined sounds dominate his speech" but concludes that this language is formed out of physical desire:

Discourses of power define the ways the subject imagines and understands its bodily desires and the generation of its language, meanings, and its own production of meaning.[16]

According to Nagy, Gollum, whose difference is inscribed upon his physical form, is emptied of his own subjectivity and constituted as one of Sauron's Others. "He is nearly completely dissolved into another system where power is a bodily concept, where language and name are corporeal *actions* (rather than something significant, symbolic)."[17] The body is then placed as "the focus of forces" that help (de)constitute Gollum's subjectivity.[18] In this instance, "Sauron's conceptualization of power is ... essentially corporeal, bodily. Power for him means *physical power* over subjects."[19] For Nagy, the body is a source of desire, and of language, a linguistic utterance even as it is twisted by the Sauronic power of the ring.[20]

In addition, Michaël Devaux's "Les Anges de l'Ombre chez Tolkien: chair, corps et corruption" thoroughly considers the physicalities-both the flesh and the bodies- of the angelic and divine spirits of Middle-earth. Devaux examines the Tolkienian distinction between angels and spirits utilizing Augustinian theology exploring also the relationships between Melkor and Sauron, and between Sauron and his Ring.[21] Valerie Rohy's insightful analysis, "On Fairy Stories," likewise pays attention to the sexualized body and the textual prohibitions and lacks surrounding it. Rohy reads *The Lord of the Rings* through the optic of Queer Theory, using Lacanian and Freudian analysis to follow the circulations of hetero- and homosexual desires and the impossibility of their fulfillment.[22] She locates a Lacanian "pleasure of desiring" in Frodo's relationship with Sam, a relationship defined by the near impossibility of any consummation.[23]

Unlike the collections that have come before, *The Body in Tolkien's Legendarium* prioritizes the issue of how bodies are constituted both in Middle-earth and in the context of Tolkien's early twentieth-century England. The contributions to the volume simultaneously further the critical conversations on subjects that have been previously engaged and break new ground. Part I: The Transformation of the Body deals with a prevalent theme throughout most of Tolkien's Legendarium, as some characters clearly metamorphose at will (Beorn, Lúthien, and Sauron) while others are physically augmented by powers beyond their control (Gollum, the Nazgûl, and Frodo). In "The Body in Question: The Unhealed Wounds of Frodo Baggins," Verlyn Flieger closely examines Frodo's physical, psychological, and metaphoric metamorphoses over the course of his journey. Flieger argues that Frodo's relationship to himself and to his environment will ultimately render him physically and psychologically wounded and permanently so. Yvette Kisor examines the insubstantiality of evil bodies in "Incorporeality and Transformation in *The Lord of the Rings*" and concludes that it is largely an illusion. The essay maintains that there exists a continuum of transformation with the Ringwraiths on one end and Gandalf on the other, and that Tolkien privileges the translucency of the latter over the invisibility of the former. And in her "Frodo's Body: Liminality and the Experience of War," Anna Smol examines the transformation and disintegration of Frodo's Self through the process of abjection, focusing upon the symbolic valence of the wounded or dead male soldier's body as it was perceived by World War I writers of England. Smol also links Tolkien's evocation of the pastoral ideal to an elegiac meditation on loss. His horrific memories of the wounded and dismembered bodies, of the uncanny terrain of dismembered body parts, produce an ambivalence that is part of the liminality of war.

Part II: The Body and the Spirit considers the meaning of physicality in relationship to the spiritual realm, exploring this intersection through the lens of Platonic and Augustinian philosophy. In his "The *Hröa* and *Fëa* of Middle-earth: Health, Ecology and the War," Matthew Dickerson appropriately begins his essay with an exploration of the complexity of Tolkien's attitude towards creation. While he did prioritize the spiritual, Tolkien recognized fecundity's importance and possessed a love for the garden-like aspect of creation. Both *hröa* and *fëa* are real and relevant in Middle-earth, and evil is manifested when there is no longer a harmony between the two. Unlike others who ascribed to the neo–Platonic idea locating the Good solely within the realm of thought and spirit, Tolkien found Good to exist in both the material and spiritual worlds. Jolanta N. Komornicka's "The Ugly Elf: Orc Bodies, Perversion, and Redemption in *The Silmarillion* and *The Lord of the Rings*" examines Tolkien's attitude towards Augustinian, Platonic and Boethian definitions of perversion and evil. Borrowing from Jeffrey Cohen's concept of the Intimate Stranger, Komornicka interrogates the relation of orcs to their own bodies, which are at once familiar in origin and monstrous. Such bodies, Komornicka concludes, are sites of social resistance and disorder.[24]

That subjectivities and bodies are constituted by and through the cultural semiotics in which they exist is a commonplace of contemporary theory. In a text, bodies are quite literally constructed out of language and also "mythologized" within the world of that text; Part III: The Discursive Body asserts this argument in different ways. In "Light (noun, 1) or Light (adjective, 14b)? Female Bodies and Femininities in *The Lord of the Rings*," Robin Anne Reid focuses on language's ability to reveal degrees of agency. Steered by recent trends in queer and feminist scholarship, Reid draws upon the verbal processes categorized by M.A.K. Halliday in order to examine how female characters are constructed at the levels of consciousness and corporeality in *The Lord of the Rings*. Gergely Nagy's "A Body of Myth: Representing Sauron in *The Lord of the Rings*" argues that Sauron is the only mythological being situated outside of Middle-earth's conventional system of signification. In an ontological mode,

Nagy explores the manner in which Sauron's physical Self is constituted through language and how a surrogate body serves to represent his subjectivity when he is disembodied.

Part IV: The Body and the Source Material explores corporeality in conjunction with texts belonging to what Tolkien referred to as his Cauldron of Story. James T. Williamson's "Emblematic Bodies: Tolkien and the Depiction of Female Physical Presence" observes how through various conventional and figural tropes female bodies within the narrative (Goldberry, Galadriel, Arwen, and Éowyn) disappear into the descriptions of physical creation: the earth, the heavens, the rhythms of cyclic time. Williamson traces this approach back to the literature of northern Europe and the British Isles. The *Volsunga Saga*, *Sir Gawain and the Green Knight*, Thomas Chestre's *Sir Lanval* all describe the female body in similar ways. Additionally, Jennifer Culver employs *Beowulf*, *The Poetic Edda*, *The Nibelungenlied*, *Sir Gawain and the Green Knight*, *The Wanderer*, and *The Wife's Lament* in her "Extending the Reach of the Invisible Hand: A Gift Looks for Gain in the Gifting Economy of Middle-earth" to demonstrate the traditional quality of the gifting economy within *The Lord of the Rings*. Culver maintains that bodies in the text serve as gifts. On one level, all mortal bodies are gifts from Ilúvatar, which must at some point be returned. On another level, bodies in service can extend the reach of a lord's authority and power or forge a union between the children of Ilúvatar. Lastly, Christopher Vaccaro's "Tolkien's Whimsical Mode: Physicalities in *The Hobbit*" notes the similarities between Tolkien's employment of bodies and that found in the fairy tale literature of Wyke-Smith's *The Marvellous Land of the Snergs*, Knatchbull-Hugessen's "Puss-cat Mew," and Grimm's "The Juniper Tree," the mythical/historical literature of *Beowulf* and Tolkien's own *The Lay of Leithian*. Vaccaro posits that it is through *The Hobbit*'s whimsical style that bodies appear at first as objects of comedy and gruesome violence, and later as objects of myth and heroism. While some traces of the earlier whimsical mode appear in *The Lord of the Rings*, it is quickly replaced by a more myth-oriented and virtue-conscious style.

Generally speaking, investigations into how bodies are constituted, employed, and mythologized have been under-utilized in Tolkien Studies. While some scholars have posed similar questions, they have done so largely tangentially. *The Body in Tolkien's Legendarium* is the first collection of essays to focus entirely on the body in Tolkien's Legendarium.[25]

Notes

1. Tolkien, *Letters*, 51.
2. J.R.R. Tolkien, *Morgoth's Ring*, ed. Christopher Tolkien (Boston: Houghton Mifflin, 1993), 399–400.
3. For a thorough consideration of Tolkien's cosmogony with regards to the necessity

of evil for the production of art see Debbie Sly, "Weaving Nets of Gloom: 'Darkness Profound' in Tolkien and Milton," 2000. Sly's analysis includes examples of divine and diabolic embodiment, which emerge out of a pythagorean conceptualization of creation.
 4. cf. Jane Chance, ed., *Tolkien the Medievalist*, 2003; George Clark and Daniel Timmons, eds., *J.R.R. Tolkien and His Literary Resonances*, 2000; Jane Chance and Alfred K. Sievers, eds., *Tolkien's Modern Middle Ages*, 2005; and Verlyn Flieger and Carl F. Hostetter, eds., *Tolkien's Legendarium*, 2000.
 5. Sarah Coakley, *Religion and the Body* (Cambridge: Cambride University Press, 1997).
 6. Brown writes, "Here were little fiery universes, through whose heart, brain, and veins there pulsed the same heat and vital spirit as glowed in the stars." Peter Brown, *The Body and Society* (New York: Columbia University Press, 1988), 17.
 7. "The aim of asceticism is a kind of effortless interiority, in which the soul is at home in the body and in control.... This effortless interiority renders the body 'transparent,' so to speak, and makes possible a community between souls that have been cut off from one another by the opacity of the fallen body." Coakley, *Religion and the Body*, 119. For an examination of a potential Augustinian influence on Tolkien's cosmology see John William Houghton, "Augustine in the Cottage of Lost Play: The *Ainulindalë* as Asterisk Cosmogony," 2003.
 8. For a critical investigation into the *corpus Christi* concept, see Sarah Beckwith, *Christ's Body: Identity, Culture and Society in Late Medieval Writings*, 1993.
 9. Bynum captures the essence of this theology of decay and resurrection of the body politic: "If corruption or fragmentation or division of the body ... is the central threat, resurrection (the reassemblage of parts into a whole) is the central victory." Caroline Bynum, "Bodily Miracles and the Resurrection of the Body in the High Middle Ages," *Belief in History*, ed. Thomas Kselman (Notre Dame: University of Notre Dame Press, 1991), 77.
 10. "Beoð þa syngan flæsc/scandum þurhwaden swa ðæt scire glæs/ ðæt mon yþæst mæg eall þurhwlitan." George Krapp, Philip Dobbie, and Elliot Van Kirk, eds., *Christ III* (New York: Columbia University Press, 1936), ll. 1281b–1283. See also *Blickling 10*: "hwonne se ælmihtiga God wille þisse worlde ende gewyrican, & þonne he his byrnsweord getyhþ & þas world ealle ðurhslyhþ, & ða lichoman þurh sceoteð, & þysne middangeard tocleofeð, & þa deadan upastandaþ, biþ þonne se flæschoma ascyred swa glæs, ne mæg ðæs unrihtes beon awiht bediglE." R. Morris, ed., *Blickling Homilies* (London: N. Trübner, 1880), 109. Thanks to Bruce Gilchrist for his aid in locating these two instances.
 11. See Michel Foucault, *The History of Sexuality*, vols. I–III, 1977; 1985; 1986. *Vol. IV: Confessions of the Flesh* was unfinished at the time of Foucault's death in 1984 and so remains unpublished. See also Michel Foucault, *Discipline and Punish*, 1977.
 12. Judith Butler, *Gender Trouble*, 1990 and *Bodies That Matter*, 1993, and Eve Kosofsky Sedgwick, *Between Men*, 1985 and *Epistemology of the Closet*, 1990. See also Diana Fuss, "Sexing the Body," 1991 and *Essentially Speaking*, 1989.
 13. See Jane Chance, *The Mythology of Power*, 2001; see also "Tolkien and the Other," 2005; "In the Company of Orcs," 2009; and "Tough Love: Teaching the New Medievalisms," 2009 for Chance's insights on alterity's effects on physicality.
 14. Chance, *The Mythology of Power*, 84.
 15. See Anna Smol, "'Oh ... Oh ... Frodo,'" 2004.
 16. Gergely Nagy, "The 'Lost' Subject of Middle-earth," *Tolkien Studies* 3, ed. Douglas A. Anderson, Michael D.C. Drout, Verlyn Flieger (Morgantown: West Virginia University Press, 2006), 61.
 17. Nagy, "The 'Lost' Subject," 61.
 18. Ibid., 63.
 19. Ibid., 64.
 20. "Gollum is a corporeal illustration of how Sauron's binary system conceives of the material existence of his subjects." Ibid., 63.

21. "Angelus enim officii nomen est, non naturae. Quaeris nomen huius naturae, spiritus est; quaeris officium, angelus est: ex eo quod est, spiritus est, ex eo quod agit, angelus est." Hipponensis Augustinus, *Enarrationes in Psalmos*, in *Patrologia latina*, ed. Jacques-Paul Migne (vol. 37, 80–144, col. 1348–1349), 103, 1, 15, http://pld.chadwyck.co.uk. See also Michaël Devaux, 2003.
22. Valerie Rohy, "On Fairy Stories," *Modern Fiction Studies* 50:4 (Winter 2004): 927–948.
23. Additionally, Rohy's unpublished "Cinema, Sexuality, and Mechanical Production" explores the representation of non-normative / artificial reproduction found in Saruman's breeding of his Uruk-hai. Rohy's essay brings to mind the five often-cited essays focused upon sexuality in *The Lord of the Rings*. See Alison Milbanck; Brenda Patridge; David M. Craig; Ty Rosenthal; and Esther Saxey.
24. See Jeffrey Cohen.
25. A special thanks to Valerie Rohy for her invaluable advice.

Works Consulted

Augustinus, Hipponensis. *Enarrationes in Psalmos. Patrologia Latina*, ed. Jacques-Paul Migne (vol. 37, 80–144, col. 1348–1349), http://pld.chadwyck.co.uk/.
Beckwith, Sarah. *Christ's Body. Identity, Culture and Society in Late Medieval Writings*. London: Routledge, 1993.
Blickling 10. *The Blickling Homilies of the Tenth Century*, ed. and trans. R. Morris, 106–115. Early English Texts Society, O.S. 58, 63, and 73. Reprinted, 1967. London: Oxford University Press, 1874–80.
Brown, Peter. *The Body and Society: Men, Women, and Sexual Renunciation in Early Christianity*. New York: Columbia University Press, 1988.
Butler, Judith. *Bodies That Matter: On the Discursive Limits of Sex*. New York: Routledge, 1993.
_____. *Gender Trouble: Feminism and the Subversion of Identity*. New York: Routledge, 1990.
Bynum, Caroline Walker. "Bodily Miracles and the Resurrection of the Body in the High Middle Ages." *Belief in History*, ed. Thomas Kselman, 68–106. Notre Dame: University of Notre Dame Press, 1991.
Chance, Jane. "'In the Company of Orcs': Peter Jackson's Queer Tolkien." *Queer Movie Medievalisms*, ed. Katherine Coyne Kelly and Tison Pugh, 79–96. Farnham, Surrey: Ashgate Press, 2009.
_____. *The Lord of the Rings: The Mythology of Power*. Lexington: University Press of Kentucky, 2001.
_____. "Tolkien and the Other: Race and Gender in Middle-earth." *Tolkien's Modern Middle Ages*, ed. Jane Chance and Alfred K. Sievers, 171–188. New York: Palgrave, 2005.
_____. "Tough Love: Teaching the New Medievalisms." *Defining Medievalism(s) II: Some More Perspectives*, ed. Karl Fulgelso, *Studies in Medievalisms*, 18 (2009): 76–98.
_____, ed. *Tolkien the Medievalist*. New York: Routledge, 2003.
_____, and Alfred K. Sievers, eds. *Tolkien's Modern Middle Ages*. New York: Palgrave, 2005.
"Christ." *The Exeter Book*. The Anglo-Saxon Poetic Records 3, ed. George Krapp, Philip Dobbie, and Elliot Van Kirk, 3–49. New York: Columbia University Press, 1936.
Clark, George, and Daniel Timmons, eds. *J.R.R. Tolkien and his Literary Resonances: Views of Middle-earth*. Westport, CT: Greenwood Press, 2000.
Coakley, Sarah. *Religion and the Body*. Cambridge: Cambridge University Press, 1997.
Cohen, Jeffrey. *Of Giants: Sex, Monsters, and the Middle Ages*. Minneapolis: University of Minnesota Press, 1999.

Craig, David M. "'Queer Lodgings': Gender and Sexuality in *The Lord of the Rings.*" *Mallorn* 38 (January 2001): 11–18.
Devaux, Michaël. "Les Anges de l'Ombre chez Tolkien: chair, corps et corruption." *Tolkien: Les racines du légendaire.* Genèva: Ad Solem, 2003.
Dickerson, Matthew. *Following Gandalf: Epic Battles and Moral Victory in* The Lord of the Rings. Ada, MI: Brazos Press, 2003.
Flieger, Verlyn, and Carl F. Hostetter, eds. *Tolkien's Legendarium: Essays on* The History of Middle-earth. Westport, CT: Greenwood Press, 2000.
Foucault, Michel. *Discipline and Punish: The Birth of the Prison*, trans. Alan Sheridan. London: Allen Lane, 1977.
_____. *The History of Sexuality, Vol. I: The Will to Knowledge (An Introduction)*, trans. Robert Hurley. New York: Pantheon, 1977.
_____. *Vol. II: The Use of Pleasure*, trans. R. Hurley. New York: Pantheon, 1985.
_____. *Vol. III: The Care of the Self*, trans. R. Hurley. New York: Pantheon, 1986.
Fuss, Diana. *Essentially Speaking: Feminism, Nature and Difference.* New York: Routledge, 1989.
_____. "Sexing the Body: Gender Politics and the Construction of Sexuality." *Inside/Out: Lesbian Theories, Gay Theories*, ed. Fuss, 233–240. New York: Routledge, 1991.
Houghton, John William. "Augustine in the Cottage of Lost Play: The *Ainulindalë* as Asterisk Cosmogony." *Tolkien the Medievalist*, ed. Chance, 171–182. New York: Routledge, 2003.
Milbanck, Alison. "'My Precious,' Tolkien's Fetishized Ring." *The Lord of the Rings and Philosophy*, ed. Gregory Bassham and Eric Bronson, 33–45. Chicago: Open Court, 2003.
Nagy, Gergely. "The 'Lost' Subject of Middle-earth." *Tolkien Studies* 3 (2006): 57–79.
Patridge, Brenda. "No Sex Please–We're Hobbits: The Construction of Female Sexuality in *The Lord of the Rings.*" *J.R.R. Tolkien: This Far Land*, ed. Robert Giddings, 179–197. London: Vision Press, 1983.
Rohy, Valerie. "On Fairy Stories." *Modern Fiction Studies* 50.4 (Winter 2004): 927– 948.
Rosenthal, Ty. "Warm Beds Are Good: Sex and Libido in Tolkien's Writing." *Mallorn* 42 (2004): 35–42.
Saxey, Esther. "Homoeroticism." *Reading* The Lord of the Rings, ed. R. Eaglestone, 124–136. London: Continuum, 2006.
Sedgwick, Eve Kosofsky. *Between Men: English Literature and Male Homosocial Desire.* New York: Columbia University Press, 1985.
_____. *Epistemology of the Closet.* Berkeley: University of California Press, 1990.
Sly, Debbie. "Weaving Nets of Gloom: 'Darkness Profound' in Tolkien and Milton." *J.R.R. Tolkien and His Literary Resonances: Views of Middle-earth*, ed. George Clark and Daniel Timmons, 109–119. Westport, CT: Greenwood Press, 2000.
Smol, Anna. "'Oh ... Oh ... Frodo!' Readings of Male Intimacy in *The Lord of the Rings.*" *Modern Fiction Studies* 50.4 (Winter 2004): 949–979.
Tolkien, Christopher, ed. *Morgoth's Ring.* London: Allen and Unwin; Boston: Houghton Mifflin, 1993.

Part I
The Transformation of the Body

The Body in Question
The Unhealed Wounds of Frodo Baggins

VERLYN FLIEGER

"Alas! There are some wounds that cannot be wholly cured," said Gandalf.

I explore Tolkien's treatment of the body of Frodo Baggins with particular attention to the drastic physical and psychological changes that take place on and in that body over the course of Frodo's journey (a journey as much metaphorical and spiritual as geographic and physical). My argument is that the changes that come about in various circumstances and situations are emblematic of Frodo's changing relationship to himself, to the "real" world around him, and to the quasi-metaphoric, quasi-psychological world of the Ring, which represents the dark side of the human personality.

Frodo Baggins would seem at the beginning of his adventure to be a pretty generic hobbit, though Gandalf's depiction of him as quoted by Barliman Butterbur enhances the picture somewhat. Barliman's description of Frodo's red cheeks, unusual height and fair skin, and bright eyes seems to lift Frodo a bit beyond his fellow-hobbits, for example Merry and Pippin. They get no such individual representation (except for their Ent draught-increased height and curling hair at the end of the story), so we can only suppose them to be as long-fingered, bright-eyed, red-cheeked, and fond of eating and drinking as their neighbors. We come to know them through their speech and behavior rather than from their looks.

With the exception of Gollum, whose wasted, aged and scrawny appearance will have a bearing on Frodo's, we get a more complete picture of Frodo's exterior than that of any other hobbit. There is a reason for this beyond authorial realism. What happens to Frodo's body over the course of his journey is the outward manifestation of his changing inner condition. It illustrates one of the bleakest motifs in the book, that Frodo's sacrifice is physical and moral as well as spiritual, that both kinds are presented as being interdependent, and that such giving-up of self and substance may or may not be rewarded. Great loss may perhaps result in great gain, but then again it may not, and neither is a foregone conclusion. The first thing to notice is a twofold circumstance: (1) that Frodo's physical self diminishes steadily and perceptibly over the course of the book, and (2) that such external alteration can be seen as an index of internal change. Although this condition may be overlooked by readers more in search of plot than theme, Tolkien takes good care to note this diminution, not frequently, but pointedly.

The brief conversation among Pippin and Frodo and Strider fairly early in the journey from Bree to Weathertop says more than at first meets the eye. Responding to Pippin's observation that he is "twice the hobbit" he once was, Frodo replies that this seems odd since it appears to him that he is actually thinning out: "I hope the thinning process will not go on indefinitely, or I shall become a wraith" (*FR*, I, xi, 196–197). In spite of a "thinning process" that is as much metaphorical as actual, Frodo is on the way to being "twice the hobbit" he has been, though it is not until almost the end of the book that Saruman, leaving the Shire, speaks the final word on what this early exchange foreshadows (*RK*, VI, viii, 299). He is right, although too few readers attend to his words, which put paid to the hopeful but careless assumption that Frodo's journey to the Undying Lands will give him eternal life. Tolkien's several statements in his letters make it clear that Frodo will die like any mortal. His journey to Valinor is, like King Arthur's to Avalon, to be healed, if he can be, of his wounds. "Frodo was sent or allowed to pass over sea to heal him — if that could be done, *before he died*" (emphasis Tolkien's).[1]

While Frodo's growth is psychological and spiritual, his girth or lack of it is physical. Yet the "thinning process" to which he refers also has a metaphorical component, and Strider, who knows more about what is going on than Frodo, is not amused. Neither we nor Frodo can understand the intensity of his reaction, for at this point we do not know that the Black Riders who have followed the hobbits from Hobbiton and will shortly surround and ambush the travelers on Weathertop are themselves wraiths — Ringwraiths. Nor have we yet any concept of what "becoming a wraith" in this sense entails — the dreadful loss of life and soul that has changed the nine kings from "mortal men doomed to die" into the deathless and bodiless servants of Sauron they have become through possession of the nine rings and submission to the One Ring.

Let us pause for a moment and consider the possible metaphoric ramifications of the Ring's one capability that we see and can measure, that of conferring invisibility. What might it mean to disappear, to lose apparent physical substance, to be seen through as if not there? I suggest that in the case of Frodo, whose bearing of the Ring carries more metaphoric meaning than anyone else's except Gollum, Tolkien is using invisibility as the outward and visible (or invisible) sign of an inward process, a progressive fading and loss of self. This does not become manifest in Frodo, however, until after his putting on the Ring at Weathertop. No apparent ill effects accrue, for example, from his wearing the Ring in the house of Tom Bombadil and again at the Prancing Pony. At the time of Pippin's comment, we probably do not heed the portent, seeing only that in Frodo's case less is more, that his outward appearance is in inverse proportion to his actual corporal substance. He is noticeably thinner (there is "a good deal less" of him than there was when he set out from Hobbiton), yet he therefore looks "twice the hobbit" that he was. He gains as he loses. Neither Frodo nor the reader can know at this point that the "thinning process" is both actual and metaphoric, an exterior manifestation of an interior and spiritual change that will indeed go on, if not "indefinitely," at least to the end of the journey and Frodo's departure over sea to Valinor.

Following Pippin's casual observation, the next evidences of Frodo's transformation come after and as a direct result of his wounding by the Morgul-knife at Weathertop. During the subsequent journey to the Ford, his perception of reality changes as he begins to fade out of the real world while at the same time the real world begins to fade before his eyes. The first indication that this is happening to him comes first as memory and then as dream (*FR*, I, xii, 214–15). What begins as an apprehension of black shapes advancing, and a dream of a dimming garden and tall black shadows, soon becomes actuality as Frodo fades farther and farther out of the physical world and deeper and deeper into the psychological and metaphorical wraith-world of the Ring. There is more than enough evidence in the text to reveal the increasing effect of his weakening hold on the world around him and the concomitant development of his perception of and participation in the shadow world.[2]

Further supporting evidence comes at the Ford of Rivendell. By this time, Frodo has not only borne (and worn) the Ring, he has been stabbed with the Morgul-knife that has left a part of itself in the wound. The result of this is both physical and psychological, making the real world appear to his eyes "shadowy and dim," while allowing the shapes of the Black Riders at the Ford (no longer dream shapes but actual) to be "dark and solid" so that he can see them clearly. It takes little imagination to see this physical change as part of Frodo's increasingly precipitous slide from one world into another — from the phenomenal world to the interior, darkly faërian world of the Ring. It is thus no accident that in the flight to the Ford, Frodo can see the Ringwraiths clearly (*FR*, I, xii, 225). The outside world, which has increasingly faded since his wounding, is now almost beyond his perception, while the previously shadowy world of the Wraiths is as clear and hard-edged as it was at Weathertop. It should not be overlooked that unlike at Weathertop, Frodo is not here wearing the Ring. He has no need to be, the wound has done its work and he now perceives the Ringwraiths as they truly are (*FR*, I, xii, 226).

Not to be overlooked in all this shadow is the fact that when he is at the Ford, Frodo can also perceive Glorfindel as he really is (*FR*, II, i, 235). Frodo may be well and truly in the Ring world, but that very circumstance has sharpened his perception of light as well as dark. The mundane world is dim and faded, but Frodo can see beyond the dark to Glorfindel "as he is upon the other side" (*FR*, II, i, 235). We may ask at this point, "The other side of what?" The phrase may refer simply to the other side of the world, to Aman/Valinor, the Land in the West at the end of the Straight Road. But it may also refer to the far edge of the Ring world, and to the possibility that by going deeply into the dark and passing through it one can come out again into the light on the other side.

This is surely the implication behind Gandalf's perception of Frodo at Rivendell. Although the Morgul-sliver has been removed from Frodo's shoulder, its effects remain, as shown by the appearance, the physical body of the convalescent Frodo:

> [T]o the wizard's eye there was a faint change, just a hint as it were of transparency about him, and especially about the left hand that lay outside upon the coverlet.
> "Still that must be expected," said Gandalf to himself. "He is not half through yet, and to what he will come in the end not even Elrond can foretell. Not to evil, I think. He may become like a glass filled with clear light for eyes to see that can."
> [*FR*, II, i, 235].

The "hint of transparency" seems to be the opposite of the shadow-transformation of the Black Riders, a movement into translucency rather than darkness, while the reference to a glass filled with clear light is an unmistakable adumbration of the Phial of Galadriel that Frodo carries into Mordor.[3] Nevertheless, Gandalf's "he may become" withholds the certain promise that such transformation will be the outcome of Frodo's ordeal. He has a long way yet to go, and to what he will come in the end no one in the story can foretell, only his creator, who is taking him deeper and deeper into the shadow side of his own heart and mind.

This becomes clearer when the Company enters Moria, where we are told that Frodo can see deeper into the darkness than any of his companions, an awareness the narrative attributes to the wound of the Morgul-knife (*FR*, II, iv, 325). It seems obvious that Tolkien is not just telling us that Frodo has excellent night-vision, but that his perception of the darkness embodied (or dis-embodied) in the Ringwraiths — a darkness that is within him as well — has sharpened. It can be no accident that it is at this point in his ordeal and in the underworld of Moria that Frodo becomes aware of his own shadow, Gollum, who is both literally and figuratively shadowing him.[4]

It is worth remembering that back in the sunlit study at Bag End Frodo had rejected Gandalf's suggestion that Gollum might be a hobbit, that there could be any relationship between himself and Gollum (*FR*, I, ii, 63). Since then he has been not only been stabbed by the Morgul-knife, he has worn the Ring not just once but three times. Although two of those instances, in the house of Tom Bombadil and at the Prancing Pony, have apparently had no consequences, the episode at Weathertop has had a profound effect. A striking contrast to the "hint of transparency" observed by Gandalf is Frodo's distorted and disturbing perception of Bilbo when at Rivendell he asks to see the Ring (*FR*, II, i, 244).

By the time Frodo gets to Moria, his ability to see into the dark has been deepened by experience. He still cannot "see" the real Gollum, who shadow-like is behind him, but he has been more than half in the Ring world since Weathertop, and he knows now that Gollum is there. His face-to-face meeting with Gollum in the Emyn Muil will be his first opportunity to confront his shadow, and it is not unimportant that he now makes a pact with it and agrees to rely on his shadow, his dark side, to guide him through the Dead Marshes and take him to the Black Gate. We may see this as the halfway mark in Frodo's journey with the darkest part still to come. The two deadliest of his physical wounds are still ahead of him—Shelob's sting, which brings him close to death, and Gollum's bite, which robs him of both finger and Ring and leaves him with only bitter self-knowledge.

The growth of Frodo's shadow side coupled with an actual wearing-away of his physical substance has the paradoxical effect of illuminating his inner being:

> [Sam] was reminded suddenly of Frodo as he had lain asleep in the house of Elrond, after his deadly wound. Then as he had kept watch Sam had noticed that at times a light seemed to be shining faintly within; but now the light was even clearer and stronger [*TT*, IV, iv, 260].

The two moments of translucency and inner light that show Frodo as others see him—first Gandalf and then Sam—are in stark contrast to his own self-awareness, which seems conscious of only loss and pain. Whatever healing may be ahead of him, his present state is at once better and worse than it was when he set out from Bag End. The inner light shines brighter, but only in contrast to the dark. Frodo may be "twice the hobbit he was" in terms of his spiritual and psychological growth, but he has still the potential to become a wraith, to fall completely under the domination of the Ring. This is, of course, exactly what happens. The implied similarity to Gollum—the one a tired, old and lonely hobbit (*TT*, IV, viii, 324), the other old and beautiful, chiseled by the "shaping years" but like Gollum far beyond the fields and streams of youth—is not accidental. His ordeal is taking its toll, and it is not over.

By the time it is over, by the time Tolkien has put his small protagonist through the punishing trials that still await him, and the final, awful test that he will fail, Frodo will have been stripped of most of what he started out with. He will have lost his innocence, his self-protective ignorance, his ordinary physical and psychological self and his home. All that on top of the greatest loss of all—the Ring. On the anniversary of his capture by the orcs at Cirith Ungol, Frodo confesses that since the Ring has been destroyed all remains "dark and empty" (*RK*, VI, ix, 304); Frodo, too, is dark and empty. The loss has saved him from wraith-hood, but left him bereft and diminished. He has grown spiritually but only by the perhaps necessary subtraction of his ordinary physical self.

Paradoxically, he may be "twice the hobbit," precisely because of all his losses. Frodo is capable of forgiving Gollum and showing mercy to Saruman. But it is worthy of notice that as the narrative draws to its close, we get no more descriptions of light from within. Gandalf's prediction, so carefully couched in the subjunctive by Tolkien, appears not to have come true. Frodo seems less like a glass filled with clear light than like a combat veteran suffering Post-Traumatic-Stress Syndrome: "There is no real going back," he tells Gandalf on the ride home, and he asks the wizard where if any place he might find rest (*RK*, VI, vii, 268).[5]

Not in the Shire, as the rest of the story makes clear. Sam worries about his master, who has no part in the great year 1420 that marks the renewal of the Shire. The shadow of "old troubles" haunts Frodo on the anniversaries of their occurrence, as Sam begins to realize:

"What's the matter, Mr. Frodo?" said Sam.

"I am wounded," he answered, "wounded; it will never really heal" [*RK*, VI, ix, 305].

It is not until "afterwards" that Sam recalls the date, October sixth, the two-year anniversary of Frodo's wounding on Weathertop. Moreover, "it" does not ever "really" heal. Frodo's illnesses, the year-marks of his wounds, are debilitating reminders of his ordeals, reminders to readers not just of the inescapable fact that Frodo does not recover, but that Tolkien does not want us to forget that he does not recover. Frodo at the end of the book is less "like a glass filled with clear light" than like a deeply damaged, battle-scarred veteran of war whose post-traumatic flashbacks are the psychic souvenirs of his physical injuries. Frodo's maimed body bears the marks and the memories of his experience, marks and memories he will carry with him to Valinor to be healed, *if that can be done*, but Tolkien leaves the question in doubt.

By the time he takes ship for the Undying Lands Frodo has faded—out of view, out of life, out of common remembrance. He has been "too deeply hurt," as he tells Sam, to enjoy the Shire (*RK*, VI, ix, 309). Such bitter knowledge is hard for readers to accept. We want a Happy Ending for Frodo, while

Tolkien uncompromisingly refuses to give us one. His letters paint an even bleaker picture than his fiction, like this to Eileen Elgar in 1963:

> [I]t was not only nightmare memories of past horrors that afflicted him, but also unreasoning self-reproach: he saw himself and all that he had done as a broken failure.[6]

Gandalf was right when he speculated at Rivendell that Frodo would not "come to evil." But neither does he come to unalloyed good, but to a painful and debilitating self-realization. Frodo's greatest unhealed wound transcends his physical maiming and loss. It is the deeper, self-inflicted wound of his "unreasoning self-reproach." The hobbit who left the washing-up for Lobelia and walked away from Bag End on September 22 has been changed both externally and internally into the maimed and battered body and damaged psyche, the "broken failure" who returns to the Shire little more than a year later only to fade out of the picture and finally to leave it altogether.

Of all the many bodies in Tolkien's Middle-earth it is Frodo's body, chiseled to beauty by the shaping years yet scarred by great struggle and greater failure, that pays the highest price and gets the least reward.

Coda

It is not hard to associate the harm done to Frodo with the damage Tolkien saw all around him in his time on the Somme, and in the palpable damage to returning soldiers that was so much a part of England after that war — the crippled, gassed, shell-shocked veterans who came home to a world that did not know what to do with them. Neither they nor those to whom they returned had any mechanism for dealing with the terrible and unforeseen results of the first "World War," of which the War of the Ring was the fictive counterpart, just as the homefolks of Hobbiton have no way of comprehending what has happened to Frodo.

Two brief passages in Tolkien's published *Letters* refer to a circumstance even more directly connected to Tolkien's own life. A letter written to Sir Stanley Unwin on 29 June 1944, barely two months after VE Day mentions that Tolkien's "son, a much-damaged soldier [is] ... trying to ... recover a shadow of his old health."[7] This comment is annotated in the editor's note # 2 to letter 74, which gives the further information that "Michael Tolkien [Tolkien's second son] had been judged unfit for further military service as a result of 'severe shock to nervous system due to prolonged exposure to enemy action.'"[8] The extent of Tolkien's grief, after coming through his own war, at seeing the effects of a second war on his son can only be imagined. His portrait of the heroic, failed, irrevocably damaged Frodo may be part oblique allusion, part oblique tribute to this other "much-damaged" soldier.

Notes

1. Tolkien, *Letters*, 328.
2. *FR*, I, xii, 215, 216, 216–217, 222, 224.
3. See *Splintered Light: Logos and Language in Tolkien's World* (Kent, OH: Kent University Press, 2002), 155–165 where I cover in greater detail the scene of Frodo's translucency.
4. The word *shadow* has a psychological as well as a metaphoric meaning as one of Carl Jung's archetypal configurations of the human psyche. In Jungian psychology the Shadow is understood as the dark or un-admitted side of the personality; that part of ourselves we do not want to see, that we reject and turn away from. For a compelling and influential Jungian reading of *The Lord of the Rings* see Timothy R. O'Neill, *The Individuated Hobbit: Jung, Tolkien, and the Archetypes of Middle-earth*, 1979.
5. Significant critical analyses have been done on the debilitating effects of PTSD on the soldiers fighting during World War I (see Joanna Bourke, *Dismembering the Male: Men's Bodies, Britain, and the Great War*, 1996) and on its effects on Frodo more specifically (see Janet Brennan Croft, *War and the Works of J.R.R. Tolkien*, 1994 and John Garth, *Tolkien and the Great War: The Threshold of Middle-earth*, 2003). In a section titled "'I am wounded, wounded; it will never really heal': Shell Shock and Other Psychological Wounds," Croft closely examines the parallels between the disorder and Frodo's condition. For further material focused primarily on the psychological distress of the trauma survivor see also Karyn Milos, "Too Deeply Hurt: Understanding Frodo's Decision to Depart," 1998 and Michael Livingston, "The Shell-shocked Hobbit: The First World War and Tolkien's Trauma of the Ring," 2006. Anna Smol also contributes to the conversation in her investigation into the ways trench-life affected male bonding and intimacy between men in her "'Oh ... Oh ... Frodo'! Readings of Male Intimacy in *The Lord of the Rings*," 2004.
6. Tolkien, *Letters*, 327–28.
7. Ibid., 86.
8. Ibid., 439.

Works Consulted

Bourke, Joanna. *Dismembering the Male: Men's Bodies, Britain, and the Great War*. Chicago: University of Chicago Press, 1996.
Croft, Janet Brennan. *War and the Works of J.R.R Tolkien*. Contributions to the Study of Science Fiction and Fantasy 106. Westport, CT: Praeger, 1994.
Flieger, Verlyn. *Splintered Light*. Kent, OH: Kent State University Press, 2002
Garth, John. *Tolkien and the Great War: The Threshold of Middle-earth*. Boston: Houghton Mifflin, 2003.
Livingston, Michael. "The Shell-shocked Hobbit: The First World War and Tolkien's Trauma of the Ring." *Mythlore* 25 (Fall/Winter 2006): 77–92.
Milos, Karyn. "Too Deeply Hurt: Understanding Frodo's Decision to Depart." *Mallorn* 36 (November 1998): 17–23.
O'Neill, Timothy, R. *The Individuated Hobbit: Jung, Tolkien, and the Archetypes of Middle-earth*. Boston: Houghton Mifflin, 1979.
Smol, Anna. "'Oh ... Oh ... Frodo!' Readings of Male Intimacy in *The Lord of the Rings*." *Modern Fiction Studies* 50.4 (Winter 2004): 949–979.

Incorporeality and Transformation in *The Lord of the Rings*[1]

YVETTE KISOR

A consideration of bodies and bodily form in Tolkien's Middle-earth leads quickly and perhaps inevitably to the question of incorporeality. Ringwraiths, Barrow-wights, the Dead of the Dwimorberg, even Sauron himself—some of the most frightening manifestations in Tolkien's Middle-earth are those whose bodies do not appear in the normal sense. Even the One Ring, though itself strongly present in material form, creates perhaps the strongest expression of incorporeality: the fading it causes in its wearer. Evil is closely associated with the Shadow of Mordor, and the growing power of Sauron is perhaps best imaged as the spreading of the Shadow.

Yet the Enemy is hardly insubstantial as encountered by the Fellowship and its allies. The arrows, swords, and axes flung at them have an intense physicality, and at every turn, it seems, the Enemy requires agents to wield its power — orcs, men, wargs — even Ringwraiths require steeds to bear them and wrappings to give them the appearance of bodily form. In fact, neither Sauron nor his principal agents the Nazgûl are entirely incorporeal. The Nazgûl can wield a sword and Sauron can wear the Ring. In fact, because of the Ring Sauron is wedded to a physical reality, and therefore a bodily form; in order to wield the Ring, he *must* be able to wear it. This necessity of embodiment created by the Ring exists simultaneously with the Ring's propensity to rob the wearer of visible bodily form, and this liminal space between embodiment and insubstantiality is occupied not only by the Ring and its maker — Gandalf too is transformed and in the process becomes something both more and less than an embodied being. This essay seeks to explore the relationship between embodiment and incorporeality by examining the function of transformation in Tolkien's Middle-earth, particularly that undergone by Gandalf and the Nazgûl, and seeing what their experience can tell us about the transformation Frodo undergoes.

Let us begin with what is perhaps the most obvious manifestation of physical transformation: the Ring and the fading it causes. As Gandalf explains to Frodo in "The Shadow of the Past," if a mortal wears the Ring frequently, he *"fades"* (*FR*, I, ii, 56).[2] The term Gandalf uses here, "fade," carries a great deal of semantic weight in Tolkien's concept.[3] This is the first use of this important term in its special sense in *The Lord of the Rings*[4] and it is emphasized here through italic type, and Gandalf immediately offers a definition of the term: to fade is to become "invisible permanently." A glance at the *OED* is instructive at this point.[5] The entry for the verb "fade" lists eleven main meanings dating back to the fourteenth century, both transitive and intransitive. Focusing on the intransitive uses, as the transitive ones are simply applications of the intransitive meanings, and eliminating specialized uses (a golf term referring to the ball's deviation from a straight course; the reduction in friction of a car's brakes) and slang (in betting), we are left with several senses all having to do with the loss of an essential quality. Thus plants are said to fade when they "lose freshness and vigour," light or color loses "brightness or brilliance," and the sound or picture associated with radio or television and cinema increases or decreases. More broadly, to fade means "to grow small or weak; to decline, decay, fail, or faint" or "to pass away or disappear gradually; vanish, die out." Looking at the first part of Gandalf's definition, to become "invisible permanently," Tolkien's concept of fading seems in line with many definitions the *OED* presents. The idea of losing brightness, and in particular of disappearing or vanishing, seems consistent with Tolkien's concept.[6]

The second part of Gandalf's definition, however, takes Tolkien's sense of "fade" further from that suggested by the editors of the *OED*. He defines fading as not only becoming "invisible permanently" but walking "in the twilight under the eye of the dark power that rules the Ring" (*FR*, I, ii, 56). This second aspect of Gandalf's definition moves beyond the idea of losing some essential quality (color, vigor, brightness) or vanishing and suggests instead moving into some other dimension, some alternate version of reality. The term "twilight" and the reference to "the dark power" place "fading" within the opposition of light and dark that helps schematize the world of Middle-earth, and suggests a kind of middle place: it is neither light nor dark but twilight.[7] In this vein it may be useful to consider Verlyn Flieger's identification of invisibility as a negative: "to be invisible is to be neither light nor dark."[8] This suggests a stronger link between the two parts of Gandalf's definition of fading, of being invisible and walking "in the twilight." The reference to Sauron, however (for "the dark power that rules the Ring" can refer to no-one else), implies that this twilight is more strongly associated with the powers of darkness than those of light. Further, this second aspect of Gandalf's definition in some sense negates the first, for rather than invisibility the one who fades experiences being seen and exists specifically "under the eye" of Sauron.

Both aspects of this definition are borne out through the experience of those who have faded.

Neither Frodo nor Bilbo, nor indeed Gollum fade, but the Men who become the Ringwraiths do, and in them we see the full effects of this fading. The hobbits experience the Nazgûl first as Black Riders seen only from a distance and known most clearly through their voice, strangely shrill and hissing, and through the sense of disquiet they create.[9] But at Weathertop, they encounter them up close, and the encounter is remarkable for its sense of disembodiedness, in which the insubstantiality of the Ringwraiths is paramount (*FR*, I, xi, 207).[10] They are described as "shadows," their presence felt rather than seen, and the passage is notable for its lack of certainty: the shadows "seem" to grow and the number of shadows is questioned, even after it is asserted that "there could be no doubt" of their presence. Yet their insubstantiality has a depth to it. They are not merely shadows, but black shadows, so black that they become "black holes," images of nothingness that suggest a tangible reality.[11]

This black depth, however, proves to be an illusion. Once Frodo puts on the Ring he sees them with other sight, and what he sees is not black but gray, not shadow but substance. The number, in doubt before, in spite of the assertion of certainty "there could be no doubt," becomes immediately clear — not "three or four" but five figures — and there is nothing insubstantial about their bodies to Frodo's eyes when he is wearing the Ring, and his experience of sight is confirmed in his body: in the stab of the Ringwraith's sword he feels indeed their bodily reality. Yet the other hobbits never see anything other than "vague shadowy shapes" (*FR*, I, xii, 209). This experience on Weathertop confirms Gandalf's words: the fading wrought by the Ring refers to invisibility, not insubstantiality. It is a question of appearance, not being. Further, when Frodo puts on the Ring, he confirms the second part of Gandalf's definition of fading as well as the first. Gandalf later explains to Frodo that he was the most vulnerable to the Ringwraiths when wearing the Ring, because then he was "half in the wraith-world" himself (*FR*, II, i, 234).[12] With the Ring on his finger he crosses over, albeit temporarily, into that twilight world Gandalf referenced, and he perceives the bodily reality of the Ringwraiths.[13] To fade is not to lose substance but to change appearance and to function in another mode of reality — the twilight world that Frodo enters when he places the Ring on his finger is one the Nazgûl cannot escape.[14] Yet to observers the invisibility of the Ringwraiths continues to manifest itself not merely as an absence of perception but as a palpable reality: it is not simply that they cannot see the Nazgûl, it is that they are *seen* as not *there*.

Tom Shippey is aware of this duality, and points to the aptness of the shadow as an image for the Ringwraiths[15]; as he observes "all the wraiths seem to be, like shadows, both material presences and immaterial absences: under their hoods and cloaks there is nothing, or at least nothing visible, but just the same they can wield weapons, ride horses, be pierced by blades or swept away by flood."[16] Shippey relates this dual nature of their faded existence, both material and immaterial, both presence and absence, to the "philosophical duality" at the heart of Tolkien's concept of evil.[17] According to Shippey, in *The Lord of the Rings* a Boethian view of evil competes with a Manichaean one, and Tolkien continually maintains aspects of both. The Boethian view of evil is the idea that "there is no such thing as evil: 'evil is nothing,' is the absence of good."[18] This Boethian view competes with a Manichaean view of evil, the idea "that Good and Evil are equal and opposite and the universe is a battlefield."[19] This "uncertainty over evil,"[20] this ambiguity that maintains both views simultaneously, is expressed through the Ring, which acts both as an external force and as a "psychic amplifier" working on the inner weakness of the possessor, and through the Ringwraiths. Shippey relates the "nothingness" of the Ringwraiths to the Boethian concept of evil as absence,[21] which coexists with their Manichaean material reality.

This tension comes to the fore in the description of the Witch-king as he opposes Gandalf at the gate of Minas Tirith (*RK*, V, iv, 103).[22] What seems so horrific in his appearance is what *should* be there, but is not — it is the crown perched atop "no head visible" and the laughter issuing from the "mouth unseen." This is quite different from the invisibility wrought by the Ring in normal circumstances; when Bilbo puts on the Ring and disappears, as far as observers are concerned he simply vanishes, though *The Hobbit* speaks of the wearer casting a watery shadow visible in bright sunlight.[23] The more permanent invisibility Gandalf terms "fading" is experienced differently by observers — not invisibility per se but rather a shadowy form, as seen on Weathertop, and a mockery of form, as seen here at the gate. This aspect is emphasized again as the Witch-king threatens Théoden and Dernhelm.[24] Again it is the empty space between crown and mantled shoulders that is underscored in this description,[25] and it is this mockery of human form that provides at least part of the sense of horror the figure produces.[26]

That figure is again substantial, though not wholly visible. His shape is "huge and threatening" and certainly he attacks Dernhelm with a bodily force that is felt in an intensely physical way. Further, Dernhelm's and Merry's attacks on the Witch-king are clearly attacks on a physical being — though perhaps not a being entirely like most bodies.[27] Merry's stroke, we are told, penetrated the "sinew behind his mighty knee" (*RK*, V, vi, 117), a description that assumes, of course, that he has both sinew and knee. This description is expanded on in a later passage detailing the virtues of the sword Merry carries from the Barrow, a sword described as having the power to cut the "undead flesh" and defeat the "spell that knit his unseen sinews to his will" (*RK*, V, vi, 120). Again, this asserts the reality of both "flesh" and "sinews," but reiterates that the sinews are "unseen" as is the head and the rest of the body.[28] Further, the flesh is "undead," reminding us of the other effect wrought by the Ring, that of immortality, or rather perpetual continuance of life, an effect we have seen in Gollum and Bilbo, and to an extent in Frodo as well, though none of these have faded. And finally this description affirms explicitly the reality of the spell wrought by the Ring and Sauron simultaneously with the assertion that the spell can be broken — and that even a hobbit can do it.

The final image of the Lord of the Nazgûl as he lies defeated by Éowyn's and Merry's dual strokes, however, returns to the picture of emptiness that was such a source of horror initially, as the once powerful, menacing figure is reduced to a fading cry. Now, what was so sinister becomes ineffectual, standing as a symbol of defeat (*RK*, V, vi, 117). The voice becomes emblematic of the physical being here, and the fact that it is described as "faded" and "bodiless" is surely significant, as is the assertion that it "died, and was swallowed up." Thus the illusion of nothingness that is a source of horror in the physical appearance of the Ringwraiths and therefore a source of power becomes a sign of the emptiness at the core of their being.

This suggestion of nothingness is imaged as well in the eye of Sauron as Frodo sees it in Galadriel's mirror (*FR*, II, vii, 379).[29] As the Ringwraiths at Weathertop seem like "black holes" the image of the Eye grows out of a "black abyss" and contains within itself "a pit, a window into nothing." This emphasis on an essential emptiness at the center is startling, yet it too is not indicative of physical reality but symbolic reality, for in spite of the depiction in Peter Jackson's film version, Sauron's physical form is not that of a fiery, disembodied eye.[30] If it were, it would make his search for the Ring ludicrous, for a giant eye cannot wear a gold ring. The probing eye is part of the reality of Sauron's presence that Frodo sees here in Galadriel's mirror and later feels on Amon Hen (*FR*, II, x, 417) and again on the slopes of Mount Doom (*RK*, VI, iii, 213). Yet Sauron has a body, and one continuous with the body he bore at the end of the Second Age when Isildur cut Ring and finger from his hand, as Gollum asserts."[31] In spite of the reality of fading, the Ring is everywhere associated with embodiedness: it necessitates its wearer maintain a physical form in order to wield it, it bestows an immortality that is really a prolonging of the body without change or growth, and the invisibility it grants is simply that — invisibility, a trick of sight that can amaze or horrify, but cannot make the body insubstantial.[32] The Ringwraiths, like all physical beings, are bound by the limitations of time and space, and require steeds to move them across a physical landscape and enough time to do it in.[33]

If the Ringwraiths' insubstantiality is, then, essentially a cheat, an illusion, and the nothingness at their core symbolic of psychic emptiness rather than literal, then the transformation wrought by the Ring is one not of essence but illusion. This suggests we must consider the physical changes Frodo appears to undergo with great care, but before we do so we must look at the other main example of apparent bodily transformation in *The Lord of the Rings*: Gandalf. When Gandalf returns in *The Two Towers*,[34] he is physically different (*TT*, III, v, 98).[35] The references to whiteness and brightness in his physical description are striking, as is the suggestion of a new power, though on the face of it the main physical change is that his formerly gray hair has turned white. Yet suggestions of a more fundamental physical change accrue, including apparent transparency (*TT*, III, v, 103). The reference is startling, not least because the likening of a body to a container filled with light is not new, a point I shall return to shortly. The association with the sun is again made strongly; not only is his glance as piercing as the suns' rays but his gaze can take in those rays directly, rays that reveal a transparency about his body. And it is not only transparency that is hinted at — as Gandalf relates the tale of his return, he narrates Gwaihir's comments as he bears him back from the peak of Celebdil, comments which suggest Gandalf now lacks both weight and solidity (*TT*, III, v, 106).[36] Transparent, apparently weightless — clearly this body is different from the body Gandalf bore previously.[37] Further, it is fundamentally different from the transformed bodies of the Ringwraiths. Where their appearance is described in terms of blackness and shadow, Gandalf's is described in terms of whiteness and bright light. Both are somehow indistinct — both shadow and transparency suggest an appearance of insubstantiality — but they are opposite in register.

Aragorn, ever wiser than most, understands that there is something different about his friend and sometime companion, making the remarkable suggestion that in his new bodily form Gandalf is not restricted by the limitations of time and space (*TT*, III, v, 104). Gandalf, however, never replies to Aragorn's question. And certainly if he can travel in this manner, Gandalf never takes advantage of it, even when he is desperately pressed for time and in urgent need of speed. He travels with great swiftness on Shadowfax, but not beyond the physical limitations of his steed or the terrain. And to Gwaihir's remark that if he let Gandalf fall, he "would float upon the wind," Gandalf neither confirms nor denies the suggestion — but he does beg him not to, affirming that he "felt life in [him] again," implying, perhaps, that he believes were Gwaihir to let him fall, that would mean his death and Gandalf does not wish to die again. Or perhaps it implies only Gandalf's unwillingness to test the suggestion.

Whatever the case, the suggestion hangs there, unanswered, as does Aragorn's. Neither is ever tested. On the surface, Gandalf's transformation seems to have brought him to a place similar to that occupied by the Ringwraiths: Both clearly have bodies, but bodies that are somehow not entirely visible, whether transparent or shadowy. Yet there the similarity breaks down. Gandalf's transparency lets light shine through, collecting and holding it, while the shadowiness of the Ringwraiths is black. Gandalf's transparency and light-holding quality ebbs and flows, and it does so in response to the power he holds and commands, shining forth, for example, at Helm's Deep (*TT*, III, vii, 147) and in rescue of Faramir at Minas Tirith (*RK*, V, iv, 94).[38] The Ringwraiths have no such control over their bodily appearance; the fading wrought by the Ring they cannot reverse nor otherwise alter or control. In spite of the horror it produces their empty appearance is effect and sign of their subjugation,[39] not their power.[40] And the possibility remains, even if it is never more than suggestion, that Gandalf the White is no longer bound by the physical limitations of time and space — if he so wishes.

The bodily transformations of the Ringwraiths and of Gandalf, then, can be seen to occupy opposite ends of a spectrum.[41] Where on this continuum can one locate the transformation Frodo undergoes? Like the Ringwraiths, he is wrought upon by the Ring, but in many features his changed physical appearance seems more in line with Gandalf's. The first hint of physical change comes after his wound is healed at Rivendell. While he carries the wound during the long march from Weathertop, Frodo is described as weary, hurt, and wounded, but not otherwise physically changed in appearance. Though we are told that at times his sight is dimmed, his physical body appears unchanged. The wounded arm is described as cold and "lifeless" (*FR*, I, xii, 215), ominous words suggestive that there is something chilling about this wound and its effects, but while the arm feels different to Frodo, to the eyes of observers it is not described as looking different. Once we see Frodo's body through Gandalf's eyes, however, after he has been healed at Rivendell, there is a difference, and it is one of transparency (*FR*, II, i, 235).[42] The fact that the change is greater in the left hand suggests that the change is effected by the Morgul-knife and the wound in his left shoulder; one assumes the transparency Gandalf notes extends to Frodo's shoulder, presumably covered by clothing so that the hand is all that is visible, though it should be noted that Frodo put the Ring on his left hand at Weathertop.[43] However, the change Gandalf notes is of transparency, not shadowiness or emptiness — in fact, in spite of its apparent agent, Ring or Morgul-knife, the transformation seems more like that Gandalf himself will experience than it does like that of the Ringwraiths, in spite of Gandalf's assertion that Frodo was "beginning to fade" (*FR*, II, i, 231). The transparency is not further defined at this point, and when Gandalf does muse on Frodo's state, it is his future state he considers. He speaks of possibility, not fact or even probability. Yet what he envisions is striking, the possibility that Frodo "may become like a glass filled with a clear light." As Gandalf the White, his own hands are described as "filled with light as a cup is with water" (*TT*, III, v, 103). What Gandalf sees as a possibility in the transparency of Frodo's hand here will later be realized in his own.[44] The transparency Gandalf sees in Frodo's hand as he lies in Rivendell, apparently healed, is itself ambiguous, able to go, perhaps, in either direction: towards the transparency of the Ringwraith, figured as black shadow and emptiness, or the light-filled transparency Gandalf himself will come to embody.[45] Gandalf glances at the first, more dire possibility when he notes that Frodo's fate is at this point an unknown, beyond even the power of one as wise as Elrond to foretell, but he asserts that Frodo will come "Not to evil, I think." He *thinks*—he does not know, and even in discarding the likelihood of evil, he acknowledges it as a possibility.

In preferring the vision of light-filled transparency Gandalf observes that it will be a selective vision, one "for eyes to see that can," and even the hint of transparency about Frodo in Rivendell is apparent specifically "to the wizard's eye"—it is not a sight available to all. This recalls Frodo's ability to see the Ringwraiths as embodied beings when he has the Ring on. Yet the Ringwraiths are not the only creatures Frodo sees differently than others do, and not only when he is wearing the Ring. As they near the Ford of Bruinen and the wound is beginning to overtake him, Frodo has another experience that recalls his differing perception of the Nazgûl. As they make their way from Weathertop Frodo's sense of reality shifts. More and more the world around him seems to him "shadowy and dim" (*FR*, I, xii, 215) and he observes repeatedly a mist or shadow that darkens his vision and separates him from his friends (*FR*, I, xii, 217, 222).[46] Glorfindel's touch can alleviate these sensations somewhat, but cannot wholly relieve them. The reality of what is happening to him is expressed in a dream Frodo has during this time in which he walks in his garden in the Shire but finds the familiar sight "faint and dim"; instead it is the "tall black shadows" peering in that have the stronger reality (*FR*, I, xii, 215). The symbolism of the dream suggests not only the threat of the Black Riders but the change that he is experiencing as the real sensory world is becoming less accessible to him than the world the Ringwraiths occupy. "You were beginning to fade" Gandalf later asserts, and what he seems to mean is not that Frodo is becoming permanently invisible—at no point does he seem anything less than solidly visible to his companions—but that he is crossing over to that twilight world.[47]

In his initial description of fading Gandalf describes those who fade as walking "in the twilight under the eye of the dark power that rules the Ring" (*FR*, I, ii, 56). Significantly, Gandalf's wording here is somewhat ambiguous. It is not entirely clear who or what is "under the eye of the dark power that rules the Ring"—is it the entirety of that twilight world where those who fade walk or is it simply those who fade? In other words, is that twilight world the domain of Sauron or is it simply a world in which he is present and can exert power?[48] It is an important distinction and Frodo's experience as he begins to fade provides some clues. When Glorfindel rides up Frodo sees him differently than the others do, as a "white light" seen through a "thin veil" (*FR*, I, xii,

221).⁴⁹ While Glorfindel certainly makes a dashing figure with his streaming cloak and shimmering golden hair, to no one else does he seem as a container of white light. Later, from the other side of the Ford, Frodo sees "a shining figure of white light" that is contrasted with "small shadowy forms waving flames" (*FR*, I, xii, 227); when he questions Gandalf later Frodo maintains the contrast between Glorfindel and his other companions, characterizing the white figure as one that "did not grow dim like the others," asking if that figure was Glorfindel (*FR*, II, i, 235).

Gandalf's answers are instructive. There are two of them. The first, his answer to Frodo's direct question, affirms that the figure of white light was indeed Glorfindel: "Yes, you saw him for a moment as he is upon the other side: one of the mighty of the Firstborn. He is an Elf-lord of a house of princes" (*FR*, II, i, 235). Later in describing what happened at the Ford he relates that the Nazgûl were "dismayed" at seeing "an Elf-lord revealed in his wrath" (*FR*, II, i, 236). This twilight world, then, is one in which not only the Nazgûl have a solid reality, but also beings such as Glorfindel, and whereas the Ringwraiths are figured in terms of shadow, one such as Glorfindel is imaged in terms of white light. All this seems to suggest, then, that while the twilight world one enters under the influence of the Ring is a domain where Sauron exerts power, it is not one where he exercises exclusive power.⁵⁰ In telling Frodo that the Elves do not fear Sauron or the Ringwraiths Gandalf states that "those who have dwelt in the Blessed Realm live at once in both worlds, and against both the Seen and the Unseen they have great power" (*FR*, II, i, 235). Gandalf does not specify exactly what he means by "both worlds"⁵¹ but the implication seems clear: one is the normal sensory world experienced by most beings of Middle-earth but the other is another dimension where sensory experience and bodily manifestation work differently, the world experienced on "the other side," in the Blessed Realm. It is also by implication continuous with the twilight world entered by those who fade, or who wear the Ring. It is a world of the Unseen and includes both light and dark, both good and evil, just as the ordinary world of Middle-earth contains both.

In examining this response of Gandalf's, it is helpful to consider Tolkien's early drafts, for this key sentence is one that changed form as Tolkien developed his concept of the "twilight world." While the notion of the "twilight world" one enters when wearing the Ring is longstanding, the exact nature of that world, who else occupies it, and who wields power within it, were not immediately apparent to Tolkien. The conversation between Gandalf and Frodo at Rivendell went through several drafts, and while the idea that beings such as Glorfindel "live at once in both worlds" appears original, exactly what that means seems to have taken some working out. In the original rough draft, Tolkien referred to "[t]he Elven-wise ones, that came out of the Far West,"⁵² which became "those that have dwelt in the Blessed Realm beyond the seas"[53] in intermediary drafts before achieving its final, simpler form. Present from the original draft is the notion, surviving unchanged, that such beings "live at once in both worlds"[54]; original as well is the idea that such beings wield power in both worlds. However, the degree and nature of that power underwent subtle changes. Tolkien originally attempted to quantify that power stating that "each world has only half power over them, while they have double power over both."[55] This confusing phrase (recalling Bilbo's description of the knowledge and esteem in which he holds his fellow hobbits during his Party speech[56]) survived unchanged in the second draft[57] but was eventually abandoned in favor of the simpler version published in *The Fellowship of the Ring*. However, while we may be grateful that Tolkien eventually rejected the mathematical ingeniousness of half and double power and what that might mean in practice, it does suggest that at some point he did try to calculate both the power exerted by beings such as Glorfindel and the power both worlds held over such beings in comparative terms. Perhaps more significantly, he saw that power as bi-directional: those who have dwelt in the Blessed Realm both exert power and are subject to it, but their ability to wield power is greater. While he retains the idea that such beings exercise power over both worlds, he no longer attempts to quantify that power and suppresses the notion of such beings being acted upon, and he now characterizes the two worlds as "the Seen and the Unseen."

Tolkien tried out other phrases to describe that "other world." In early drafts of the material that became "The Shadow of the Past" Gandalf, in describing the effect of the Rings of Power on their possessors, refers to the normal sensory world as "the world under the sun"[58] and the other world as alternately "the phantom world" and "the world of shadow,"[59] before settling on "the other side in which invisible things move."[60] His rejection of terms like "phantom" and "shadow" to describe that world suggests that he did not want to associate it too strongly with Sauron, preferring the more neutral "in which invisible things move" and eventually, in the published version, the ambiguous "twilight," not solely dark nor light, but both. Further, note that the discussion here concerns Rings, plural. It took Tolkien some time to crystallize his concept of Frodo's Ring as the One Ring, the Ruling Ring, and for a while he considered many rings, wielded by many wearers. As he developed his concept of a "twilight world" associated with both the Rings of Power and Elf-lords like Glorfindel he considered a number of manifestations. At one point Tolkien, in a series of notes, suggests "perhaps Elves — if corrupted — would use rings differently: normally they were *visible in both worlds* all the time and equally with a ring they could appear *only in one* if they chose."[61] This was ultimately rejected, but it shows Tolkien wrestling with the concept of two worlds, and trying to work out the differing appearances bodies had within them, including the notion that some beings could control how they appeared in either world. It leads him to the notion that "the high-elves of the West, of whom some still remain in the middle-world, perceive and dwell at once both [in] this world and the other side without the aid of rings."[62] Those who have dwelt in the Blessed Realm occupy both realms simultaneously; for beings of Middle-earth such as Frodo, the Ring acts as the bridge, the conduit, between worlds, or, as Jane Chance suggests, the "Ring with its power to cross dimensions, as it were, carries with it the double danger of two worlds. When the other world becomes immanent within this one, it is through the ability to cross one mode into another, or the power of the Ring, that Frodo becomes apparent in that world, though invisible in the normal world."[63]

In his discussion of the bodily effects of Sauron's power, Nagy explains this other world as follows: "It does not matter that the 'invisible world' is there to duplicate the real one; its sights are articulated in physical terms as well and in terms of physical perceptions. This world is just as physically coded (and described) as the other; it is simply that it opens up this physicality/visibility for persons in privileged positions of power."[64] He is speaking here specifically of Sauron's power and his action on those who come under the influence of the Ring, as well as the kind of power the Ring allows its possessor to access; one of the ways the Ring works is by "taking the subject out of the visible and into the invisible world ... [into] this 'Other' reality."[65] However, it does not exclude the possibility that the invisible world can be inhabited by other beings of power. Though Nagy does not assert this specifically, it remains possible that the invisible world is not exclusively Sauron's domain. Nagy hints at this, in fact, in a note to his statement quoted above as he considers the implications of Gandalf's remark that "those who dwell in the Blessed Realm live at once in both worlds," though he is bothered by the fact that "even such elven-lords do not actually see Frodo wearing the Ring."[66] His is a valid concern, and it suggests that as the maker of the Ring and its ultimate master Sauron does wield a power in that other world that is different from that held by other beings who inhabit both worlds. The unseen world is not created by Sauron, who cannot create *ex nihilo*, and it existed before the Ring, but through the Ring Sauron gains access to that world and wields a power within it — but not over it.

In noting the hint of transparency about Frodo's appearance as he recovers in Rivendell and considering the possibility that he "may become like a glass filled with a clear light" (*FR*, II, i, 235), Gandalf seems to be thinking of elven-lords like Elrond and Glorfindel as those who may have that power of sight. What the reader later discovers, of course, is that Sam too has eyes that can see such things — and not only in the future. As Sam watches Frodo sleep in Ithilien, he is reminded of Frodo's appearance when he lay sleeping in Rivendell, recovering from his wound, when Sam sometimes observed a faint light shining within him. Sam notes that the light seems to shine more brightly now, and he describes Frodo's face as "peaceful" but "old," though also "beautiful," and still unmistakably Frodo's (*TT*, IV, iv, 260).[67]

Sam's eyes seem even more prescient than Gandalf's. He had seen, already, in the house of Elrond, not only transparency, but a light-filled transparency. What Gandalf saw only as possibility was already realized in Sam's sight. Further, as Sam saw it, it did not predominate in Frodo's left hand but was a quality of Frodo himself. And for Sam it is associated with the love he bears his master, a love that transcends the presence of the light. Sam's power of sight comes not from having dwelt in the Blessed Realm nor from having worn the Ring, which at this point in the narrative he has not yet done, but from his love for Frodo.[68]

So what, then, can we make of Frodo's transformation? In *The Lord of the Rings*, it is incomplete, potential and not actuality, and is associated with his suffering.[69] It is connected both with his experience of evil and his experience of love, and partakes of both fading, like that undergone by the Ringwraiths, and the more essential transformation typified by Gandalf. It brings him into the twilight world where the Nazgûl walk, but that world is one that other beings of power also occupy. The invisible world is a dimension where both light and dark obtain, and though it is originally strongly associated with Sauron and powers of darkness, there are hints that it is a realm where many powers walk. It is another reality, and one where physical, bodily transformation is possible. If the transformations undergone by Gandalf and the Nazgûl occupy a spectrum, as suggested earlier, then Frodo's transformation encompasses the range of their experiences, pulled first in the direction of the faded Ringwraiths but revealing the potential to move in the other direction: from shadow and darkness and subjugation towards light and brightness and power.

Notes

1. An early version of this essay was presented at the Forty-first International Medieval Congress at Western Michigan University, Kalamazoo, Michigan in May 2006 as part of Session 289: The Body in Middle-earth.

2. Italics original. A consideration of Tolkien's earliest drafts is instructive. While he does not use the term "fade" the earliest sketching out of these ideas contains the main features that survive into the published work: "the Ring overcomes you, you yourself become permanently invisible — and it is a horrible cold feeling. Everything becomes very faint like grey ghost pictures against the black background in which you live ... you are under the command of the Lord of the Rings." *The Return of the Shadow*, 75. Not only are the concepts of permanent invisibility and being under the power of Sauron already present, but so too is the germ of the idea of existing in two worlds at once.

3. As Steve Walker notes, "Tolkien makes words serve entirely new semantic functions, as when *fade* comes to mean, in addition to its usual denotation, the specific psychophys-

iological withering induced by wearing the ring." See Steve Walker, *The Power of Tolkien's Prose: Middle-earth's Magical Style* (New York: Palgrave, 2009), 125.

4. As related to the action of the Ring; Tolkien uses "fading" twice earlier in the chapter in reference to the coming of night: "a cool pale evening was quietly fading into night" (*FR*, I, ii, 55) and "twilight was fading" (*FR*, I, ii, 55). This is a more ordinary usage of the term, though it could be argued that given the importance of the term in *LotR*, its use here just prior to Gandalf's introduction of "fading" in its specialized sense, is significant. Tolkien also uses the term "fade" in conjunction with the elves and the decay of Arda, specifically in reference to their diminishment since the Elder Days and the possibility of their further diminishment. For example, Sam begs for "a tale about the Elves before the fading time" (*FR*, I, xi, 203) and Galadriel refers to the possibility that "Lothlórien will fade, and the tides of Time will sweep it away" if Frodo should succeed in destroying the Ring (*FR*, II, vii, 380). Similarly, Elrond believes that if the One Ring is destroyed "the Three will fail, and many fair things will fade and be forgotten" (*FR*, II, ii, 282). Whereas the One Ring causes "fading" in the wearer the three Elven rings arrest the "fading" that results from the process of time.

5. *OED Online*, s.v. "fade, *v.*'" *The Oxford English Dictionary*, 2d ed. (Oxford University Press, 1989), accessed March 12 2011, http://www.oed.com/view/Entry/67571?rskey=J5pNyt&result=6&isAdvanced=false. As is well known, Tolkien worked at the *OED* from 1918–20. For a discussion of Tolkien's work on the *OED* and how it influenced his vocabulary, see Peter Gilliver, Jeremy Marshall, and Edmund Weiner, *Ring of Words: Tolkien and the Oxford English Dictionary* (Oxford: Oxford University Press, 2006).

6. While none of these definitions are explicitly negative, some critics do view invisibility in this way, focusing on its unnaturalness. For Robley Evans "invisibility is a perversion of the natural state of things, and is associated with evil and disorder." See Robley Evans, *J.R.R. Tolkien*, Writers for the 70's (New York: Warner, 1972), 51.

7. "Twilight" is another loaded term in Tolkien's usage, particularly in its capitalized form, associated not only with the opposition of light and dark but with the process of time whereby the progression of a people or Middle-earth itself is likened to the progress of a natural day (from morning to night). For example, Faramir calls the Rohirrim "Middle Peoples, Men of the Twilight" in opposition to "the High, or Men of the West, which were Númenoreans" and "the Wild, the Men of Darkness" noting that the Númenoreans like himself "are become Middle Men, of the Twilight, but with memory of other things" (*TT*, IV, v, 287). It is an image of deterioration here, yet Tolkien is not consistent in his usage. At other times he associates Twilight with the Elder Days in the beginning of the world; for example, in his discussion of the evolution of Trolls and their speech he contrasts the more recent descendents with "the older race of the Twilight" and refers to "their beginning far back in the twilight of the Elder Days" (*RK*, App. F, 410). In yet another related sense he associates Twilight specifically with the elves in opposition to both the Shadow of Mordor and the mortality of men, most clearly in the part of the Tale of Aragorn and Arwen found in Appendix A (*RK*, App. A, 337–44).

8. Verlyn Flieger, *Splintered Light: Logos and Language in Tolkien's World*, 1983, rev. ed. (Kent, OH: Kent State University Press, 2002), 157.

9. Sniffing or snuffling and the Black Breath are also features, both of which imply sensory presence.

10. This is the aspect of the Ringwraiths most emphasized by critics. To Katharyn Crabbe they are without form, "strange, formless, black-cloaked riders"; to Patricia Meyer Spacks they are without faces, "the faceless Black Riders, the Ringwraiths, who are faded into physical nothingness by their devotion to evil"; to Robley Evans they are shadows, "frightening shadows swooping about the dark roads and skies of Middle-earth"; to Roger Sale they are "the very definition of shadow." See Katharyn W. Crabbe, *J.R.R. Tolkien*, 1981, rev. ed. (New York: Continuum, 1988), 67; Patricia Meyer Spacks, "Power and Mean-

ing in *The Lord of the Rings,*" Understanding The Lord of the Rings: *The Best of Tolkien Criticism,* ed. Rose A. Zimbardo and Neil D. Isaacs (Boston: Houghton Mifflin, 2004), 52–67 at 56; Evans, *J.R.R. Tolkien,* 50; and Roger Sale, "Tolkien and Frodo Baggins," *J.R.R. Tolkien,* Modern Critical Views, ed. Harold Bloom (Philadelphia: Chelsea House, 2000), 27–63 at 41.

11. Though most of the description is little changed from the earliest draft, the reference to the blackness of the Ringwraiths' shadows is a later addition (see *The Return of the Shadow,* 185). It is unlikely that Tolkien is thinking of black holes in the astronomical sense, regions of intense gravitational pull from which light cannot escape, however appropriate that might be to the imagery of light and dark that pervades *The Lord of the Rings*; according to the *OED* that meaning is first recorded only in 1968. The older meaning (eighteenth century), however, of prison may have been in Tolkien's mind. See *OED Online,* s.v. "black-hole, n.," *The Oxford English Dictionary,* 2d ed. (Oxford University Press, 1989), accessed 3 January 2012, http://www.oed.com/view/Entry/19728?rskey=jhKCJM& result=1&isAdvanced=false.

12. Tolkien's revisions here are noteworthy; the original draft reads: "For while the ring was on, you yourself were in the wraith-world, and subject to their weapons" (*Return of the Shadow,* 208); Tolkien has reduced Frodo's presence in the wraith-world by half and eliminated the idea that only when he wears the Ring is he subject to the weapons of the Nazgûl. The wording is changed to that in the published version in the second draft. See 217n6.

13. As Christopher Tolkien observes: "The significance of the Ring, in its power to reveal and be revealed, its operation as a bridge between two worlds, two modes of being, has been attained, once and for all" (*The Return of the Shadow,* 189).

14. It should be noted that when the Ring slips on Frodo's finger at the Prancing Pony there are no Nazgûl present so there are no faded beings to describe. Further, though they bear aspects in common, wearing the Ring is NOT equivalent to fading. See *FR,* I, ix, 172. Gergely Nagy also notes the difference of Frodo's experience at the Prancing Pony when "Frodo accidentally slips on the Ring" referring to it as "a clever narrative device on Tolkien's part." Gergely Nagy, "The 'Lost' Subject of Middle-earth," *Tolkien Studies* 3 (2006): 57–79, at 76n31. It is a point well taken; certainly Frodo's experience of the wraith-world is much more effectively revealed at Weathertop than at the inn in Bree.

15. "Shadows are the absence of light and so don't exist in themselves, but they are still visible and palpable just as if they did." T.A. Shippey, *The Road to Middle-earth,* 1982, rev. ed. (Boston: Houghton Mifflin, 2003), 146–7. As Shippey has suggested elsewhere, "Wraiths then are not exactly 'immaterial' ... in this they are like shadows." T. A. Shippey, "Orcs, Wraiths, Wights: Tolkien's Images of Evil," *J.R.R. Tolkien and His Literary Resonances: Views of Middle-earth,* ed. George Clark and Daniel Timmons, Contributions to the Study of Science Fiction and Fantasy 89 (Westport, CT: Greenwood Press, 2000), 183–98, at 190.

16. Shippey, *The Road to Middle-earth,* 148.
17. Ibid., 142.
18. Ibid., 140.
19. Ibid., 141.
20. Ibid., 145.
21. Ibid., 214.
22. The original draft contains already the image of the crown set atop "no visible head"; the later addition of the reference to his unseen mouth serves to further emphasize the horror already present in the original conception (see *The War of the Ring,* 337).
23. *The Annotated Hobbit,* 136, 226.
24. *RK,* V, vi, 115. Though the wording undergoes revision, all the elements are present in the original draft of this scene (see *The War of the Ring,* 365). The idea that the black

mantle covers emptiness has already been suggested; Gandalf tells Frodo that "they wear [black robes] to give shape to their Nothingness" (*FR*, II, i, 234).

25. Shippey refers to "a state of nothingness like that of 'the haggard king' of Minas Morgul" (*Road*, 148).

26. In discussing the gradual way Ringwraiths are revealed to the reader, Walker observes how "a black hole absence become[s] a terrifying presence" and notes the effectiveness of "this gradual incarnation of bodiless presence." See Walker, *The Power of Tolkien's Prose*, 24.

27. Thus I take issue with critics who assert that the Nazgûl are formless or without bodies; Steve Walker, for instance, claims, "Even without a body, the Lord of the Nazgul, however much 'Death' in the abstract, is very much an individuated being" and Robley Evans focuses on "the dissolution of form into formlessness, in his figure of the Black Prince, the leader of the Ringwraiths or Nazgûls, who leads the attack on Minas Tirith; the Black Prince wears a crown but no face is to be seen beneath it." See Steve Walker, *The Power of Tolkien's Prose*, 57 and Robley Evans, *J.R.R. Tolkien*, 134. Much better is Michael Stanton who affirms, "Yet they have physical bodies — those black robes they wear enclose something — they have voices," and Tom Shippey, who asserts that though the Lord of the Nazgûl "is also in a sense insubstantial, like a shadow ... yet there must be something there." See Michael N. Stanton, *Hobbits, Elves, and Wizards: Exploring the Wonders and Worlds of J.R.R. Tolkien's* The Lord of the Rings (New York: Palgrave, 2001), 136; and Shippey, "Orcs, Wraiths, Wights," 190.

28. I take issue with Shippey's characterization of the Ringwraiths here as fleshless, though elsewhere Shippey discusses the ambiguous nature of their physical reality: "The Ringwraiths are fleshless and 'faded' from addiction, and privation, and from being caught by Sauron" (Shippey, *Road*, 369n6 to chap. 5). In a similar vein, Nagy asserts that "the Nazgûl, subjects to the Nine Rings of Men, are totally under Sauron's control but have no physical bodies any more" (Nagy, "The 'Lost' Subject," 65). I would qualify that by asserting rather that they do have bodies, but not in the same physical sense as they did before they faded.

29. This passage is, according to Christopher Tolkien, almost unchanged from its original draft except that in the earlier version "the black slit of its pupil" is described as opening on a "pit of malice and despair" rather than "a pit, a window into nothing" (*The Treason of Isengard*, 254). The change aligns with both Tolkien's emphasis on emptiness and an unwillingness to assign an emotion like despair so explicitly to Sauron.

30. Against this idea there is the description of Sauron provided by Gollum in "The Black Gate Is Closed" that I reference here as well as Tolkien's discussion of "the incarnation of great spirits in a physical and destructible form" (Tolkien, *Letters*, 332). In addition Tolkien refers to Sauron as being "diminished" by the destruction of Númenor, and needing "time for his own bodily rehabilitation" (Tolkien, *Letters*, 280).

31. *RK*, IV, iii, 250. Nagy is somewhat unclear on this question of Sauron's physical form, referring at one point to the "lack of the physical appearance that he cannot assume any more" ("The 'Lost' Subject," 69) and in a note referencing the assertion in *The Silmarillion* that Sauron "could never again appear fair to the eyes of Men (*Sil*, 347)" (78n45); perhaps Nagy's point is not that he cannot assume a physical appearance but that Sauron is limited as to the nature of that appearance.

32. Throughout *The Hobbit* in his many adventures wearing the Ring, Bilbo is frequently concerned that he will be discovered by someone stumbling into him; this comes up again in an early draft of *The Lord of the Rings* when Bingo (an early version of Frodo) hides in a cupboard after disappearing from his party in order "to avoid being bumped into, being totally invisible" (*The Return of the Shadow*, 33). This distinction is not made carefully enough by some critics; Robley Evans, for example, claims that "[t]o become invisible is to be without form" (153); this is not specific enough, as the invisible lack only *visible* form.

33. As Tom Shippey notes, "the Ringwraiths do have physical capacities ... [the Lord of the Nazgûl] and his fellows can act physically, carrying steel swords, riding horses or winged reptiles, the Lord of the Nazgûl wielding a mace. But they cannot be harmed physically, by flood or weapon — except, coincidentally, by Merry's blade of Westernesse, wound round with spells for the defeat of Angmar: it is the spells that work, not the blade itself" ("Orcs, Wraiths, Wights," 190, 191).

34. He does not simply return, but is "sent back" (*TT*, III, v, 106), an important distinction.

35. His earliest notes outlining the story from Moria show Tolkien developing these ideas: "[Does?] Gandalf *shine* in the sun. He has a new power after overcoming of Balrog? *He is now clad in white*" (*The Treason of Isengard* 211, italics original).

36. When Gandalf calls Gwaihir to him in *The Return of the King* he notes that "[y]ou will not find me a burden much greater than when you bore me from Zirak-zigil, where my old life burned away" (*RK*, VI, iv, 227–8). See *Sauron Defeated* 45 for an earlier draft, repeated almost word for word.

37. Anne C. Petty observes that "he is light, nearly transparent, as the original Gandalf has been burned away." See Anne C. Petty, *One Ring to Bind Them All: Tolkien's Mythology* (Tuscaloosa: University of Alabama Press, 1979), 66.

38. These scenes are present in early outlines and drafts, consistent with other notes and drafts that suggest Tolkien's concept of Gandalf returning with new power imaged through a shining whiteness was longstanding; see *The War of the Ring* 274 and 326.

39. "While the nine are loyal thanes indeed, the reciprocity, the key aspect of the *comitatus* relationship symbolized through ring-giving, has been lost, and the Ring becomes a symbol not of mutual obligation but of servitude." Yvette Kisor, "Ring-giving," *The J.R.R. Tolkien Encyclopedia: Scholarship and Critical Assessment*, ed. Michael Drout (New York: Routledge, 2006), 570–1, at 571.

40. Nagy suggests that "the body is accordingly distorted by the physical effects of the Ring, one of which is the conferral (or illusion) of bodily power" ("The 'Lost' Subject," 64). Christopher Vaccaro observes that "supernatural and unnatural, [the Ring] promises greater power while offering, in reality, an undoing of one's being and one's accomplishments." Christopher Vaccaro, "Rings," *The J.R.R. Tolkien Encyclopedia: Scholarship and Critical Assessment*, ed. Michael Drout (New York: Routledge, 2006), 571–2, at 572. For a further consideration of the effects of the One Ring, see William Senior, "One Ring, the," *The J.R.R. Tolkien Encyclopedia*, 483–4.

41. In a page of notes that includes the phrase "Wizards = Angels," possibly the first written record of this concept, Tolkien penned a series of notes on what happened to Gandalf after the fall in Moria and what he is like when he reappears. It includes the following, italics original: "*He has thus acquired something of the awe and terrible power of the Ringwraiths, only on the good side. Evil things fly from him if he is revealed — when he shines*" (*The Treason of Isengard*, 422). This description suggests that Tolkien indeed saw the transformations undergone by Gandalf and the Ringwraiths as akin, but opposed.

42. In his description of his father's second draft of this chapter, Christopher Tolkien notes that the concept of Frodo's changed physical appearance was apparently a later addition (*The Return of the Shadow*, 212).

43. *FR*, I, xii, 208. Flieger observes this as well, noting that "the hint of transparency suggests that Frodo may be fading because of his contact with evil, because of the wound from the Morgul-knife and the burden of the Ring. This is to some extent the case, of course, although it is not the whole story" (Flieger, *Splintered Light*, 157).

44. In her assessment of this scene, Flieger connects Gandalf's consideration that Frodo may become "like a glass filled with a clear light" with the Phial of Galadriel, which contains "the light of Eärendil's star, set amid the waters of [Galadriel's] fountain" (*FR* II, viii, 367). That light is the last remaining Silmaril and "the Phial as it is — a glass filled

with clear light — is in its being what Frodo may attain in his becoming. It anticipates his future" (Flieger, *Splintered Light*, 159).

45. Paul Kocher sees Frodo's transparency as associating him with the elves: "Although Frodo cannot actually turn into an elf, his innate spiritual kinship to them is revealed by his physical state after recovery from the wound inflicted by Angmar on Weathertop." Paul H. Kocher, *Master of Middle-earth: The Fiction of J.R.R. Tolkien* (New York: Ballantine, 1972), 118.

46. Tolkien's revisions emphasize the progression of Frodo's descent into this shadowy world; the first two of these references are not present in earlier drafts (see *The Return of the Shadow*, 193).

47. In discussing the importance of the early drafts of this chapter, Christopher Tolkien notes: "Moreover the idea has now entered that the wound of the Ring-wraith's knife produces, or begins to produce, a similar effect to that brought about by putting on the Ring" (*The Return of the Shadow*, 199). The effect on his perception is a lasting one, as Frodo notes along the journey (*FR*, II, iv, 325).

48. Too often critics have failed to appreciate this ambiguity and simply assumed that this twilight world is Sauron's, ignoring the presence of other beings like Glorfindel within it. So, for example, Randel Helms, who speaks of "putting on the Ring and thereby entering their realm and power, the dominion of Sauron," and Robley Evans, who claims, "The Ring 'stretches' the soul until it passes invisible barriers into the realm of the Dark Lord," and identifies that realm as the domain of those who are slaves to Sauron, asserting that "the servants of the Ring enter a world invisible to those as yet free." In a similar vein, Paul Kocher sees Mordor as "blend[ing] imperceptibly into the wraith world of the Ring [because] ... the Ring, being only an extension of Sauron's personality and power, makes a world like its master's" asserting unequivocally that Sauron has created a region "to house himself and those he has made like him." See Randel Helms, *Tolkien's World* (Boston: Houghton Mifflin, 1974), 84; Evans, *J.R.R. Tolkien*, 154 and 174; and Kocher, *Master of Middle-earth*, 62.

49. Significantly, this sentence is absent from early drafts of this scene, indicating that Tolkien's concept of the twilight world one enters when wearing the Ring and/or fades was one that developed over time (see *The Return of the Shadow*, 194).

50. Paul Kocher sees the power of Glorfindel and his ilk as indicative of how the "elves have learned to penetrate also into that ambiguous region where life verges upon death. The Valar have taught them how" (99).

51. Stanton takes him to mean the two geographic realms mentioned or implied, that of Eldamar and Middle-earth, observing that "those who have lived in the West can easily live in two realms, spiritually astride the limits of mere geography" (101).

52. *The Return of the Shadow*, 212.
53. Ibid., 364.
54. Ibid., 212, 364.
55. Ibid., 212.
56. "I don't know half of you half as well as I should like; and I like less than half of you half as well as you deserve" (*FR*, I, i, 38).
57. *The Return of the Shadow*, 364.
58. Ibid., 258, 270n19.
59. Ibid., 270n19.
60. Ibid., 258.
61. Ibid., 225, italics original. This occurs in a series of notes Tolkien entitled "Queries and Alterations." It includes as well the comment "See note about their 'being in both worlds'" but as Christopher Tolkien notes, no such note can be found, and he associates it with Gandalf's comment to Frodo at Rivendell that the Elves "live at once in both worlds," discussed above. See notes 52–57.

62. Ibid., 260-1.
63. Jane Chance, *The Lord of the Rings: The Mythology of Power*, 1992, rev. ed. (Lexington: University Press of Kentucky, 2001), 46.
64. Nagy, "The 'Lost' Subject," 65.
65. Ibid., 67.
66. Ibid., 76n32.
67. This passage appears to be absent from the earliest known draft; see *The War of the Ring*, 134. It seems likely that both this passage and the corresponding one in which Gandalf observes Frodo's "transparency" in Rivendell (*FR*, II, I, 235) are late additions.
68. Critics have tended to associate Frodo's transparency solely with fading and his role as Ring-bearer, and have not made the connection to the light-filled transparency exhibited by Gandalf after his transformation. Tom Shippey sees the fact that "Frodo [is] starting to become transparent" as indicative of his "becoming a wraith" and Rose Zimbardo notes that "even after the Ring has been destroyed, the effects of having exercised its power remain. Frodo, who has endured the full temptation of the Ring's power and who has had to war with himself before it could be destroyed, has become, as Sam tells us, almost transparent." See Shippey, "Orcs, Wraiths, Wights," 192 and Rose A. Zimbardo, "Moral Vision in *The Lord of the Rings*," *Understanding* The Lord of the Rings: *The Best of Tolkien Criticism*, ed. Rose A. Zimbardo and Neil D. Isaacs (Boston: Houghton Mifflin, 2004), 68–75 at 73. While I agree that the change in Frodo's appearance is related to the morgul-knife wound and his bearing the Ring, that is, as I argue in this essay, only part of the story.
69. Flieger sees this potentiality as more tenuous, finding in the designation of "The Sea-bell" as *Frodos Dreme* the possibility that what awaits Frodo across the sea is not healing but rejection; see Flieger, *Splintered Light*, 161–5. This is an important and recurring idea in Flieger's work; see also *Interrupted Music: The Making of Tolkien's Mythology* (Kent, OH: Kent State University Press, 2005), 82–3 and *A Question of Time: J.R.R. Tolkien's Road to* Faërie (Kent, OH: Kent State University Press, 1997), 207–25 and 238–9.

Works Consulted

Anderson, Douglas A. *The Annotated Hobbit*. Boston: Houghton Mifflin, 2002.
"black hole, *n.*" *OED Online*. December 2011. Oxford University Press. Web. 3 January 2012. http://www.oed.com/view/Entry/19728?rskey=jhKCJM&result=1&isAdvanced= false.
Chance, Jane. *The Lord of the Rings: The Mythology of Power*. Lexington: University Press of Kentucky, 2001.
Crabbe, Katharyn W. *J.R.R. Tolkien*. 1981. Rev. ed. New York: Continuum, 1988.
Evans, Robley. *J.R.R. Tolkien*. Writers for the 70's. New York: Warner, 1972.
"fade, *v.*¹" *OED Online*. December 2011. Oxford University Press. Web. 3 January 2012. http://www.oed.com/view/Entry/67571?rskey=J5pNyt&result=6&isAdvanced=false.
Flieger, Verlyn. *Interrupted Music: The Making of Tolkien's Mythology*. Kent, OH: Kent State University Press, 2005.
———. *A Question of Time: J.R.R. Tolkien's Road to* Faërie. Kent, OH: Kent State University Press, 1997.
———. *Splintered Light: Logos and Language in Tolkien's World*. 1983. Rev. ed. Kent, OH: Kent State University Press, 2002.
Gilliver, Peter, and Jeremy Marshall, and Edmund Weiner, eds. *Ring of Words: Tolkien and the Oxford English Dictionary*. Oxford: Oxford University Press, 2006.
Helms, Randel. *Tolkien's World*. Boston: Houghton Mifflin, 1974.
Kisor, Yvette. "Ring-giving." *The J.R.R. Tolkien Encyclopedia: Scholarship and Critical Assessment*, ed. Michael Drout, 570–1. New York: Routledge, 2006.

Kocher, Paul H. *Master of Middle-earth: The Fiction of J.R.R. Tolkien.* New York: Ballantine, 1972.
Nagy, Gergely. "The 'Lost' Subject of Middle-earth." *Tolkien Studies* 3 (2006): 57–79.
Petty, Anne C. *One Ring to Bind Them All: Tolkien's Mythology.* Tuscaloosa: University of Alabama Press, 1979.
Sale, Roger. "Tolkien and Frodo Baggins." *J.R.R. Tolkien.* Modern Critical Views, ed. Harold Bloom, 27–63. Philadelphia: Chelsea House, 2000. Excerpt from *Modern Heroism: Essays on D. H. Lawrence, William Empson, & J.R.R. Tolkien*, ed. Roger Sale. Berkeley: University of California Press, 1973. Rpt. in *Tolkien and the Critics: Essays on J.R.R. Tolkien's "The Lord of the Rings,"* ed. Neil D. Isaacs and Rose A. Zimbardo, 247–88. Notre Dame: University of Notre Dame Press, 1968.
Senior, William. "One Ring, the." *The J.R.R. Tolkien Encyclopedia: Scholarship and Critical Assessment*, ed. Michael Drout, 483–84. New York: Routledge, 2006.
Shippey, Tom A. "Orcs, Wraiths, Wights: Tolkien's Images of Evil." *J.R.R. Tolkien and His Literary Resonances: Views of Middle-earth*, ed. George Clark and Daniel Timmons. Contributions to the Study of Science Fiction and Fantasy 89, 183–98. Westport, CT: Greenwood Press, 2000.
_____. *The Road to Middle-earth.* 1982. Rev. ed. Boston and New York: Houghton Mifflin, 2003.
Spacks, Patricia Meyer. "Power and Meaning in *The Lord of the Rings*." *Understanding* The Lord of the Rings: *The Best of Tolkien Criticism*, ed. Rose A. Zimbardo and Neil D. Isaacs, 52–67. Boston: Houghton Mifflin, 2004. Rpt. of "Ethical Patterns in *The Lord of the Rings*." *Critique* 3 (1959): 30–42. Rpt. in *Tolkien and the Critics: Essays on J.R.R. Tolkien's "The Lord of the Rings,"* ed. Neil D. Isaacs and Rose A. Zimbardo, 81–99. Notre Dame: University of Notre Dame Press, 1968.
Stanton, Michael N. *Hobbits, Elves, and Wizards: Exploring the Wonders and Worlds of J.R.R. Tolkien's* The Lord of the Rings. New York: Palgrave, 2001.
Tolkien, J.R.R. *The Return of the Shadow*, ed. Christopher Tolkien. The History of *The Lord of the Rings* 1. The History of Middle-earth 6. Boston: Houghton Mifflin, 1988.
_____. *Sauron Defeated*, ed. Christopher Tolkien. The History of *The Lord of the Rings* 4. The History of Middle-earth 9. Boston: Houghton Mifflin, 1992.
_____. *The Treason of Isengard*, ed. Christopher Tolkien. The History of *The Lord of the Rings* 2. The History of Middle-earth 7. Boston: Houghton Mifflin, 1989.
_____. *The War of the Ring*, ed. Christopher Tolkien. The History of *The Lord of the Rings* 3. The History of Middle-earth 8. Boston: Houghton Mifflin, 1990.
Vaccaro, Christopher. "Rings." *The J.R.R. Tolkien Encyclopedia: Scholarship and Critical Assessment*, ed. Michael Drout, 571–72. New York: Routledge, 2006.
Walker, Steve. *The Power of Tolkien's Prose: Middle-earth's Magical Style.* New York: Palgrave, 2009.
Zimbardo, Rose A. "Moral Vision in *The Lord of the Rings*." *Understanding* The Lord of the Rings: *The Best of Tolkien Criticism*, ed. Rose A. Zimbardo and Neil D. Isaacs, 68–75. Boston: Houghton Mifflin, 2004. Rpt. in *Tolkien and the Critics: Essays on J.R.R. Tolkien's "The Lord of the Rings,"* ed. Neil D. Isaacs and Rose A. Zimbardo, 100–108. Notre Dame: University of Notre Dame Press, 1968.

Frodo's Body
Liminality and the Experience of War[1]

ANNA SMOL

"I am wounded by knife, sting, and tooth, and a long burden," says Frodo on the way home to the Shire, aptly summarizing his major injuries inflicted by the Ringwraith, Shelob, Gollum, and the carrying of the Ring (*RK*, VI, vii, 268). His quest involves other physical trials as well, such as capture by the Watcher at the gates of Moria, bruising by the orc-chieftain's spear in the mines, and whipping by orcs in the Tower of Cirith-Ungol. Although all of the hobbits share some of Frodo's earlier trials in the Old Forest and in the Barrow, and other characters are wounded or killed in the course of the story, it is Frodo who is the real target, as Glorfindel gently reminds him in their flight from the Black Riders. In *The Lord of the Rings*, no one except Frodo is subjected to a continuous physical assault throughout the story of the quest and its aftermath. Frodo's body is under attack: externally, it is wounded, injured, and maimed; internally, it is subjected to a battle of will as Frodo strives to control his own sensations and his own actions in opposition to the lure of the Wraith-world and the domination of the Ring.

Frodo's body is the territory on which he battles to maintain his physical and psychological integrity. As a liminal figure — as someone who has crossed the boundary between a familiar peaceful world and an unknown world of war — Frodo struggles to resist the disintegration of other boundaries that shore up his sense of self: those between human and animal, animate and inanimate, life and death. The relentless process of "fading" that Frodo undergoes reveals the permeability of those boundaries, bringing him face to face with the uncanny and the abject. His experiences have much in common with those of World War I soldiers who, in their writings, describe physical and psychological trauma and the difficulty of reintegrating into peacetime society. Like many soldiers who left home to witness almost indescribable horrors on the Front, Frodo enters a liminal space where he is suspended on the thresholds of other worlds and where we watch his gradual disintegration and inability to reconstitute himself after the quest.

Critics have pointed out how Tolkien's experiences in the Battle of the Somme influenced his fiction,[2] and Tolkien himself suggests in the second edition of *The Lord of the Rings* that readers look to the First World War as a possible biographical reference point.[3] Although Tolkien only published the book in 1954, he wrote most of it during the Second World War when two of his sons were serving in the military, and in his letters to them he relives some of his own wartime memories. The "animal horror" of trench life is an experience Tolkien shared with other World War I writers.[4] Most of them recorded their reactions and memories either during the war or in the twenties and thirties. Publishing decades later, Tolkien may be considered, as Brian Rosebury suggests, the last of the Great War writers.[5] These writers varied, of course, in their attitudes to the war and in their beliefs about life. As John Garth points out, Tolkien resists in many ways the dominant literary model of trench writing, which features disenchantment, passive suffering, and ironic and cynical action, in order to acknowledge, for example, heroism, honor, and camaraderie.[6] Nevertheless, because Tolkien and other writers were generally exposed to similar situations and endured similar trials, common elements of their experiences emerge in their poetry, letters, stories, or diaries. Tolkien's *The Lord of the Rings* adds another genre to this roster of Great War literature, which allows us to see how the war experience could be transformed to become myth. And even though Tolkien explores different attitudes to war in a range of his characters, it is particularly in the character of Frodo that Tolkien gives us an intimate representation of the physical and psychological experience of war.

If any character in the book is to represent the "lost generation" of young men who went to war in 1914, it is Frodo who, even before he becomes involved in the quest, is already marked by loss. The first time that we hear about Frodo is when we are told of Bilbo's adoption of him, the need for which is explained by some of the patrons at *The Ivy Bush* who, many years later, still have not tired of gossiping about the loss of Frodo's parents in a boating accident. The first direct words that Frodo speaks in the story are "Has he gone?" in reference to Bilbo's disappearance,[7] followed by a wish that he could have seen him off, and he spends the next day giving away designated gifts to friends and relatives and fending off others who are attempting to plunder his property. The dispersal of these material goods does not affect Frodo's physical well-being at this point, but the process of loss that is established in these early chapters does contribute to the establishment of an elegiac mood that will be the prevailing atmosphere in which Frodo's body is gradually divested of normal life.

In order to show adequately the physical deterioration that Frodo's body undergoes, Tolkien establishes a contrasting beginning point so that we can judge how the healthy, red-cheeked hobbit can become the blind, twitching, slumped and starved body, unable to move on his own, on Mount Doom. The hobbit who laughs with pleasure at the smell of mushrooms rising from Mrs. Maggott's basket or the lively fellow who saves the best wine for himself and his closest friends, downing the last glass of Old Winyards with gusto as he says good-bye to Bag End becomes, when he reaches his goal, the being who cannot smell, taste, hear, or see anything except the Wheel of Fire. Gandalf and Bilbo might have thought very highly of Frodo, but he starts off the quest being critical of his reflection in the mirror, while Pippin teases him about having to lose some weight. After the first day of tough walking and a night of uncomfortable sleep out in the wild, Frodo regrets the comfortable bedding he left behind and wishes he had decided to drive. As he does throughout the story, Tolkien makes us well aware of how much food, water, and sleep the travelers can get; in early days, the hobbits encounter few problems in obtaining these necessities. They even eat two evening meals in one night, one at the Maggott farm and then another plentiful spread at Crickhollow. The excess of water in the Crickhollow baths, with Pippin spouting fountains of water onto the floor, contrasts sharply with the parched conditions that Frodo and Sam will eventually endure in Mordor. Perhaps barely realizing it, the reader is shown in the opening chapters a plenitude of such physical comforts that will be pared down gradually until all are lost and will need to be restored.

Even these glimpses of normal hobbit pleasures occur under the pall of Gandalf's warnings and the increasing dread of the Black Riders. As the story proceeds and the dangers become clearer and more immediate, scenes of ordinary life are fleetingly recalled in the midst of events that are far more dire. These memories form brief elegiac images of what has been lost. Like Aragorn's elegiac verses, modeled on the Old English elegy "The Wanderer," which lament the loss of a previous life, Frodo's recall of elements from the past that are now missing heightens the sense of loss in the present. Frodo's memories typically focus on the Shire, Bag End, and Bilbo. In the Mines of Moria, Frodo's thoughts move backwards in time to when he lived peacefully in Bag End with Bilbo. Wounded and pursued by Black Riders, Frodo dreams faintly that he is back in the Shire in his garden. Later, imprisoned in the orc tower, Frodo tries to recreate images of his past in the Hobbiton. Frodo's memories coalesce around the natural world of the Shire and its associations with Bilbo. Even after waking up in Rivendell, Frodo feels that his reflection in the mirror resembles his younger self who used to go hiking with Bilbo in the Shire, only with the difference that his eyes reveal a thoughtfulness that comes from experience. In contrast, Sam's memories typically include family and friends; when Sam's thoughts turn to Bywater, he thinks of Rosie and his father and sister.

Sam's memory of his past life even intersects, we might assume, with Frodo's; waking Frodo in the Tower of Cirith Ungol, Sam attempts to recreate the cheerfulness of his interactions with his master back in Bag End. However, there is a difference between the two. Sam's memories generally include people and a life that are still potentially waiting for him; Frodo's elegiac memories are more attached to the land of the Shire itself, which will be severely damaged, and to Bilbo, who is no longer there. While both Sam's and Frodo's recollections remind us of a pastoral Shire, Frodo's memories, unlike Sam's, do not return to his group of friends but to Bilbo and a youthful, innocent past that Frodo has already lost.

The evocation of a pastoral ideal as a meditation on loss is a centuries-old literary theme, but one particular historical moment in which the pastoral acquired significance was the First World War. According to literary historian Paul Fussell, in British Great War literature reference to the pastoral was a way to comfort oneself with memories of home as well as a way "to hint by antithesis at the indescribable."[8] What most often seems to be indescribable is the horror of the dead or wounded body. For example, in the poem "To His Love," Ivor Gurney skirts round what has happened to a killed soldier, first by only hinting through negative statements at the condition of the dead man: "His body that was so quick/Is not as you/Knew it"[9] but then pleading with increasing fervency to "cover him over" with flowers, pastoral images that will hide the reality of the dead body. Even then, however, what the speaker is trying to forget escapes into words in the very last lines:

> Cover him, cover him soon!
> And with thick-set
> Masses of memoried flowers —
> Hide that red wet
> Thing I must somehow forget.[10]

What Gurney and other soldiers in the First World War had to face — and perhaps try to forget — were unprecedented numbers of casualties. Because of the military development of weapons that proved "more effective instruments of dismemberment"[11] than ever before, fragmented bodies were a constant feature of the landscape, more likely to turn a pastoral scene into what Samuel Hynes calls "landscape-with-corpse," a typical wartime revision of the conventions of Romantic nature poetry.[12] The horror of witnessing the dismembered body is unmistakable in scenes such as that described by a desperate soldier in Edmund Blunden's "Third Ypres":

> For God's sake send and help us,
> Here in a gunpit, all headquarters done for,
> Forty or more, the nine-inch came right through,
> All splashed with arms and legs, and I myself
> The only one not killed nor even wounded.[13]

But it is not only the dead who presented a dreadful vision of fragmented bodies. Wounded soldiers with amputated limbs, some of them fitted with prosthetics, became a common sight during and after the war. According to historian Joanna Bourke, amputations in the First World War were performed "on a scale never seen before, or since," not only because of the nature of injuries suffered in battle and doctors' eagerness to experiment with new techniques but also because surgeons' stations could not be kept clean, leading frequently to gas gangrene, with amputation as the only possibility of survival.[14] Tolkien's vision of the War of the Ring includes nightmare elements that prominently feature dismembered bodies. Gollum reminds us that Sauron's hand had only four fingers due, of course, to Isildur's cutting off of the Ring (*TT*, IV, iii, 250), although Sauron's presence is generally felt more as a disembodied enemy than someone with actual limbs; he is seen as the Eye of Sauron or heard through the creature who serves as the Mouth of Sauron. Needless to say, Nine-Fingered Frodo does not escape maiming, and neither do some of Tolkien's other heroes who appear in earlier stories, such as Beren Erchamion and Mædhros in *The Silmarillion*. The frequent occurrence of dismemberment in Tolkien's work seems to be a constant feature of his imagination, quite possibly a reflection of the reality of injuries caused by shelling in the trenches.

The ubiquity of body parts in the landscape of war renders the earth ambivalent, according to Eric Leed, who discusses how soldiers might look to their entrenchment in the ground as a place of safety but at the same time would encounter death there either in killed bodies around them left to decompose in the earth or in the sight of the enemy rising out of their trenches in the ground. Such ambivalence, according to Leed, is part of the liminality of war, a transitional space in which clear distinctions are transgressed, such as those between life and death or self and other.[15] What might seem like a familiar landscape becomes, for example, "landscape-with-corpse"; it becomes unfamiliar, giving rise to a feeling of uncanniness. The uncanny as a response to the trauma of war, particularly the dismemberment of the body, is discussed by Roxanne Panchasi, who points out that Freud's essay on the uncanny was published in 1919, "at the same moment that European society was faced with a profound collective experience of the uncanny, confronted by the loss of millions of lives and the return of huge numbers of wounded and mutilated soldiers from battle."[16] Freud defines the uncanny as a core of feeling that can give rise to fear, dread, or horror in presenting us with something unfamiliar (*unheimlich*) that was once familiar (*heimlich*) but then repressed or surmounted. Panchasi identifies the fragmented body in war as uncanny: "Human bodies were transformed into 'uncanny' parts, recognizable as arms, hands or fingers because of certain familiar cues, but terrifying because they had taken on a character all their own. Wrenched from the soldier's body, these parts functioned in wartime and postwar narratives as signposts of death and destruction strewn across the physical and psychic landscapes of battle."[17] Freud points out that the uncanny arises when distinctions between categories such as animate and inanimate, human and automaton, life and death become uncertain, and as literary examples he cites "dismembered limbs, a severed head, a hand cut off at the wrist ... feet which dance by themselves ... all these have something peculiarly uncanny about them, especially when, as in the last instance, they prove capable of independent activity in addition."[18] Frodo also encounters a landscape that rapidly becomes *unheimlich*, populated by uncanny body parts, in the Barrow-downs episode, his first major test in which he must surmount his fear of death and act to bring his friends back from the threshold of death to life.

John Garth sets up the scene on the Barrow-downs as a transmuted version of Tolkien's war experience: the unidentified dikes and trenches in the countryside and the chalk terrain are reminiscent of the Somme landscape, while the fog that entraps and paralyzes the hobbits, along with the pale green light that they see in the Barrow, are similar to accounts of poison gas attacks.[19] Garth's general view of the episode as being uncharacteristically surreal for Tolkien can be explained, however, if one looks at how the landscape suddenly transforms from pleasant and pastoral to frightening and unfamiliar, leading to the introduction of the uncannily animate body parts that threaten to attack Frodo.

The surrealism of the Barrow-downs scene, in fact, is what most closely identifies this episode as a typical Great War narrative. The hobbits are making their way through a pleasant, grassy landscape of hills and valleys and feeling heartened by their progress — as Tom Shippey points out, "they are still moving in a very familiar landscape, all of it within a day's walk of Tolkien's own study."[20] When they decide to stop for a rest, however, Frodo catches a glimpse of standing stones that looked teeth rising up out of gums. This sense of the landscape as a grotesque human part is reinforced when the hobbits sit down for a meal by one of these stones that looks like a finger guarding something or warning onlookers. Not heeding any disquieting feelings, the hobbits eat and then unintentionally fall asleep. They wake suddenly and are alarmed to find a transformed landscape in which they feel trapped in a fog that encloses them. In this suddenly unfamiliar landscape, Frodo loses the other hobbits. When he calls out to them, he hears a deep voice that seems to come from the ground. The voice of the barrow-wight telling Frodo that he is waiting for him seems to be the voice of the landscape waiting to capture and betray Frodo. Verlyn Flieger aptly captures the eeriness of this scene in which "dreaming and waking are interwoven"[21] in her description of the barrow-wight as "a dark presence out of a dream lost on waking, a vague, ominous faceless memory on the edge of awareness, sensation without shape or substance."[22]

In this waking nightmare, Frodo finds his friends arrayed as for a funeral, with a longsword lain across their necks. Listening to the wight's incantation, Frodo feels dread, and then he is faced with a macabre representation of the uncanny: a long arm walking on its fingers, heading towards the unconscious Sam. Frodo's own fear of death and horror of possibly witnessing the dismemberment of his friends, surfacing at this moment, is aptly represented by the uncanny. His first instinct is to save his own life by running away, but he surmounts his fears and forces himself to act by cutting off the hand of the crawling arm. The severed body part that seems to act on its own raises questions about the boundaries between animate and inanimate, life and death, human and inhuman. This surreal experience is over when Frodo calls on Tom Bombadil, who like a parent dispelling nightmarish visions, brings the hobbits out of the dark and carries the hidden treasures in the Barrow into the light of the sun. Frodo's last glimpse of the interior of the barrow offers an image of the uncanny losing its power; the severed hand is still twitching, but presumably it is finally destroyed when Tom goes back in to stomp on it.

Bombadil's freeing of the treasure, leaving it for anyone to take who wishes, is his final step in breaking its long spell; through this act, he allows the unfamiliar to become an acknowledged part of the world again, thus destroying its uncanny powers. Although Frodo and his friends have encountered several trials before the barrow-wight, only at the end of this episode, when they are given knives by Tom Bombadil, do they realize that fighting might have to be part of their adventure. Frodo's encounter here with the uncanny constitutes his first real taste of the experience of war.

At this point, Frodo still leads the company and remains unharmed, but later in the story, when Frodo's physical and psychological well-being begin to deteriorate, and only he and Sam are left with Gollum as their guide, they encounter another uncanny landscape that Tolkien admitted was at least partly based on No Man's Land: the Dead Marshes.[23] Once again, John Garth sets out some of the parallels between the Dead Marshes and the battlefield of the Somme, including the dead bodies left behind on the field, visible in the mud and ooze of a scarred landscape, and the acute fear of surveillance as the Eye scans the landscape,[24] while Barton Friedman cites several British descriptions of No Man's Land that are strikingly like Tolkien's.[25] Decomposing and dismembered bodies were common sights that haunted soldiers: "When you see millions of the mouthless dead/Across your dreams in pale battalions go"[26] writes Charles Hamilton Sorley about the phantoms that so many soldiers had to deal with — often phantoms of the men they had killed, or of the friends that they had lost. Tolkien's friend, G.B. Smith writes of his own ghosts in his poem "Memories":

> Shapes in the mist, ye see me lonely,
> Lonely and sad in the dim firelight:
> How far now to the last of all battles?
> (Listen, the guns are loud tonight!)[27]

As Roxanne Panchasi notes, "Frightful images of the undead, phantoms, and animated corpses appeared throughout biographical, autobiographical, and fictional accounts of the war."[28] Fussell's account of how various superstitions and legends of supernatural events flourished on the Front only emphasizes further the liminality of No Man's Land, a place where the boundary between the familiar and the unfamiliar, the natural and the supernatural disintegrates. In fact, Hynes calls some of the descriptions of the place "oddly phantasmagorical, because their reality is."[29]

As Frodo and Sam follow Gollum into the Marshes, carefully picking their way through the mud and water in the dark, Sam sees some ghostly, mysterious lights. After Gollum explains that the dead faces Sam sees in the pools belong to people of many races who fought a great battle in that place hundreds of years ago, Sam wonders what kind of evil power has created apparitions of the dead who cannot really be there. Sméagol cannot give him an answer, leaving the question uneasily open, without an explanation of how something that seems so unnatural could occur.

In this uncanny confrontation between natural and supernatural, alive and dead, another threshold is crossed as well, the boundary between one's own body and what is outside it. Eric Leed notes that many soldiers complained of the smell of the dead, the presence of corpses, the rats that fed on them, and the inability to keep clean: "Pollution and the sense of having no control over the access of substances, animals, and other men to one's own body"[30] could become a serious concern, as in the case that Leed cites of a soldier who fell into the distended abdomen of the corpse of a German soldier, swallowing the entrails: "It would be difficult to find a more complete violation of the distinctions which separate the dead from the living, friend from enemy, rotten from edible, than this experience which left a lasting mark of pollution upon the young officer."[31] Although Tolkien's description of events in the Dead Marshes is not as graphically disgusting, Sam does experience — through sight, smell, and touch — the horror of coming close to the dead bodies in the water: his hands fall into a smelly, sticky substance, and his face comes close to the water, which looks like a dirty window. Sam springs back with a cry of horror when he realizes that there are dead faces in the water.

In discovering the dead bodies through Sam's point of view, we share his horror at the pollution of the self coming into contact with them. What becomes apparent, however, is that Frodo has already found the dead bodies. Moments before Sam sees the dead faces, he comes across Frodo who is looking at the lights, his hands covered in watery slime from the pools. Frodo responds to Sam's call as if he is being awakened from a dream, and when Sam asks who or what the dead faces could be, Frodo answers almost as if he were chanting poetry, in lines that feature balanced rhythms and repetitions, internal rhymes, and alliterative accents:

> They lie in all the pools, pale faces, deep deep under the dark water. I saw them: grim faces and evil, and noble faces and sad. Many faces proud and fair, and weeds in their silver hair. But all foul, all rotting, all dead [*TT*, IV, ii, 235].

Unlike Sam who immediately recoils and wants to move on, Frodo seems to linger over the uncanny vision. The water and slime on his hands are the signs of his transgression of the boundaries between the living and the dead; he speaks as if he too has become a phantom like those he has seen under the water. Without a doubt, Frodo has touched the "antipastoral deathscape" of war[32]; in fact, it is not just a "landscape-with-corpse" but a place in which the margins between land and corpse are fused so that the landscape itself becomes a sick, corrupted body. Wilfred Owen's description of No Man's Land — "It is pock-marked like a body of foulest disease and its odour is the breath of cancer"[33] — is similar to Tolkien's Dead Marshes and the "Nomanlands" (*TT*, IV, ii, 239) leading up to Mordor, which are described as a diseased landscape. Here, the mounds of rock, which are compared to rows of gravestones, recall the sight of war cemeteries.

The loathsome quality of the landscape and the defilement that Sam feels in his contact with it characterize abjection. Julia Kristeva defines the abject as that which is violently rejected or expelled in order to maintain a sense of self, of the "I." According to Kristeva, the abject is "[a] massive and sudden emergence of uncanniness, which, familiar as it might have been in an opaque and forgotten life, now harries me as radically separate, loathsome. Not me."[34] The corpse provides one example of abjection, states Kristeva: "refuse and corpses *show me* what I permanently thrust aside in order to live,"[35] but the corpse does not respect boundaries: "It is death infecting life."[36] Sam's horror and sense of pollution are feelings associated with abjection, as is the emotion underlying one trench soldier's description of the typical corpse in No Man's Land as "a fetid heap of hideous putrescence."[37] Kristeva emphasizes the abject's permeable borders; abjection, she writes, is caused by "what disturbs identity, system, order. What does not respect borders, positions, rules. The in-between, the ambiguous, the composite."[38] In the Dead Marshes, the dead faces do not seem to respect boundaries between the dead and the living, between inside and outside, between landscape and self, not even the usual borders between different sides of the battle between good and evil. Frodo reports seeing different races together in the Dead Marshes, a fact that Gollum confirms. But the ambiguity of abjection, its "in-between" quality, means that it creates a shifting boundary line that is necessary to define the self, or subject. Frodo, standing in the Dead Marshes with water and slime dripping from his hands, is drawn to the abject, lured into becoming abject himself, which would signify his total loss of self, of the "I" that defines itself against the borders of abjection.

There is, however, another figure of abjection in the scene, and that is Gollum, who first comes into full view in the preceding chapter, "The Taming of Sméagol." Loathing the hobbits' civilized, cooked food, this creature who was once something very like a hobbit but now has devolved into an animal-like being compared variously to an insect, a spider, a frog, and a dog, Gollum embodies further qualities of abjection as defined by Kristeva. He cannot even speak of himself with the first-person pronoun "I" and his idiosyncratic speech, characterized by "a general phonetic and syntactic simplicity," "repetitiousness," and "body-determined sounds," as Gergely Nagy points out,[39] suggests that Gollum is regressing to what Kristeva would call an archaic space that is largely pre-linguistic, before the boundaries between self and other are established. Expressing similar views of Gollum, though in different terms, Verlyn Flieger points out: "as the narrative progresses, Frodo gradually comes apart, his nature splitting into component light and dark. We see this process externally embodied in his relationship with Gollum, and even more vividly in Gollum's relationship with himself."[40] Sam's revulsion makes him plead for the necessity of expelling Gollum from their company, but Frodo, now lapsing into the "in-between," recognizes a connection with Gollum, which the narrator comments on when telling us that their minds could reach one another. According to Flieger, Gollum "is Frodo turned inside out."[41] Frodo's attempts, described by Gergely Nagy, to reconstitute Gollum as Sméagol succeed up to a point; Frodo's desire to bring "Sméagol" back arises from his fear that he too will lose himself the way Gollum has. That danger is present for all three of the company in the landscape of war, particularly the Dead Marshes. They must follow Gollum's style of stooping and crawling like animals, unsuccessfully avoiding the cesspools until they are as foul-smelling and slimy as he is. Sam sardonically thinks to himself that they will all become Gollums sooner or later if they have to continue in this way.

The events in the passage of the Dead Marshes epitomize what is happening to Frodo throughout the quest: physically and psychologically, the boundaries of his self are disintegrating as he gets closer to Mount Doom. Frodo retreats more often to a world of sleep and dream, while his waking self finds even walking under the weight of the Ring more difficult. In the trek through the marsh, a landscape that marks a transition to the gates of Mordor, Frodo's condition worsens significantly. Sam becomes increasingly anxious about Frodo, keeping him in front of him because he often stumbles or lags behind, and Frodo becomes more aware of the weight of the Ring and the surveillance of the Eye. It is not surprising that this chapter narrating

Frodo's encounter with the dead also includes his first direct experience of the Wraiths on wings, airborne enemies who swoop down on the company, and ends with him and his companions hiding in a hole, entrenched, as it were, against their unseen enemies.

The dream-like condition in which Frodo encounters the war-dead is an altered state of being which usually signifies that Frodo has drifted into another level of reality where he has access to a vision different from what the ordinary, conscious self can see or understand. Although Frodo's dreams, as Flieger points out, vary in significance from being prophetic to being caused merely by anxiety,[42] he does lapse more frequently into a dream state as the story progresses. Near the beginning of the quest, Frodo makes decisions as the leader of the small band of hobbits, who cheer him on as their captain, but by the time that company has dwindled to just Frodo and Sam, Sam increasingly must take the lead, his point of view coming to the fore. In numerous episodes, the onward march can only begin after Sam wakes Frodo up, bringing him back to the world their conscious selves inhabit. The effect is to make Frodo seem like a ghost of the self that Sam once knew, like someone who is being drawn into a phantom world that is elsewhere. Gandalf calls the condition "fading," and he means more than just Frodo's gradual withdrawal from the narrative focal point.[43]

"Fading" is a term that encompasses Frodo's physical and psychological disintegration, and its process is most extensively described in the chapters recounting Frodo's wounding by a Morgul knife on Weathertop and the ensuing events until he reaches Rivendell. Here, the descriptions of Frodo's lifeless arm going cold and his impaired vision insistently draw our attention to the frailty of the flesh, as in many accounts of World War I casualties. For example, Wilfred Owen's well known poem "Dulce et Decorum Est" details the effects of a poison gas attack on one soldier without his protective mask who is flung into a wagon where his companions have to "watch the white eyes writhing in his face" and his blood "[c]ome gargling from the froth-corrupted lungs"[44] as the troops continue on their march.

Whether tended to in the trenches or watched over in a bed, as in Siegfried Sassoon's "The Death-Bed," in which the speaker observes a man's pain that "[l]eapt like a prowling beast, and gripped and tore/His groping dreams with grinding claws and fangs,"[45] these writers are intensely aware of the fragility of the body as they are forced to witness almost unspeakable scenes of suffering and to feel the futility of not being able to allay their companions' pains. Similarly, Tolkien frequently reminds us of Frodo's physical condition: his shivering body lying on the ground, his numb left arm, the icy grip of pain in his side and shoulder, and his intermittent consciousness which sometimes only allows him to see dimly a shadowy landscape around him. Aragorn and the hobbits try to care for Frodo after he is wounded by the

Nazgûl blade, bathing the injury, watching over him, treating him with *athelas*, and trying to get Frodo as quickly as possible to Elrond, who has more potent means of curing the poison. The long march of Frodo's companions to the point of exhaustion, the anxiety over Frodo's worsening condition, and at the end the sprint to escape the enemy and to reach Elrond's house all convey the same kind of desperation expressed by soldiers trying to save the wounded in hopeless circumstances.

Of course, circumstances do seem much more hopeless and Sam's despair completely warranted when he and Frodo are in Mordor. Here, Sam must watch Frodo's decline being unable to do anything to stop the cause and very little to alleviate the symptoms as he watches Frodo slumped over with his head between his knees, his arms dangling beside him, his hands twitching with exhaustion. Sam's attitude is very like the dominant view in World War I literature, where the shattered body, not a glorified heroic one, is kept at the forefront of the imagination, and there is little that can be done to respond to that physical reality.

Tolkien's description of Frodo's condition also helps to explain how Frodo is affected psychologically by Sauron's weapons. The poison in the Morgul knife blade aids in the work that the Ring is already performing by luring Frodo across a threshold leading into the Wraith-world, where all autonomy is surrendered to Sauron. Before the attack on Weathertop, Frodo jokes to Pippin that he is losing weight and doesn't want to become a Wraith. Aragorn reacts quickly to stop Frodo's flippant comments, since he alone of the company has some knowledge of the nature of the Wraiths; he later explains that they are drawn by the Ring, and that their perceptions differ from that of normal beings. The Wraiths see our world as if through a veil, with the forms of ordinary beings casting shadows in their minds, but darkness reveals things to them that ordinary beings cannot see. The power of the Ring, when Frodo puts it on, thrusts him past that veiled threshold and allows him to see clearly into the Wraith-world with altered vision. As if reversing black for white, he sees beneath their black clothing to their white faces and grey hair, their grey clothes and silver helmets and swords. The vision is gone once the Ring is taken off, but the knife poison allows the process of "wraithing," as Tom Shippey calls it,[46] to continue at a slower pace. Frodo's vision worsens, as if a mist is blocking his vision, and when he finally collapses shortly after Glorfindel's arrival, he feels pain and cold and sees a shadow between him and the rest of the company. We see Frodo in transition here, sliding into the world of darkness belonging to the Wraiths; and only when Glorfindel tends to his wound does he slip back into the world of ordinary perception where he can see his friends more clearly. Frodo wavers on the boundary line between normal reality and the Wraith-world; it is significant that he is in a dreamlike state when he envisions the Black Riders looking for him. At the same time, however, he also has an enhanced perception of Glorfindel's elvish nature when he sees a white light shining through him as if through a thinly veiled barrier.

Frodo's vacillation between two worlds leaves him open to the call of the Wraith-world, where selfhood is subsumed under the power of Sauron. With the Black Riders in pursuit, Glorfindel commands Frodo to ride on, but he is seized by an inexplicable hesitation and while the landscape becomes misty in his eyes, he recognizes that the Nazgûl are commanding him to wait. Though he breaks away, the pursuing Riders again command him to stop at the Ford of Bruinen, a boundary marking Elrond's territory, and by this point, Frodo can no longer refuse. The fact that, even so, he still tries to resist makes this one of Frodo's greatest heroic moments. First, he cries out in a shrill voice telling the Riders to go back, and then, with the advancing Riders laughing at him and still calling, Frodo only manages the same command in a whisper. Finally, with the Riders steadily coming towards him calling for the Ring, Frodo's last response is to vow by Elbereth and Lúthien the Fair that the Riders will not have him or the Ring, though the physical effort of resistance overwhelms him and he falls senseless to the ground. Frodo needs more than his own powers to defeat such enemies, as becomes evident in later encounters in Shelob's Lair, in the Orc Tower, and on Mount Doom.

Frodo's acquiescence to the silent commands of the Riders and then his conscious resistance dramatize the liminality of his position. Wavering on the boundary between two realms, the Wraith-world and Rivendell, Frodo must exert his greatest powers of will in order to make a choice, but the dangers of surrendering his autonomy to the overpowering forces of Sauron are abundantly clear, and the battle is far from over, since the poisoned knife blade is only one weapon that attempts to accelerate the slower and more insidious work of the Ring itself. By the time Frodo is imprisoned in the Tower of Cirith Ungol, whipped and tormented by his orc captors, he has even less control of his own will and his own perceptions. There, Sam finds Frodo wounded and stripped of everything he owns. When he hears Sam, Frodo wants to know if he's still dreaming; he does not seem to know which reality he is perceiving, thinking that the orc that was whipping him has transformed into Sam. In the red glare of the orc lamp, Frodo looks as if he is on fire, an appearance so unlike the white light that Sam has seen elsewhere shining from within Frodo that it seems entirely fitting that moments later Frodo should suffer from a vision in which he thinks that Sam has changed back into an orc, and Frodo accuses him of stealing the Ring. When his eyes clear and his perceptions return to reality, Frodo asks for forgiveness, correctly attributing his outburst to the greater hold that the Ring now has on him. Garth sees this episode as evidence that Frodo is suffering from a split personality due to the Ring's mastery of his perceptions.[47] The split enables Frodo's self to slide over the threshold separating his conscious reality from the world of Mordor. But the closer Frodo gets to Mordor and the longer he carries the Ring, the more likely he is to cross that threshold into Sauron's power, possibly forever. Early on, the Ring's power is almost unnoticeable — at Bag End, when Frodo makes a movement to throw the Ring away he finds that he puts it back in his pocket instead — but in front of the gates of Minas Morgul, his will is totally overmastered, and he stumbles forward with his hands held out and his head drooping from side to side. At this point, the Ring's power manifests itself by transforming Frodo into a grotesque automaton, an uncanny creature who, though alive, is under someone else's control as if he were a puppet or a machine.

John Garth identifies the Ring, "a device for magnifying power and achieving domination," as "the arch–Machine" — a "symbol of the evils that Tolkien saw at their worst in the mechanized First World War."[48] Samuel Hynes points out that one of the dominant ideas to emerge in World War I narratives is that war is a machine that victimizes its soldiers.[49] In his letters, Tolkien applies the term "Machine" to the Rings of Power because, like all "machinery," they "attempt to actualize desire, and so to create power in this World" which Tolkien believes will inevitably "turn to new and horrible evil."[50] Although not referring to the First World War but to the Second, Tolkien declared in his letters that at the end of it there was "only one thing triumphant: the Machines."[51] This image of the machine in war writing, according to Eric Leed, refers mainly to the issue of "human and individual autonomy."[52] Fighting an unseen enemy through increasingly mechanized weapons of war, or advancing into No Man's Land under orders only to be shot down by the enemy's machines, many trench soldiers felt dehumanized, as if they had become unwilling and inevitable victims of an immense power. Similarly, Tolkien's Ring is a device, a machine that drains individuals of their ability to act on their own. It promises the actualization of desire, but its possessors find that instead of satisfying their own wishes, the Ring consumes their autonomy in order to fulfill its own desire (which is one and the same with Sauron's): to dominate all life.[53] Gandalf's prognosis for any ringbearer is not hopeful, revealing that in the end the dark power will triumph no matter how strong a resistance one can muster.

Gollum puts it another way, crying out that Sauron will eat everyone if he gets the Ring. The idea of Sauron, through the Ring or his agents, eating or consuming his victims is consistently maintained as the dominant image of how selfhood is surrendered. For example, Frodo lurches grotesquely and through no will of his own towards the gate of Minas Morgul, which looks like a mouth about to devour him. The monstrous Shelob, though not interested in Sauron's machinery, serves his purposes by feasting on living things. And finally, the entrance into Mount Doom looks like a mouth that leads into the dark, hot, rumbling interior of the mountain. In this heart of Sauron's realm, Sam hears the noises of what sound like engines, leaving the impression that he and Frodo are being swallowed by a living entity that is at the same time a machine.[54] Even in a relatively early adventure, after Frodo's wounding on Weathertop, Sam's comic poem about troll cannibalism reflects in a localized, milder way the desire of evil to consume its victims; by the end of the novel, Grima Wormtongue's behavior in Bag End represents a loathly, degraded version of the same act.

Near the end of the quest, Frodo is almost totally consumed, physically and psychologically, by the Ring. No elegiac memories can comfort him; he has been stripped of everything he once had; all of his senses are destroyed, and his vision has been drawn far past the threshold of Sauron's realm, with no veil to separate him from it. Yet, even so, Frodo resists, much as he did when the Black Riders were beckoning to him, but now only in a barely audible whisper, repeatedly calling on Sam to control his own body for him by holding his hand. Although Frodo is not taking a stand with sword drawn as he did at the Ford of Bruinen, his attempts to prevent his hand from touching the Ring even when he has lost autonomy over his own body must be acknowledged as an immense effort of heroic will.

When Sam does take Frodo's hands, Tolkien gives us a brief but exemplary moment that negotiates equality between the two, the culmination of a process that has been slowly ongoing throughout the quest in which Frodo's self is emptied and Sam gradually takes his place. The handholding gesture is reminiscent of the medieval ritual of swearing fealty to a lord: traditionally, the vassal would kneel before his lord and put his hands together in a prayer position; the lord would put his hands around the vassal's as a sign of protection and exert some pressure to show his dominant position; the vassal would then kiss the lord's hands. Tolkien rewrites the ritual so that Frodo and Sam act as both vassal and lord. Sam kneels, but he is still above Frodo, who has been stricken to the ground. Then, "Sam took his master's hands and laid them together, palm to palm, and kissed them; and then he held them gently between his own" (*RK*, VI, iii, 220). Sam, in the role of the lord, takes the hands offered to him, the hands, paradoxically, of his "master." It is Sam, however, who kisses the hands as a vassal would, signifying love and service. And Sam does not exert pressure to indicate his dominance but holds Frodo's hands gently. This unique version of the lord — vassal relationship contrasts starkly with a previous episode, which Jane Chance calls "the most medieval, feudal, scene of oath-swearing in the epic"[55] when Gollum grovels at Frodo's feet to swear that he will never let Sauron have the Ring. At that time, Sam imagines that Frodo has turned into a tall and commanding lord with a whining servant below him. Such hypermasculine domination, however, is not a feature of Frodo and Sam's relationship generally, and certainly not at this point in their journey. On Mount Doom, Frodo's acknowledgement of Sam as his leader and protector is a precursor to the moment when social status and power are completely exchanged in Frodo's final bequest to Sam, when he calls him his heir and leaves everything from his past and in his future to him.

This exchange between Frodo and Sam on Mount Doom is also part of the last stage of their journey to destroy the Ring, by which point Sam in effect stands in for the body that Frodo barely seems to inhabit. Not only does Sam control Frodo's hands, but he also becomes his eyes as he searches for the doorway, and his legs as he carries him on his back. Their physical closeness reaches this point after gradually increasing over the course of the quest. By the last night on Mount Doom, looking on the shivering Frodo, Sam regrets leaving his blankets behind while trying to warm Frodo's body. This act is a long way from when Sam blushes in embarrassment at stroking Frodo's hand after he awakens from his illness in Rivendell, but as the quest progresses, such gestures become part of their tender physical interactions. They fall asleep hand in hand, they creep through Shelob's lair holding hands, they kiss each other's hands, and Frodo sleeps on Sam's lap on the Stairs of Cirith Ungol or in his embrace in the Tower. In Tolkien's delineation of the close bond between Frodo and Sam, characterized by tender gestures, he represents yet another aspect of the experience of war. Sam takes on the nurturing role of Frodo's batman, not only packing supplies and preparing food but also fighting and standing ready to die by his master; in fact he experiences a great crisis when he struggles to wrench himself away from Frodo's side in Shelob's lair after he thinks that Frodo is dead. Fussell points out that such strong feelings were not unusual, often developing into romantic "crushes" particularly between an officer and his batman[56]; other critics have examined how in such relationships the binary oppositions defining gender roles and sexual identities blurred during the war, resulting in a queering of heteronormative masculinity.[57] According to Santanu Das, for example, gestures of friendship between men in the trenches can best be understood in terms of a continuum that "goes beyond strict gender divisions, sexual binaries, or identity politics."[58] Examining how "non-genital tactile tenderness" was expressed by men in the First World War, Das finds "norms of tactile contact between men changed profoundly" and that this "new level of intimacy and intensity"[59] represented a "very different order of male experience, one that accommodated fear, vulnerability, support, succor, and physical tenderness."[60] In addition to this new kind of emotional experience, trench friendships could also constitute a new kind of social experience. As Mark T. Hooker points out: "The change in the relationship between Sam and Frodo as the quest progresses reflects a change in the English class structure that was brought about by World War I."[61] The love between Frodo and Sam, then, develops in the liminal space of war, where the boundaries between master and servant, between conventional masculine and feminine roles, and between homosexual and heterosexual identities begin to crumble.

Sam's gentle touching of Frodo, as opposed to the rougher pawing of Gollum, present two parallel modes of relating to Frodo. Just as Frodo wavers on the boundary between the Wraith-world and Rivendell, his disintegrating self has two competing claims made on him, the abjection of Gollum or the love and protection of Sam. Moments before entering the Sammath Naur, Frodo says farewell to Sam, looking at him as if he were far away. In leaving Sam and entering the heart of Sauron's realm, Frodo chooses to claim the Ring. However, in an ironic reversal of expectations, it is Gollum who saves Frodo and ensures the destruction of the Ring. In a matter of moments, the madness of Gollum prevails, Frodo's body is maimed, and circumstances change so suddenly that victory over Sauron is assured. Fussell discusses the irony of circumstances that characterizes many war narratives, where nothing turns out quite as it was expected,[62] and such irony defines the climactic point of Tolkien's quest story as well. At that moment, the abject Gollum is violently expelled, leaving Frodo with a clearer sense of the boundaries of his own self. It is left to Sam to comment, though perhaps too optimistically, that Frodo had once again returned to his old self of the Shire. Frodo tells Sam that he's glad to be there with him, but he also reminds Sam that they should forgive Gollum, who played his part in the destruction of the Ring. Though Gollum is gone, Frodo has an abiding sense of his own abjection, as it was embodied in Gollum, and he follows Gandalf's lead in showing mercy and pity, feelings that Sam is only beginning to understand.

What Sam does see and understand more easily, however, is the nobler, self-sacrificing side to Frodo. In Rivendell, Gandalf's concern over Frodo's "fading" leads him to discern a transparency about his injured hand. Gandalf muses to himself that Frodo may become a kind of vessel filled with a light. Gandalf seems to recognize that, even in the best of circumstances, Frodo will become transparent, like a glass, as if emptied of his present contents. The loss of self that this entails may be replaced by light, a consistent symbol in Tolkien's mythology for the divine. Flieger discusses how Frodo is a microcosm for Tolkien's larger mythology, extending beyond *The Lord of the Rings*, in which light is continually fragmented, with the hope that it may be remade."[63] Sam is one person who does have the eyes to see this light in Frodo. In Ithilien, he looks at Frodo asleep and remembers watching him in Rivendell as well; in both instances, Sam can see that light. Unlike Gandalf, Sam does not have a clear explanation for the phenomenon, though he recognizes that he loves Frodo. Sam can see Frodo with this visionary power; for example, at the entrance to the Cracks of Doom, Frodo appears to Sam as if he is dressed in white robes with a wheel of fire at his breast. The figure in white recalls the light that shines from within, but the image could also be reminiscent of traditional iconography of Christ with a bleeding heart. John Garth considers various allusions in Tolkien's use of the wheel image, including one to Christ and the Cross.[64] As do other World War I literary historians, Garth points out, "[i]n First World War writings, the comparison of suffering, self-sacrificial soldiers to Christ is routine."[65]

The inability of Frodo's mind and body to maintain autonomy results in a condition that has been equated with shell shock and post-traumatic stress disorder. Several critics comment on how Frodo manifests many of the symptoms of shell shock, such as sudden blindness, the loss of other senses, uncontrollable twitching or trembling, recurrent dreams and visions.[66] More recently, a broader diagnosis of post-traumatic stress disorder has also been suggested for Frodo's recurrent illnesses after the quest is over, which occur on significant anniversaries of his injuries.[67] Cases of shell shock, or neurasthenia, "accounted for forty percent of casualties in combat zones" in 1916,[68] the year that Tolkien served in the trenches. It is likely that he would have seen men with the disorder during and after the war. According to Wilfred Owen, "These are men whose minds the Dead have ravished,"[69] and he describes the cause of their condition: "Always they must see these things and hear them, /Batter of guns and shatter of flying muscles."[70] Later during the Second World War and closer to home, Tolkien would have witnessed his son Michael, whom he called "a much damaged soldier,"[71] trying to recover after being discharged from military service because of "severe shock to nervous system due to prolonged exposure to enemy action."[72] Frodo, too, suffers from his "long burden" and, like shell-shocked men in the First World War, one of the causes may be attributed to an enforced experience of impotence and passivity in the face of overwhelming powers that one can do nothing about. Shell shock is, in a sense, a loss of autonomy. As in other war narratives, Frodo becomes a picture of the "damaged man" that Hynes identifies as the dominant figure in post-war literature.[73]

Just as war neuroses did not end with the declaration of peace in 1918, so too Frodo's wounds persist even after the victory celebrations on the Field of Cormallen. Arwen is one of those wise enough to foresee that Frodo's self sacrifice is a loss too great from which to return. She gives him a gift to help him face both physical and psychological pains, both of which trouble Frodo as he gets closer to the Shire again. On the anniversary of his wounding at Weathertop, he tells Gandalf that his wound is aching and he is suffering from the memory of the attack. Frodo realizes even then that he cannot go back to the Shire as he once was. Frodo's inability to return successfully to peacetime life is figured as an inability to awaken fully into the old life he once led. He continues to be suspended in the liminal position that he experienced throughout the quest. Contributing to this impression is the awakening scene on the Field of Cormallen, a moment of eucatastrophe that belongs much more fully to Sam than it does to Frodo. In Rivendell, it is Frodo who awakens after an encounter with Mordor asking about his location and the time, to be answered by Gandalf; in Ithilien, it is Sam who awakens to ask Gandalf where he is and what time and day it is, emphasizing yet again the exchange of places between Frodo and Sam. Although we are told that Frodo had awakened earlier in the day, Sam's (and our) first view of Frodo is of someone still asleep until roused by Sam. Later, the hobbits having bid all their other companions farewell upon returning to the Shire, Merry comments on how their adventure seems like a fading dream; Sam, too, when thinking back on the beginning of the quest, comments that it seems like a dream to him. However, Frodo does not experience the same awakening and return to reality: "To me it feels more like falling asleep again" (*RK*, VI, vii, 276). The last stroke of the war occurs on Frodo's doorstep, his home already having been invaded by Saruman. Even at Bag End, where Frodo expects to cross the threshold into his old life, the transition is infected by the infiltration of Mordor. Instead of leaving behind his experiences, Frodo relives in successive bouts of illness what he has gone through, and at such times he appears to be in a partial dream-like state or looking at things far away. The abject figure of Gollum may have been expelled, but Frodo continues to feel abjection within. For example, on one occasion, Farmer Cotton finds him lying ill in bed, feverishly lamenting the loss of the Ring. Frodo's gradual withdrawal from Shire activities makes him seem even more like the Kristevan figure of the deject, the stray who lives on the margins of society, in contrast to Sam, who successfully reintegrates into Hobbiton, marrying, begetting children, and occupying himself in socially useful tasks. Kristeva believes that the catharsis that literature provides is one way in which the abject can be purified; significantly, only when Frodo immerses himself in his own abjection by writing down his experiences, then bequeathing his book to Sam, is he ready to leave Middle-earth for the possibility of healing in the West before his death.

In the end, Tolkien does not rest with a totally disillusioned vision of war experience. He allows Sam to step in for Frodo and to live a full life. Frodo's self sacrifice entails an emptying of the self, but the white light that shines through him signifies a claim made on him by other powers than those of Mordor, powers that could possibly redeem his loss. Frodo does not cross the threshold back into the Bag End of old, nor does he take the last steps into the Wraith-world; his final, decisive move is to sail into the blessed lands of the West, reunited with Bilbo, and with the possibility of Sam following him in the remote future. Tolkien, however, makes no promises; the book ends with Sam returning to his family with the poignant memory of the sea and of his last sight of Frodo's ship on the horizon. Frodo, however, unable to awaken into ordinary life, sails out of it, into the dreamworld he has been halfway inhabiting all through the quest — in this case, into the dream he once had in Bombadil's house. The veil of this last threshold is removed — "the grey rain-curtain turned all to silver glass and was rolled back" — and a pastoral paradise, where "he beheld white shores and beyond them a far green country under a swift sunrise" (*RK*, VI, ix, 310), finally seems to be within reach.

Notes

1. Research for this essay was supported by a Mount Saint Vincent University Research Grant. I would also like to acknowledge my colleagues on The Reading Room discussion boards at *TheOneRing.net*, who never cease to broaden my views, to question my ideas, and to insist on the most rigorous standards of close reading.

2. Tom Shippey discusses the influences of both world wars on Tolkien's fiction and argues that Tolkien is one of a group of twentieth-century writers who experienced war directly and attempted to understand the evil they had witnessed through the genre of fantasy. Brian Rosebury's *Tolkien: A Cultural Phenomenon* (2003) assesses Tolkien's place as a twentieth-century writer and *The Lord of the Rings* as an example of war literature. Janet Brennan Croft, in *War and the Works of J.R.R. Tolkien* (2004), applies some of the themes and characteristics of World War I writings as defined by Paul Fussell's *The Great War and Modern Memory* (1975) primarily to Tolkien's published works. She also considers Tolkien's military training as an influence on his battle descriptions. John Garth's book, *Tolkien and the Great War* (2003), focuses on how Tolkien's involvement in the First World War influenced his earliest mythical writings, but he also includes a final chapter suggesting ways in which *The Lord of the Rings* can be seen in the context of Tolkien's war experiences. In his later article "Frodo and the Great War" (2006), Garth outlines further ways in which the Great War is transmuted into myth in Frodo's story.

3. In the Foreword to the second edition of *The Lord of the Rings*, Tolkien objects to earlier readings that saw the work as an allegory of the Second World War. Rejecting allegorical and topical interpretations, Tolkien does, however, suggest that his experiences in the First World War might provide a biographical context for the work. Mark T. Hooker cites Carpenter's biography, in which he quotes Tolkien comparing Sam to the privates and batmen that he had known in the war.

4. Tolkien, *Letters*, 72.

5. Brian Rosebury, *Tolkien: A Cultural Phenomenon* (Houndmills, Basingstoke: Palgrave Macmillan, 2003), 139–140.

6. John Garth, *Tolkien and the Great War: The Threshold of Middle-earth* (London: HarperCollins, 2003), 287–313.

7. *FR*, I, i, 44. Lynne Evans, "A Dream Narrative: Loss and Recovery in *The Lord of the Rings*," April 17, 2006, unpublished paper, 3.

8. Paul Fussell, *The Great War and Modern Memory* (New York: Oxford University Press, 1975), 235.

9. Ivor Gurney, *Collected Poems of Ivor Gurney*, ed. P.J. Kavanagh (Oxford: Oxford University Press, 1982), 41.

10. Ibid.

11. Joanna Bourke, *Dismembering the Male: Men's Bodies, Britain and the Great War* (Chicago: University of Chicago Press, 1996), 34.

12. Samuel Hynes, *A War Imagined: The First World War and English Culture* (New York: Atheneum, 1991), 192–94.

13. Edmund Blunden, *Undertones of War* (London: R. Cobden-Sanderson, 1929), 291.

14. Bourke, *Dismembering the Male*, 33–34.
15. Eric J. Leed, *No Man's Land: Combat & Identity in World War I* (Cambridge: Cambridge University Press, 1979), 20–21.
16. Roxanne Panchasi, "Reconstructions: Prosthetics and the Rehabilitation of the Male Body in World War I France," *Differences: A Journal of Feminist Cultural Studies* 7.3 (1995), 111.
17. Ibid., 120.
18. Sigmund Freud, "The 'Uncanny,'" *An Infantile Neurosis and Other Works* (London: Hogarth Press, 1975), 244.
19. Garth, "Frodo," 46–47.
20. Tom Shippey, *J.R.R. Tolkien: Author of the Century* (London: HarperCollins, 2001), 64.
21. Verlyn Flieger, *A Question of Time: J.R.R. Tolkien's Road to* Faërie (Kent, OH: Kent State University Press, 1997), 200.
22. Ibid.
23. *Letters*, 303.
24. Garth, "Frodo," 47–48.
25. Barton Friedman, "Tolkien and David Jones: The Great War and the War of the Ring," *Clio* 11.2 (1982), 115–116.
26. Charles Sorley, *Marlborough and Other Poems* (Cambridge: Cambridge University Press, 1932), 78.
27. Geoffrey Bache Smith, *A Spring Harvest* (London: Erskine Macdonald, 1918), 63.
28. Panchasi, "Reconstructions," 120.
29. Hynes, *A War Imagined*, 116.
30. Leed, *No Man's Land*, 18.
31. Ibid., 19.
32. Sandra Gilbert, "'Rats' Alley': The Great War, Modernism, and the (Anti)Pastoral Elegy," *New Literary History* 30.1 (1999), 185.
33. Wilfred Owen, *Wilfred Owen: Collected Letters*, ed. Harold Owen and John Bell (Oxford: Oxford University Press, 1967), 429.
34. Julia Kristeva, *Powers of Horror: An Essay on Abjection*, trans. Leon S. Roudiez (New York: Columbia University Press, 1982), 2.
35. Ibid., 3.
36. Ibid.
37. Hynes, *A War Imagined*, 112.
38. Kristeva, *Powers of Horror*, 4.
39. Gergely Nagy, "The 'Lost' Subject of Middle-earth: The Constitution of the Subject in the Figure of Gollum in *The Lord of the Rings*," *Tolkien Studies* 3 (2006), 59–60.
40. Verlyn Flieger, *Splintered Light: Logos and Language in Tolkien's World*, 2d ed. (Kent, OH: Kent State University Press, 2002), 149–50.
41. Ibid., 151.
42. Flieger, *Question*, 175–206.
43. Yvette Kisor effectively speaks to Tolkien's use of this term in her essay contained in this collection.
44. Owen, *Collected Letters*, 55.
45. Siegfried Sassoon, *Collected Poems 1908–1956* (London: Faber and Faber, 1964), 35.
46. Shippey, *J.R.R. Tolkien*, 121–28.
47. Garth, "Frodo," 50.
48. Ibid.
49. Hynes, *A War Imagined*, 439.
50. *Letters*, 87–88.
51. Ibid., 111.

52. Leed, *No Man's Land*, 150.
53. Gerely Nagy suggests that the Ring is "the perfect example of Kristeva's abject" ("The 'Lost' Subject," 70) because it represents a borderline of the subject in Gollum, who both loves it and hates it. My reading emphasizes more Gollum's function as abject in the constitution of Frodo's subjectivity, while Nagy's comments suggest Gollum's interiorization of abjection. Nagy's Lacanian reading does not explore further Kristevan possibilities. His view of the corporeal nature of Gollum's language, for example, could be identified as Kristeva's semiotic as opposed to symbolic language, while Gollum's relationship to Shelob would be productive territory for a Kristevan reading of Gollum's connection to the semiotic chora. Frodo and Sam's journey into Shelob's lair through dark tunnels to face a female embodiment of primitive appetites which threatens to consume them could also be read in Kristevan terms as a regression into an archaic maternal space from which the subject has to separate in order to survive.
54. This reading of the Mount Doom episode was first suggested to me in a post by "squire" on *The Reading Room* message boards at TheOneRing.net on March 3, 2006. http://archives.theonering.net/rumour_mill/rpg/viewer/readingroom/44230C770002446 C.html.
55. Jane Chance, "Tough Love: Teaching the New Medievalisms," *Studies in Medievalism* 18 (2010): 85.
56. Fussell, *The Great War*, 270–86.
57. David Craig's article, "Queer Lodgings," draws attention to the love between Frodo and Sam and, following Paul Fussell's study of World War I literature, reads it in the light of the homoerotic relationships described by some soldiers in the war. Jane Chance also reads Tolkien's text, among others, as a "critique of and interrogation of masculinity and male bonding" ("Tough Love, " 80), but she discusses the queering of the hobbits in Tolkien's book mainly in relation to the Orcs: "The Orc, as repressed sexuality amid brute animality, in queer terms represents the hypermasculine polar opposite of the Hobbit as a form of desexualized and even idealized feminine" ("Tough Love," 88). My reading here and in my essay "'Oh ... oh ... Frodo!' Readings of Male Intimacy in *The Lord of the Rings*" suggests that Frodo and Sam's physical intimacy and emotional relationship (seen in the context of representations of male relationships in the First World War) provide sufficient evidence for a queering of masculinity in Tolkien's *Lord of the Rings*.
58. Santanu Das, "'Kiss Me, Hardy': Intimacy, Gender, and Gesture in World War I Trench Literature," *Modernism/Modernity* 9.1 (2002), 56.
59. Ibid., 52.
60. Ibid., 69.
61. Mark T. Hooker, "Frodo's Batman," *Tolkien Studies* 1 (2004), 130.
62. Fussell, *The Great War*, 3–35.
63. Flieger, *Splintered Light*, 147–65.
64. Garth, "Frodo," 50–51.
65. Ibid., 50.
66. Janet Brenna Croft, *War and the Works of J.R.R. Tolkien* (Westport, CT: Praeger, 2004), 133–135; Garth, "Frodo," 49–50.
67. Croft, *War*, 135–36.
68. Bourke, *Dismembering the Male*, 109.
69. Owen, "Mental Cases," *Collected Poems*, 69.
70. Ibid., 69.
71. *Letters*, 86.
72. Ibid., 439.
73. Hynes, *A War Imagined*, 304.

Works Consulted

Blunden, Edmund. *Undertones of War*. London: R. Cobden-Sanderson, 1929.
Bourke, Joanna. *Dismembering the Male: Men's Bodies, Britain and the Great War*. Chicago: University of Chicago Press, 1996.
Chance, Jane. "Tough Love: Teaching the New Medievalisms." *Studies in Medievalism* 18 (2010): 76–98.
Craig, David. "'Queer Lodgings': Gender and Sexuality in *The Lord of the Rings*." *Mallorn: Journal of the Tolkien Society* 38 (2001): 11–18.
Croft, Janet Brennan. *War and the Works of J.R.R. Tolkien*. Contributions to the Study of Science Fiction and Fantasy 106. Westport, CT: Praeger, 2004.
Das, Santanu. "'Kiss me, Hardy': Intimacy, Gender, and Gesture in World War I Trench Literature." *Modernism/Modernity* 9.1 (2002): 51–74.
Evans, Lynne. "A Dream Narrative: Loss and Recovery in *The Lord of the Rings*." April 17, 2006. Unpublished paper.
Flieger, Verlyn. *A Question of Time: J.R.R. Tolkien's Road to Faërie*. Kent, OH: Kent State University Press, 2001.
——. *Splintered Light: Logos and Language in Tolkien's World*. 1983. Rev. ed. Kent, OH: Kent State University Press, 2002.
Freud, Sigmund. "The 'Uncanny.'" *An Infantile Neurosis and Other Works: The Standard Edition of the Complete Psychological Works of Sigmund Freud*. Translated from the German under the General Editorship of James Strachey. In collaboration with Anna Freud. Assisted by Alix Strachey and Alan Tyson. Vol. 17, 218–256 (1917–1919). London: Hogarth Press, 1975.
Friedman, Barton. "Tolkien and David Jones: The Great War and the War of the Ring." *Clio* 11.2 (1982): 115–36.
Fussell, Paul. *The Great War and Modern Memory*. New York: Oxford University Press, 1975.
Garth, John. "Frodo and the Great War." *The Lord of the Rings 1954–2004: Scholarship in Honor of Richard E. Blackwelder*, ed. Wayne G. Hammond and Christina Scull, 41–56. Milwaukee: Marquette University Press, 2006.
——. *Tolkien and the Great War: The Threshold of Middle-earth*. London: HarperCollins, 2003.
Gilbert, Sandra. "'Rats' Alley': The Great War, Modernism, and the (Anti)Pastoral Elegy." *New Literary History* 30.1 (1999): 179–201.
Gurney, Ivor. *Collected Poems of Ivor Gurney*, ed. P.J. Kavanagh. Oxford: Oxford University Press, 1982.
Hooker, Mark T. "Frodo's Batman." *Tolkien Studies* 1 (2004): 125–36.
Hynes, Samuel. *A War Imagined: The First World War and English Culture*. New York: Atheneum, 1991.
Kristeva, Julia. *Powers of Horror: An Essay on Abjection*, trans. Leon S. Roudiez. New York: Columbia University Press, 1982.
Leed, Eric J. *No Man's Land: Combat & Identity in World War I*. Cambridge: Cambridge University Press, 1979.
Nagy, Gergely. "The 'Lost' Subject of Middle-earth: The Constitution of the Subject in the Figure of Gollum in *The Lord of the Rings*." *Tolkien Studies* 3 (2006): 57–79.
Owen, Wilfred. *The Collected Poems of Wilfred Owen*, ed. C. Day Lewis. London: Chatto & Windus, 1964.
——. *Wilfred Owen: Collected Letters*, ed. Harold Owen and John Bell. London: Oxford University Press, 1967.
Panchasi, Roxanne. "Reconstructions: Prosthetics and the Rehabilitation of the Male Body in World War I France." *Differences: A Journal of Feminist Cultural Studies* 7.3 (1995): 109–140.

Rosebury, Brian. *Tolkien: A Cultural Phenomenon.* Houndmills, Basingstoke: Palgrave Macmillan, 2003.
Sassoon, Siegfried. *Collected Poems 1908–1956.* London: Faber and Faber, 1964.
Shippey, Tom. *J.R.R. Tolkien: Author of the Century.* London: HarperCollins, 2001.
Smith, Geoffrey Bache. *A Spring Harvest.* London: Erskine Macdonald, 1918.
Smol, Anna. "'Oh ... oh ... Frodo!' Readings of Male Intimacy in *The Lord of the Rings.*" *Modern Fiction Studies* 50.4 (Winter 2004): 949–79.
Sorley, Charles. *Marlborough and Other Poems.* Cambridge: Cambridge University Press, 1932.

PART II

The Body and the Spirit

The *Hröa* and *Fëa* of Middle-earth
Health, Ecology and the War

MATTHEW DICKERSON

About the nature of Middle-earth, J.R.R. Tolkien writes in his commentary on the *Athrabeth Finrod Ah Andreth*: "There are on Earth 'incarnate' creatures, Elves and Men: these are made of a union of *hröa* and *fëa* (roughly but not exactly equivalent to 'body' and 'soul')."[1] In writing this, Tolkien is affirming a *Weltanschauung* in which both body and spirit are real and relevant.[2] More generally, the world of Middle-earth has both a *seen* reality and an *unseen* reality, and the sentient creatures that dwell in it are part of both.

In some ways, such an explicit statement in Tolkien's commentary (or in this paper) is unnecessary. The spiritual nature of elves and men — this union of *hröa* and *fëa* and the presence of both the seen in the unseen — can be discerned throughout all of the Legendarium (though it is somewhat more evident, for example, in *The Silmarillion* than in *The Hobbit*). What is more interesting is what Tolkien makes of this. After a brief summary of the evidence of the unseen world in *The Lord of the Rings*, this paper explores the implications of Tolkien's concept of *hröa* and *fëa* upon three human concerns: health, ecology, and war. We see that the reality of the *fëa* impacts how man[3] relates to man, how man relates to the earth and the rest of creation (specifically Arda and its *olvar* and *kelvar*),[4] and how man relates to the creator, Ilúvatar.

Glimpses of the Unseen: Spirit in Middle-earth

The twentieth-century philosopher and mathematician Bertrand Russell, a well-known contemporary of J.R.R. Tolkien, in his essay "Why I Am Not a Christian" articulately summarizes the basic premise of materialism, one of the dominant worldviews of modernity:

> Materialists used the laws of physics to show, or attempt to show, that the movements of human bodies are mechanically determined, and that consequently everything we say and every change of position that we effect fall *outside* the sphere of any possible free will.... If, when a man writes a poem or commits a murder, the bodily movements involved in his act result solely from physical causes, it would seem absurd to put up a statue to him in the one case and to hang him in the other.... My own belief is that ... physicists will in time discover [these] laws governing minute phenomena, although these laws may differ very considerably from those of traditional physics.... Whatever may be thought about it as a matter of ultimate metaphysics, it is quite clear that nobody believes in [free will] anymore.[5]

In another essay titled "What I Believe," he gives a slightly different paraphrase of the same ideas:

> Man is a part of nature, not something contrasted with nature. His thoughts and his bodily movements follow the same laws that describe the motions of stars and atoms.... The total number of facts of geography required to determine the world's history is probably finite; theoretically they could all be written down in a big book to be kept at Somerset House with a calculating machine attached, which, by turning the handle, would enable the inquirer to find out the facts at other times than those recorded.[6]

It would be difficult to find a worldview in sharper contrast with Tolkien's than that expressed by Bertrand Russell. As mentioned in the opening paragraph, there is in Middle-earth both a seen reality and an unseen reality: a material plane whose "motions" are subject to what some call "laws" of cause and effect and which are thus theoretically calculable, and a spiritual plane not subject to any *material* laws of physics. It does not require any keen work of scholarship to detect the presence of the spiritual in Tolkien's work, and the observation of it is by no means original. Yet given the prevalence, especially in academic circles, of the alternative worldview of materialists such as Russell, some mention of where and how the spiritual reality is seen, especially in *The Lord of the Rings*, is nonetheless useful in order to place the rest of this paper in context. The spiritual reality is most plainly to be seen in *The Silmarillion*, especially in the *Ainulindalë* and the *Valaquenta*, but even later in the *Akallabêth*. Before *Eä*, the material world, even comes into existence, we read of the creation of the Ainur, the Holy Ones: beings of pure spirit who are the offspring of the thought of the Creator, Eru Ilúvatar. Even when Eru himself is not explicitly mentioned in the narrative for long passages, the presence and influence of his angelic servants, the Valar and the Maiar, is never long forgotten. Neither is the presence of the demonic foes of Eru who are also beings of spirit: Morgoth and his servants, Sauron and the Balrogs (or Valaraukar). The Valar are fundamentally of the unseen world; their visible form is only a "raiment" that they take (or discard without loss), coming from "their knowledge of the visible World, rather than the World itself.... Therefore the Valar may walk, if they will, unclad, and then even the Eldar cannot clearly perceive them."[7] It is safe to say, then, that much of the narrative of *The Silmarillion* takes place either at the level of the unseen, or where the events in the material realm are profoundly influenced by events and beings from the spiritual realm. Most of the narrative of *The Lord of the Rings*, by contrast, appears to take place at the level of the seen, or material reality. The spiritual reality — at least at first glance — is harder to discern. For example, Eru Ilúvatar, the creator of Middle-earth, is not mentioned once in *The Lord of the Rings*! The closest the narrator or any of the characters come to a reference to Eru is when Faramir's folk pause before a meal and remember Elvenhome, and "that which is beyond Elvenhome and will ever be" (*TT*, IV, v, 285). Elvenhome, presumably, is Valinor or its chief city Valmar, home of the Valar. "That which is beyond," then, must be the realm of Eru himself: that is, Heaven, the great spiritual realm. But Faramir's comment is never explained, and only readers of *The Silmarillion* or Tolkien's other Legendarium writings might guess what this means. As for the passage in the second chapter of *The Fellowship of the Ring* when Sam says to Gandalf "Lor bless you" (*FR*, I, ii, 72), the reader may hear this as "Lord bless you," but the comment comes across more as an act of habit on the part of the young Gamgee than as a theological statement.

Other than the Vala Elbereth, the Valar are mentioned only twice in the narrative of *The Lord of the Rings*, once by a character within the tale and once by the narrator. In the skirmish when Faramir's men ambush the Southrons, and Mûmakil come charging in, Damrod in his dismay cries out an explicit prayer: "May the Valar turn him aside!" (*TT*, IV, iv, 269). Later, when Théoden leads the Rohirrim into the Battle of Pelennor Fields, the narrator compares the charge of the King of Rohan upon his horse Snowmane to the charge of the Vala Oromë ages past when the world was young (*RK*, V, vi, 113). To hear more of the Valar, the reader must read *Appendix A, I, i*. The spiritual realm of Valinor, the undying land, and its chief city Valmar, city of the Valar, is also mentioned a small number of times, and the reader may guess, especially from the scene at *The Grey Havens*, that it is a heavenly realm now physically separated from Middle-earth.[8] But little is said explicitly that would tie that spiritual realm to the events in the history of the material realm.

Acknowledging all of this, there are still numerous hints throughout *The Lord of the Rings* that there is a spiritual plane as well as a physical plane, and that what happens in the unseen world has profound influence on the seen. There are numerous references to Elbereth, known also as Varda, the Queen of the Valar. She is not only named in song on numerous occasions, she is also called upon in prayers for aid, including by Frodo on Weathertop and by Sam when he faces Shelob. And, as the narrator makes clear, these cries for Elbereth's aid are never in vain. Aragorn even comments to Frodo after his near-fatal encounter on Weathertop when he stabs the Ringwraith, that the spoken name of the Vala Elbereth was more deadly to the enemy than his blade had been (*FR*, I, xii, 210). Bradley Birzer summarizes the clearly spiritual role of Elbereth as follows:

> Elbereth serves as another Marian figure in the Legendarium. The angelic wife of Manwë and maker of light and stars, she serves, like Mary in Roman Catholic theology, as the "Queen of Heaven." As noted earlier, the Elves invoke her in prayer and revere her more than any other of the Valar. In turn, she listens to their prayers. She also answers the prayers of hobbits, including Sam's pleas for aid during battles with Shelob. Together with Manwë, it is Elbereth who sends Gandalf to aid in Middle-earth against Sauron.[9]

The connotations here are very spiritual, and deal with matters of the *fëa* as well as the *hröa*.

Still, one might argue that understandings like this, even if correct, are only accessible to those familiar with Tolkien's Catholicism or at least more generally with the Christian faith. Explicit discussions of God, angels, or heaven are not to be found in *The Lord of the Rings*. Given Tolkien's dislike for intentional allegory and explicit religion in a work of fantasy this is not surprising.[10] We might ask whether there is any evidence of the unseen reality for the reader not steeped in any religious thought. Again, the answer is yes. There are many such indications, coming from several different characters including Elrond, Galadriel, Aragorn, and Faramir, as well as in the descriptions of Saruman and Sauron.

Perhaps the clearest suggestions of the spiritual world come from Gandalf. For now we mention three; others will be described in the context of subsequent sections of this essay. One of the first hints in the book of the unseen reality in Middle-earth comes from something Gandalf tells Frodo early on about the history of the One Ring and Bilbo's finding of it. After saying that something was at work beyond Sauron's designs, Gandalf adds—in language he considers as plain and clear as possible—that "Bilbo was *meant* to find the Ring, and *not* by its maker. In which case you also were *meant* to have it" (*FR*, I, ii, 65). What Gandalf is speaking of are the powers at work in the world. One of these powers is Sauron. But as Gandalf has just told Frodo, "There was more than one power at work" (*FR*, I, ii, 65). What power is that? Again, the readers of *The Silmarillion* might well guess that it is Eru, either at work directly or indirectly through his servants, the Valar. But the casual reader needs neither to know this, nor to be aware of biblical allusions; it is clear that these powers are not material, fleshly powers. Whatever was happening was not happening at the physical plain; it was something unseen.

In case the reader misses this, Tolkien spells it out even more clearly a few chapters later through something Gandalf says about the Elven warrior Glorfindel, who had come to Frodo's aid when the he was pursued by the Ringwraiths on route to Rivendell. He refers to Glorfindel as having dwelt in the Blessed Realm of Valinor, and thus living at once in both worlds. As a result he has great power "against both the Seen and the Unseen." Frodo, Gandalf says with an heir of mystery, managed to catch a glimpse of Glorfindel as he is "upon the other side" (*FR*, II, i, 235). Here Gandalf's reference to the unseen world is both explicit and clear. Both worlds are real, and Glorfindel seems to live at once in both. He also has power in both. Though the narrator does not use the term *fëa* in *The Lord of the Rings*, we understand that Glorfindel is powerful in both *hröa* and *fëa*—and that these are two different things. Even the phrase "the other side," apart from the reference to the Unseen, suggests something about a different world.

What we are seeing, put simply, is that Tolkien, a devout Catholic, held views consistent with his faith in that he was most certainly not a materialist; he did not believe that physical matter was the *only* reality. Of course some worldviews such as deism acknowledge the possibility that the spiritual world is real, but not that it is relevant. For Tolkien, however, the spiritual world was both real and relevant. Again, this is seen powerfully in an observation that Pippin makes about Gandalf at one of the darkest moments in the tale shortly after they have entered Minas Tirith when the dark clouds of Mordor have presaged the coming siege. Despite the dismaying news he has just heard, Gandalf laughs. Pippin looks at Gandalf in surprise and wonder, for the laugh was gay and merry and yet it is care and sorrow that visibly line the wizard's face. As he looks at the wizard more intently, Pippin finally perceives something. What does he perceive? Joy. Great joy. A veritable fountain of mirth. He perceives that were it to gush forth from the wizard, it would be enough to set an entire kingdom laughing (*RK*, V, i, 31). Gandalf's peculiar joy at this moment is best described as a spiritual joy, or joy of the *fëa*: a joy that comes from his underlying knowledge of the unseen reality behind the seen. Which is to say, to Gandalf the unseen is visible. He has, after all, passed through fire and death. He has died, and been sent back. He, like Glorfindel, has seen the other side. And what he sees of the spiritual realms gives him hope in the material realm, because he knows the realms are not isolated one from the other.

Healing the Body and the Soul

Perhaps the most obvious implication of the reality of both body and spirit is to the question of what it means to be healthy. Since incarnate creatures are a union of body and soul, it also stands to reason that goal of true health is the nurturing of both a healthy body and a healthy soul. Nowhere is this more evident than in the words spoken by Aragorn at the healing of Éowyn. He acknowledges that he *might* have the power to heal her body and to recall her from the dark valley of death, but he goes on to say that she might awake to despair rather than to hope, and that if she wakes to despair she will need a different kind of healing than any that he can bring her (*RK*, V, viii, 143–44). Aragorn's words here speak to the reality and importance of the *fëa* as well as the *hröa*. The significance of the physical body is attested to by Aragorn's effort to heal Éowyn's body — as well as his numerous other efforts at the healing of others, including Frodo, Sam, Faramir, and Merry. One of the first signs of Aragorn's right to kingship is his ability to heal the body. But as Aragorn himself points out very clearly, healing the body alone is not enough. The spirit or soul, the *fëa*, is also important. If Éowyn's body is healed but her spirit is not, then her physical healing is in vain. True health involves *hröa* as well as *fëa*.[11]

We also see implications of *hröa* and *fëa* in the treatment of both Sméagol and Saruman by Gandalf and later Frodo. Gandalf speaks of his hope — slim though that hope is — that Sméagol might be *cured* before he dies. He then speaks of the kindness that the elves are showing Sméagol, even though they have him in prison (*FR*, I, ii, 69). It is clear from the context that the cure of which Gandalf speaks is not a bodily cure, but a healing of Sméagol's spirit: a rescuing of him from the power of the Ring. Others including Aragorn and later Frodo also undertake to help with this spiritual healing of Sméagol. Something similar is at work with Saruman; again both Gandalf and Frodo hope for a spiritual healing of the White Wizard. When Gandalf confronts him at Isengard, he is in part hoping for Saruman's aid in the war against Sauron, but he also desires to help Saruman (hopeless though the effort seems). And, as was the case with Sméagol, the help Gandalf wants to provide is spiritual; it is help for Saruman's soul. Gandalf always seems as concerned for the spiritual wellbeing of others as for their physical wellbeing; with regard to Saruman he grieves that a wizard who once had so much potential for good now just sits in a tower festering (*TT*, III, x, 190).

We might ask, precisely what sort of *treatment* is good for the *fëa*? The first part of the answer, explicit in Gandalf's words, is "kindness." But it goes much deeper than *mere* kindness, coming closer to a concept loosely associated with *pity*, in modern connotation more accurately and completely known as *mercy*. The practice of mercy is fundamental to the health not only of the recipient, but of the giver. Bilbo's mercy shown to Gollum not only allows the possibility of healing for Sméagol, but also proves critical to the health of Bilbo's own *fëa*. Gandalf makes this clear to Frodo. He speaks of Bilbo's having shown pity and mercy to Gollum, and notes that it is precisely because of his practice of pity that Bilbo took "so little hurt from the evil, and escaped in the end" (*FR*, I, ii, 68–69). In a personal letter, Tolkien makes a similar point about Frodo's choice to show mercy to Sméagol: "By a situation created by his 'forgiveness,' he was saved himself, and relieved of his burden."[12] Tolkien's use of the word "salvation" suggests a profoundly spiritual concept.

Sadly, it is a lack of compassion on the part of Samwise Gamgee toward Sméagol that ultimately hinders the healing of the Sméagol's soul. In another personal letter, Tolkien explains his own thoughts on the interaction between Sam and Sméagol:

> For me perhaps the most tragic moment in the Tale comes ... when Sam fails to note the complete change in Gollum's tone and aspect ... [Gollum's] repentance is blighted and all Frodo's pity is (in a sense) wasted.[13]

Of course Frodo's pity is not completely wasted, because it helps keep Frodo's own soul healthy, as already noted. But the results of Sam's treatment of Sméagol, or Gollum, or Slinker and Stinker, illustrates profoundly the implication of Tolkien's view of *hröa* and *fëa*, and what helps bring healing to the complete person.

One of the most striking tragedies in the entire Legendarium, though one little discussed in the critical literature, is the tale of Míriel, mother of Fëanor. The tale is relevant to our discussion. As recounted in *The Silmarillion*, after Míriel gives birth to Fëanor she is "consumed in spirit and body" and yearns "for release from the labor of living."[14] The very wording of this speaks of the importance of both bodily and spiritual health; both body and spirit can suffer, or be "consumed." Both are meant to be healthy. So central is bodily health to creation that elves are not even subject to disease. But Míriel actually "tries to *die*"— not only to destroy her body, but "to abandon being." She "refused rebirth." In one letter, Tolkien describes this event as "disastrous" and leading "to the 'Fall' of the High-elves."[15] The import of this suggestion should not be overlooked: the "Fall of the High-elves" was in some way precipitated by an unhealthy separation of *hröa* from *fëa* in the person of Míriel, and perhaps a denial of both.

And this leads to a final note in this section. In emphasizing the spiritual reality, Tolkien does not diminish the physical; the importance of the health of the *fëa* does not deny the significance of the health of the *hröa*. If one of the elven race is slain in Middle-earth, if their body is destroyed, their spirits do not remain disembodied. They are "rehabilitated and reborn" and eventually even recover "memory of all their past; they remain identical."[16] In the same essay in which Tolkien introduces the *hröa* and *fëa*, he makes this point clear: the *hröa* and *fëa* "were designed each for the other, to abide in perpetual harmony." He adds that "the separation of *hröa* and *fëa* is 'unnatural,' and proceeds not from the original design, but from the 'Marring of Arda,' which is due to the operations of Melkor."[17] This is part of what make's Míriel's case so strange and so tragic.

Body, Spirit, and Tolkien's Environmentalism

Tolkien's view of body and spirit, seen and unseen, affects nearly every aspect of his writing. One of many implications in the Legendarium of the reality of the spiritual realm as well as of the material realm is upon the ecology of Middle-earth and the appropriate land-use ethics of its people. Paul H. Kocher may have been the first scholar to identify this aspect of Tolkien's work when he wrote in 1972 that "Tolkien was [an] ecologist."[18] However Kocher did not go much beyond this intuitive comment to actually explore Tolkien's ecology. Recently more attention has begun to be given to the environmental aspects of the Middle-earth writings. Scholars including Don Elgin, Patrick Curry, Alfred Siewers, Christina Ljungberg Stücklin, and Verlyn Flieger have written paper-length treatments dealing explicitly with the environmental perspective implicit in Tolkien's works.[19] However the first book-length treatment of this as a significant aspect of Tolkien's work, *Ents, Elves, and Eriador: The Environmental Vision of J.R.R. Tolkien* by Matthew Dickerson and Jonathan Evans, did not appear until 2006.[20] Though Tolkien's life predated the modern environmental movement, and he was not known as a "nature writer," we can nonetheless discern in his writings a strong trace of environmentalism, and an expression of many of the ideas suggested by environmental writers and thinkers of the past four decades. The practical applications of his environmentalism can be seen in several places in *The Lord of the Rings*, most notably in the threefold vision of environmental degradation in Mordor, Isengard, and Sharkey's Shire, as well as in positive visions in Lothlórien, the Shire's positive agrarianism, and the Ents' restoration of Isengard. We also see how Tolkien's ecology is firmly rooted in his *Weltanschauung* of body and spirit. The reality and importance of the physical realm avoids the dangers inherent in Gnosticism or neo–Platonism, while the significance of the spiritual provides a transcendent basis for self-sacrificial environmentalism.

Let us return for a moment to our central quote with which we began this paper. Tolkien describes elves and men as "made of a union of *hröa* and *fëa* (roughly but not exactly equivalent to 'body' and 'soul.'" Tolkien is not original or unique in his portrayal of human (and elvish) nature as being one of body and soul. It is a fundamentally Christian understanding. In a statement that also has profound implications for the previous section of this paper, Jesus asks, "For what doth it profit a man, if he gain the whole world and suffer the loss of his own soul? Or what exchange shall a man give for his soul?"[21] Were we reading Tolkien in another time and culture, this aspect of his writing might be so commonly accepted as not to necessitate any comment. As mentioned, however, Tolkien's view contrasts sharply with a prevalent modern western materialist worldview which affirms only the body (the material) and denies the soul or spiritual self.

It would be tempting, then, to draw a close parallel between the *Athrabeth* and the *Phaedrus* where Plato writes, "And this composition of soul and body is called a living and mortal creature."[22] Certainly the two are in agreement about some fundamental aspect of the human condition, and Tolkien references Plato for partial understanding. However it is clear from Tolkien's Legendarium that he also did not accept the form of thought associated with the first-century Gnostics or with modern neo–Platonism. This derivation of Platonic philosophy sees goodness only in the world of thought and idea, and not in the physical earth: the mind or spirit is said to be good, but the body is not. Tolkien, by contrast, though he affirmed the reality of the spiritual world, also affirmed the value and goodness of the material world. As we saw at the end of the previous section, the *hröa* and *fëa* were *meant* for each other. Thus just as the worldview that informs Tolkien's Middle-earth writing is in contrast with materialism that denies the spiritual, it also contrasts with these various forms of Eastern mysticism as well as Gnosticism which affirm some invisible world (thought and ideas, or soul and spirit), but deny either the goodness, relevance, or even ultimate existence of the body. Expanding the notion of *hröa* and *fëa* to the broader concept of the physical world and the spiritual, it is in the affirmation both of the reality of soul and spirit and in the goodness and value of the material world that we find Tolkien's ecology rooted.

A few aspects of Tolkien's "environmental vision" as it relates to the topic at hand are worth mentioning, beginning with a few observations about the hobbits and the Shire. That hobbits are creatures close to the earth is hard to miss. Not only their bare feet, but their very style of dwelling keeps them in contact with the soil, as we see from the opening sentence of *The Hobbit*. Readers also soon learn of hobbit homes that "the best rooms were all on the left-hand side (going in), for these were the only ones to have windows, deep-set round windows looking over his garden, and meadows beyond, sloping down to the river."[23] Thus hobbits value nature; their "best rooms" are not the largest ones or the most luxuriously furnished (despite their love for comfort), but the ones with the clearest views of nature, both cultivated (gardens) and wild (meadows and rivers). We see their love of nature also in the nature names they give to their children, especially daughters who are often named after flowers: Rose, Elanor, etc. This is the advice Frodo gives to Sam for naming his first child.[24]

There is more here than merely sentimentality. This points to deeper values held by the hobbits: two values in particular. They see the created physical earth as inherently valuable, independent of any economic use or pragmatic utilitarian value, and they also value simplicity. As bodily creatures in a physical world, they work with their own hands, caring for the physical earth: the land and the things that grow upon it. They value food, and cheer, and song, simple pleasures again associated with the stuff of the earth. And, as Tolkien suggests in the dying words of Thorin toward the end of *The Hobbit*, if more of us valued these things, the world would be a merrier place.

Again we see the Hobbits' delight in these simple things for their own sake, and not merely as means to some other ends, or as vehicles for achieving power. This is perhaps why they are able to resist the seductive power of the Ring for so long; they are not fundamentally concerned with power, or with the manipulations of power, and thus they are able to take things for what they are, and not merely as means. It also explains why Frodo is able to make the sacrifice he makes. He speaks of his desire to save the Shire, and his willingness to give up his own firm foothold there and take to a life of wandering, "as long as the Shire lies behind, safe and comfortable" (*FR*, I, ii, 71). His self-sacrifice is a spiritual virtue, one associated in Tolkien's Christian faith with Jesus' incarnation and death on the cross. But the sacrifice is motivated not merely by the other residents of the Shire, his friends and neighbors, but also by the Shire itself, the land; there is a goodness in the created earth, the bodily beings who inhabit it, and the "firm foothold" it provides.

Perhaps the clearest expression of the importance of both the physical and spiritual informing Tolkien's ecology can be seen in Yavanna's creation of the plants and animals of Middle-earth, and the mythic origins of life on Arda. Yavanna's creation is what Tolkien called "sub-creation,"[25] attended to as her part of the song of the Ainur, which itself is part of Ilúvatar's creation of Eä. Yavanna's work is a fulfillment of her sacred duty to "show forth [her] powers in adorning [Ilúvatar's] theme ... with [her] own thoughts and devices."[26] Of the things she creates, she later says, "All have their worth ... and each contributes to the worth of the others." Even Aulë, when explaining the use his Dwarves will make of the earth, acknowledges to Yavanna: "The things of thy realm have worth in themselves, and would have worth if no Children were to come."[27] The existence of Ents is owed to the inherent worth of plants, and their worthiness to be protected.

Furthermore, the most important mythic symbols in all of the history of Middle-earth are trees: the Two Trees of Valinor. The very ground on which they were grown was said to have been "hallowed"—made holy, or sacred—by Yavanna. Furthermore, she set in the Two Trees "all her thought of things that grow in the earth."[28] So the Two Trees are not only sacred but are symbolic of all life on earth, thereby implying a sacredness to all of life represented in the trees. We are told that "Of all things which Yavanna made they have most renown, and about their fate all the tales of the Elder Days are woven."[29] What we see, then, is that the things of Arda — plants, animals, skies, seas, rivers, mountains, etc.— are understood to be good and worthwhile as material aspects of creation apart from any utility to man, elf, or dwarf. A vital aspect of good stewardship, then, as portrayed by Tolkien through wise figures like Gandalf, Galadriel, and Treebeard, is good creation-care: taking care of the earth including leaving good soil for those who come after us to till.

Indeed, Yavanna's work is more than just good; it is of spiritual value. The things of the earth are seen as *sacred* in the deepest sense of that word. They have both a sacred origin in the purpose of Ilúvatar, and a sacred duty. Tolkien wrote in a letter in 1969 that the chief purpose of life may be to be moved "to praise and thanks" for the creation of the world and all within it.[30] It is not surprising, then, that Tolkien portrays it as evil to destroy the created earth. Treebeard describes, as the central manifestation of Saruman's evil, the white wizard's wanton felling of trees. It is worth noting that this is seen as an evil whether the wood is put to use or not. Whether the trees are cut down and left to rot as an act of orc-mischief, or chopped up and hauled off to burn for energy in Orthanc, the act of felling these trees is bad (*TT*, III, iv, 77). The most damning statement, though, is that Saruman, "does not care for growing things" except to the extent that they can be used — or, one might say, exploited (*TT*, III, iv, 76). Similarly, the downfall of Númenor in the Akallabêth and the evil that causes it is closely tied to both the deforestation of Middle-earth and to the killing of its symbolic tree Nimloth, the White Tree of Númenor.[31]

Of course "good" and "evil" are spiritual terms, ultimately owning their objective definition to Ilúvatar. One of the central ideas in all of Tolkien's writing is that morality is objective: good and evil are not arbitrary categories.[32] As Dickerson and Evans note, "Our use of our time and our treatment of the earth are not merely matters of personal preference: there are right and wrong ways to fulfill our duties as stewards of the earth. Tolkien would have us do the right."[33] One of the "right ways" is the use of agrarian practices that are indefinitely sustainable. Another is the preservation of wilderness as inherently valuable, independent of utilitarian or pragmatic purposes.

In short, then, Tolkien's portrayal of the reality and goodness of the physical body comes from a worldview in which the material world has inherent value. But the reality of the spiritual world adds a sacredness to nature, and also provides a transcendent basis by which good and evil can be defined: a basis by which the morality of our interaction with the created world can be judged, and by which we can speak of healthy care of the earth as good and right, and of exploitation as not just inconvenient but as evil. The final chapter of *Ents, Elves and Eriador* ends with a note about the "environmental principles" evident in Tolkien's "imaginative vision of ecology harmony." It states that Tolkien, "offers us an inspiring, imaginative portrayal of how we might fulfill the responsibilities of environmental stewardship that are our burden and privilege to bear."[34]

Not Against Flesh and Blood

Lastly, we turn to Tolkien's view of war presented in the *The Lord of the Rings* and how it is shaped by his view of *hröa* and *fëa*. Much of the warfare in the trilogy can be understood as a working out of a passage of St. Paul's writing, which speaks of the body and spirit in terms of warfare: "For our wrestling is not against flesh and blood; but against principalities and powers, against the rulers of the world of this darkness, against the spirits of wickedness in the high places."[35] This sheds light on the real nature of war in Middle-earth, and in many ways ties together all three of the themes of this paper, explaining why Gandalf displays power when and as he does, why Boromir's death was a victory and not a defeat, why Galadriel refuses the One Ring (though her refusal brings about the fall of Lothlórien), and why "The Scouring of the Shire" is not an afterthought but one of the most important scenes in the trilogy.

As careful readers are aware, the Istari (wizards) in general and Gandalf in particular are spiritual beings who have taken incarnate form. Like Melian, mother of Lúthien, they are of the order of the Maiar. Tolkien describes them as angelic beings. Gandalf "is not, of course, a human being (Man or Hobbit)," but rather "an *incarnate* 'angel.'"[36] As such, Gandalf is not on earth to fight physical battles against beings of flesh. Throughout all of *The Lord of the Rings*, he almost never displays any power or prowess in battle against mortal foes, but reserves his real power for confrontations with other beings of similar spiritual nature: the Balrog, Saruman, and the Nazgûl.[37] For example, we think of the normal foe of angels as being demons. This is precisely what the Balrogs are described as: "Dreadful among these *spirits* were the Valaraukar ... demons of terror."[38] However the main point here is not to explore the few instances where Gandalf *does* show his might, but to point out the countless instances where he does *not*, but instead does something very different: encouraging the people of Middle-earth to choose hope and good over despair and evil. It is this, not the fighting of orcs, nor even the fighting of balrogs, that is the very thing he came to do. Tolkien himself explains the nature of wizards, and why these spiritual beings would take physical form and limit their own potency choosing rather to motivate and inspire the enemies of Sauron.[39] Gandalf and the Powers who sent him understand the nature of a spiritual battle. In Christian thought, a spiritual battle is not won with swords or bows;

it is won at one level by making moral choices, and more specifically by resisting sin. In our primary world in Tolkien's Christian worldview, the spiritual foe is Satan, the devil. And Satan works by temptation and deception.[40] Thus it is the spiritual act of that choosing — the choosing of good — that Gandalf hopes to encourage and inspire. This is why he doesn't simply appear and win the battles for the people of Middle-earth, or, more specifically, why the one who sent him did not give him the power to do that. For Gandalf to win the battles for the people of Middle-earth would have taken away their power of choosing.

In helping Théoden understand that he still has strength to choose, Gandalf brings a spiritual healing that enables the King of Rohan to fight the battles he is meant to fight. There were two battles for Théoden: the one on the field fought with his sword, and the earlier one in Meduseld that he wins with his choosing the moment he rises and casts off his prop. The earlier one fought in Meduseld was ultimately more important for Théoden's *fëa*. Likewise, the "Scouring of the Shire" illustrates most clearly what Gandalf had come for: to train the people of Middle-earth to fight the right battles in the right way, to help them to grow up, or mature, in the wisdom necessary to do it.[41]

A similar point about the importance of spiritual battles could be made with regard to Boromir's death. Boromir's dying words are an expression of personal failure. In every physical way, Boromir was right to say he had failed (*TT*, III, i, 16). At the time of his death, he had failed at everything he set out to do. He did not bring either Isildur's Bane (the Ring) or the Sword that was Broken (Aragorn) back to Minas Tirith to aid his people. He failed to protect Merry and Pippin from capture. He failed simply to live. Yet both Aragorn and Gandalf speak clearly of the victory Boromir had won, and of his escape in the end (*TT*, III, i, 20; *TT*, III, v, 99). Though his *hröa* had failed, Boromir's *fëa* had won the crucial battle: he had confessed to Aragorn his attempt at the ring, and repented. Boromir might not have understood that there was a battle against spiritual wickedness, but Aragorn and Gandalf did, and they knew that in the end Boromir won that battle.

Galadriel also understood what the real battle was. One of the most profound moments of the tale is when she refuses the temptation of the Ring. Though she speaks with great passion of the enduring love that the Elves have for their land and their works, a love deeper than the seas, she says they would rather cast it all away than serve Sauron (*FR*, II, vii, 380). What would it profit her, she seems to be asking, if she saved the whole of the world (or even of Lothlórien), and yet suffered the loss of her own soul? Faramir makes a similar comment, again echoing the teaching of Jesus in Matthew 16:26. When speaking to Frodo of Isildur's Bane, he claims that he would refuse to use the Dark Lord's weapon even if it came to him freely, lying beside the highway, and it was his only hope of saving his beloved city of Minas Tirith (*TT*, IV, v, 280). He understands that it would profit him nothing to save Minas Tirith, if the cost of that triumph were the soul he would certainly lose by using the weapon of the Dark Lord. A victory for the flesh does not justify the defeat of the soul; Tolkien makes this clear. The battle of the *fëa* is the most important.

But of course the physical battles still must be fought. Elves and men are not disembodied beings; as we have pointed out, the reality and importance of the *fëa* does not negate the importance of the *hröa*. It is not merely that life must be lived out on the physical plane — though that itself is important — but that there is goodness in the material world. Thus Gandalf can honestly tell Denethor that he cares for all worthy things that are in peril. That is, quite literally, he thinks of all worthy things as being in his care. And even the smallest thing is worth the effort to save. Even if all of Gondor perishes, Gandalf says, he will not have been a total failure if even a single living thing survives (*RK*, V, i, 30–31). In speaking of worthy things, Gandalf is referencing the physical world, thus the added comment to that which can "bear fruit and flower again." Choosing to care for the earth, rather than to exploit it, is part of the spiritual battle Gandalf calls those around him to fight. In short, the spiritual (or moral) battle of making right choices has implications on the material plane, and that is part of its significance. And of course our actions on the material plane have spiritual consequences; it is what we choose to do with our *hröa* that defines our morality and thereby the health of the *fëa*.

Conclusion

Not surprisingly, all of the three areas explored in the previous three sections are closely related — indeed inseparable. Tolkien's notion of *hröa* and *fëa* is a fundamental aspect of his Christian worldview, and though he avoids explicit religion or allegory in *The Lord of the Rings*, that worldview undergirds and informs all of his thinking, which is why he called *The Lord of the Rings* "a fundamentally religious and Catholic work."[42] Of course this suggests, as Tolkien himself suggests in many places, an important applicability to our world of these principles seen in Middle-earth. Certainly part of what makes the environmental ideas discussed in section three of this chapter so valuable is that many of them may be translated to our world. In his famous BBC radio interview, Tolkien associated the Shire with the central Midlands English countryside, and its "good water, stones and elm trees and small quiet rivers and so on."[43] The same can be said of the applications to health and to war.

And as with many of the most important ideas in the Legendarium, a key to understanding begins with Tolkien's creation myth in *The Silmarillion*. Readers of that myth may have wondered about the "Secret Fire," a phrase Tolkien uses interchangeably with "Flame Imperishable" and "Imperishable Flame." What is the Flame Imperishable? What does the name mean or to what does it refer? There are only a few hints in the *Ainulindalë*, and though the uses of these names are consistent with the version of the creation myth in *Morgoth's Ring: The Later Silmarillion*, the Secret Fire is not mentioned outside these few creation myth accounts. In the *Ainulindalë*, readers are told that the Fire, or Flame "is with Ilúvatar,"[44] that the Ainur were kindled with it,[45] and that it was sent to burn at the heart of the World.[46] Christopher Tolkien suggests that the Flame Imperishable "appears to mean the Creative activity of Eru (in some sense distinct from or within Him)." He goes on to clarify, and adds that it refers to "the mystery of 'authorship,' by which the author, while remaining 'outside' and independent of his work, also 'indwells' in it, on its derivative plane, below that of his own being, as the source and guarantee of its being."[47]

Clyde Kilby, however, gives a slightly different explanation, recalling conversations with Tolkien while he was helping him prepare *The Silmarillion* for publication. "Professor Tolkien talked to me at some length about the use of the word 'holy' in *The Silmarillion*. Very specifically he told me that the 'Secret Fire sent to burn at the heart of the World' in the beginning was the Holy Spirit."[48] At first glance, these two answers, the one suggested by J.R.R. Tolkien's son, and the other given to Kilby, may appear to be different. In the Christian Trinitarian doctrine of God, however, they are fully compatible. In the Christian understanding, the Holy Spirit is the Third Person of the Trinity sent to dwell on earth and in the hearts of those who follow God. When Jesus (God incarnate, God the Son, the Second Person of the Trinity) departed the earth to return to the right hand of the throne of God the Father (the First Person of the Trinity), he promised that the Holy Spirit would come to believers.[49] The coming of the Holy Spirit, described in Acts 2:1–4 is one of the most important passages of the Christian New Testament. But many Christians also understand that the spirit hovering over the deep in Genesis 1 is the Holy Spirit through whom God's creative hand was at work. If we associate the Flame Imperishable with the Holy Spirit, there are two implications to Tolkien's mythology, both of which are fully compatible with what we have seen so far. The first relates the nature of Ilúvatar's Children (elves and men) with Ilúvatar himself. In particular, the spiritual nature of men and elves — the fact that the *fëa* is real and important — is an aspect of their having been created in the image of the Creator, Ilúvatar; man and elf are spiritual because God is spiritual. The spiritual nature of the Children comes from the Holy Spirit in whom they were kindled. This is a reflection of the Judeo-Christian creation account that speaks very clearly of man having been created in God's image.[50] The Holy Spirit is then given to indwell those in a relationship with God, as described above. This is the path toward true spiritual health. Of course Tolkien, though he implies much about man's spiritual nature, and about the importance of spiritual health, says nothing in the Legendarium about the Christian doctrine of the Holy Spirit. This is part because he was seeking to avoid explicit religion in his works, and in part because (as numerous scholars have addressed) he was writing (like the *Beowulf* poet) as a Christian describing a pre–Christian time, and the Holy Spirit was given to man after Christ.

But there is another aspect of the author's indwelling in his work — that is, of Ilúvatar's indwelling in Middle-earth, and God's indwelling in our world — that Tolkien did specifically address, and it is Tolkien's ultimate answer to the question of the spiritual battle. We began this paper with a passage from Tolkien's commentary on the *Athrabeth Finrod Ah Andreth*. The *Athrabeth Finrod Ah Andreth* itself is (as the title proclaims in Elvish) a dialogue between Finrod, the great and wise Elven King of Nargothrond in the First Age, and a wise mortal woman Andreth who has fallen in love with Finrod's brother. Although this dialogue did not appear in the first published version of *The Silmarillion*, Tolkien's notes indicate that the dialogue was considered complete and final, and that he intended it, along with the commentary, to be published as part of *The Silmarillion*. In the dialogue, Andreth raises an old human hope that one day the Creator, Eru Ilúvatar, would enter into his own creation in order to finally defeat the enemy Melkor. She asks Finrod if he thinks this possible. Finrod's response is central to Tolkien's Christian understanding of the hope for Middle-earth.

> If Eru wished to do this, I do not doubt that he would find a way, though I cannot foresee it.... [I]f He will not relinquish His work to Melkor, who must else proceed to mastery, then Eru must come in to conquer him.... If any remedy for [Melkor's evil] is to be found, ere all is ended, any new light to oppose the shadow, or any medicine for the wounds: then it must, I deem, come from without.[51]

What Finrod and Andreth are speaking of is the incarnation of Eru — a time when the Creator will take on the form of flesh: will take to himself the *hröa* of man. In doing so, he will defeat Melkor from within his creation. It is that victory in the spiritual war that will make possible health for both *fëa* and *hröa* because it will free Middle-earth from the corruption of Melkor. But such action also hallows all of Middle-earth. All of nature becomes not only the creation of the Creator but his dwelling place. Therefore our care for the earth is not just our care for our own dwelling place but our care for the dwelling place of God. The reality of the *fëa* doesn't diminish the significance of the *hröa*, and of the physical earth, but makes environmentalism itself a spiritual activity.

Notes

1. J.R.R. Tolkien, *Morgoth's Ring: The Later Silmarillion, Part One*, ed. Christopher Tolkien, The History of Middle-Earth *10* (Boston: Houghton Mifflin, 1993), 330.

2. The English *spirit* and *soul* are used interchangeably here. Their etymology and (at times subtle) different historical uses is beyond the scope of this paper. Readers should note that Tolkien's usage of "soul" in this passage is explicitly distinguished from a strictly Platonic idea, and we may assume it is more in keeping with a Christian, and specifically Catholic view. For example, it is clear from Tolkien's entire mythology that the *fëa*, though associated with the English *soul* in the cited passage, is related to an eternal *spiritual* entity whose existence continues even if the associated *hröa* dies. Thus names like *Fëanor* are glossed as "spirit of fire."

3. *Man* is used here to refer to the race in Middle-earth. There are important differences between elves and men regarding the *fëa* and the *hröa*. One concerns their after-death fates. *The Silmarillion* hints that at the end of time elves and men will be joined in making a new music to Ilúvatar. While Eä lasts, however, the after-death fates of men and elves are sundered.

4. Respectively, *plants* and *animals*.

5. Bertrand Russell, "Why I Am Not a Christian," *Why I Am Not a Christian* (New York: Simon & Schuster, 1967), 37–39.

6. Russell, "What I Believe," *Why I Am Not a Christian*, 48–49.

7. *Sil*, 21.

8. Of course Valinor is also a bodily realm, a realm of real material substance, and the elves who dwell there have *hröa* (are embodied). But it is also a spiritual realm: the place where the Valar dwell and where the *fëa* of departed elves may go to the Halls of Mandos.

9. Bradley Birzer, *J.R.R. Tolkien's Sanctifying Myth* (Wilmington, DE: ISI Books, 2003), 64.

10. See, for example, the fourth paragraph of Tolkien's famous letter 144 to Milton Waldman in Tolkien, *Letters*. Though it also must also be noted that Tolkien himself at times wrote stories that are best understood as allegorical ("Leaf by Niggle," for example), and even allegory that is clearly intentional (the story of the tower "The Monsters and the Critics").

11. One might argue here that Aragorn is speaking only of Éowyn's *emotions* and that emotions are merely bodily responses: chemical reactions in the brain. Though this may be, at least in part, an accurate statement from the point of view of modern psychology, to force that interpretation upon Tolkien's works presupposes a materialist worldview that is not present.

12. Tolkien, *Letters*, 234.

13. Ibid., 329–30.

14. *Sil*, 63.

15. *Letters*, 286.

16. Ibid.

17. Tolkien, *Morgoth's Ring*, 330–331.

18. Paul Kocher, *Master of Middle Earth: The Fiction of J.R.R. Tolkien* (Boston: Houghton Mifflin, 1972), 26.

19. See the following: Patrick Curry, "'Less Noise and More Green': Tolkien's Ideology for England," 1995 and Patrick Curry, "Middle-earth: Nature and Ecology," 2004; Don D. Elgin, *The Comedy of the Fantastic*, 1985; Verlyn Flieger, "Taking the Part of Trees," 2000; Christina Ljungberg Stücklin, "Re-enchanting Nature: Some Magic Links Between Atwood and Tolkien," 1999; and Alfred Siewers, "Tolkien's Cosmic-Christian Ecology," 2005.

20. Matthew Dickerson and Jonathan Evans, *Ents, Elves, and Eriador*, 2006. A more thorough exploration of ideas in this section can be found in this book.

The Hröa *and* Fëa *of Middle-earth* (Dickerson) 81

21. Matthew 16:26 (*Douay-Rheims*).
22. Plato, *Phaedrus*, trans. Benjamin Jowett, 246c. http://classics.mit.edu/Plato/republic.html.
23. *Hobbit*, 29.
24. See Dinah Hazell, *The Plants of Middle-earth*, 2007 for more on where hobbit names come from.
25. See, for example, Tolkien's use of the word sub-creation and the treatment of this in "On Fairy Stories."
26. *Sil*, 15.
27. Ibid., 45.
28. Ibid., 38.
29. Ibid.
30. *Letters*, 400.
31. See *Sil*, 269, 272 and *Unfinished Tales*, 262.
32. Numerous scholars have commented on this aspect of Tolkien's works. See, for example, Chapter 11 (pp. 173–191) of Peter Kreeft, *The Philosophy of Tolkien*, 2005. Other elucidations of the objective nature of morality in Tolkien's works can be found in: Birzer, *Sanctifying Myth*, 2003, 67–68, 107; Matthew Dickerson, *Following Gandalf*, 2003, 115–136; Richard Purtill, *Myth, Morality, and Religion*, 1984; and Tom Shippey, *Author of the Century*, 2000, 132–133.
33. Dickerson and Evans, *Ents*, 49.
34. Ibid., 258.
35. Ephesians 6:12 *(Douay-Rheims)*.
36. *Letters*, 201.
37. II/v, III/x, V/iv.
38. *Sil*, 31, emphasis added.
39. *Letters*, 202.
40. See, for example, Genesis 3:1–13 and Matthew 4:1–11.
41. Gandalf's words to the hobbits as he prepares to leave them before they enter the Shire illustrates this: "'You must settle its affairs yourself; that is what you have been trained for. Do you not yet understand?'" (*RK*, VI, vii, 275).
42. *Letters*, 172.
43. J.R.R. Tolkien, Interview with Dennis Gerrolt, "Now Read On..." BBC, Radio 4, January 1971.
44. *Sil*, 16.
45. Ibid., 15.
46. Ibid., 20.
47. Tolkien, *Morgoth's Ring*, 345.
48. Clyde Kilby, *Tolkien and The Silmarillion* (Wheaton, IL: Harold Shaw, 1976), 59.
49. John 1:33; Luke 24:48–49; Acts 1:7–8.
50. Genesis 1:26–27.
51. Tolkien, *Morgoth's Ring*, 332.

Works Consulted

Birzer, Bradley. *J.R.R. Tolkien's Sanctifying Myth*. Wilmington, DE: ISI Books, 2003.
Curry, Patrick. "'Less Noise and More Green': Tolkien's Ideology for England." *Proceedings of the J.R.R. Tolkien Centenary Conference 1992*, ed. Patricia Reynolds and Glen Good-Knight, 126–138. Altadena, CA. and Milton Keynes, Buckinghamshire: The Mythopoeic Press and The Tolkien Society, 1995.
_____. "Middle-earth: Nature and Ecology." *Defending Middle-earth*, ed. Patrick Curry, 48–86. Boston: Houghton Mifflin, 2004.

Dickerson, Matthew. *Following Gandalf: Epic Battles and Moral Victory in* The Lord of the Rings. Grand Rapids: Brazos Press, 2003.

_____, and Jonathan Evans. *Ents, Elves, and Eriador: The Environmental Vision of J.R.R. Tolkien*. Lexington: University Press of Kentucky, 2006.

Elgin, Don D. *The Comedy of the Fantastic: Ecological Perspectives on the Fantasy Novel*. Westport, CT: Greenwood, 1985.

Flieger, Verlyn. "Taking the Part of Trees: Eco-conflict in Middle-earth." *J.R.R. Tolkien and His Literary Resonances: Views of Middle-earth*, ed. George Clark and Daniel Timmons, 147–158. Westport, CT: Greenwood Press, 2000.

Goetz, Stewart, and Charles Taliaferro. *A Brief History of the Soul*. Malden, MA: Wiley Blackwell, 2011.

Hazell, Dinah. *The Plants of Middle-earth*. Kent, OH: Kent State University Press, 2007.

Kocher, Paul. *Master of Middle Earth: The Fiction of J.R.R. Tolkien*. Boston: Houghton Mifflin, 1972.

Kreeft, Peter. *The Philosophy of Tolkien*. San Francisco: Ignatius Press, 2005.

Nagy, Gergely. "Saving the Myths: The Re-Creation of Mythology in Plato and Tolkien." *Tolkien and the Invention of Myth*, ed. Jane Chance, 81–100. Lexington: University of Kentucky Press, 2004.

Plato. *Phaedrus*, trans. Benjamin Jowett, 246c, 18 April 2011. http://classics.mit.edu/Plato/republic.html.

Purtill, Richard. *J.R.R. Tolkien: Myth, Morality, and Religion*. San Francisco: Harper and Row, 1984.

Russell, Bertrand. "Why I Am Not a Christian." *Why I Am Not a Christian*. New York: Simon & Schuster, 1967.

Shippey, Tom. *J.R.R. Tolkien: Author of the Century*. New York: Houghton Mifflin, 2000.

Siewers, Alfred. "Tolkien's Cosmic-Christian Ecology." *Tolkien's Modern Middle Ages*, ed. Jane Chance and Alfred K. Sievers, 139–153. New York: Palgrave, 2005.

Stücklin, Christina Ljungberg. "Re-enchanting Nature: Some Magic Links between Atwood and Tolkien," *Root and Branch: Approaches Towards Understanding Tolkien*, ed. Thomas Honegger, 151–162. Zurich: Walking Tree, 1999.

Tolkien, J.R.R. Interview with Dennis Gerrolt. "Now Read On..." BBC, Radio 4, January 1971.

_____. "On Fairy Stories." *The Tolkien Reader*, 33–99. New York: Del Rey, 2003.

The Ugly Elf
Orc Bodies, Perversion, and Redemption in The Silmarillion *and* The Lord of the Rings[1]

JOLANTA N. KOMORNICKA

Against the nuanced presentation of hobbit, elf and man, the orc at first glance has little to recommend it. Often found in a band, swarming over the lands of Middle-earth, an orc is rarely glimpsed as an individual. At the word, the imagination conjures forth a fleshy, dark host, even though the fullest descriptions of orc bodies appear not in *The Silmarillion* or *The Lord of the Rings*, but in J.R.R. Tolkien's notes, published by Christopher Tolkien throughout *The History of Middle-Earth*. It is no accident that orcs are the recurring henchmen in *The Silmarillion* and *The Lord of the Rings*.[2] In them, Tolkien unfolds before us the three ages of Eä, from Creation to Decline. Throughout, an over-riding concern rests in both the nature of evil, as its form impacts how the individual may combat it, and in how redemption can be gained. Redemption often concerns the heroes, those who successfully combat the external evil or that of their forbearers (as Aragon seeks to redeem himself from the legacy of Isildur in the fight against Sauron). In the orc, however, Tolkien provides both evil's most prevalent manifestation and the truest expression of the hope that personal and generational evil cannot just be overcome, but absolved and rehabilitated. Through employing medieval tropes of the monstrous and the body, Tolkien explores Christian theological ideas of evil being and evil action to provide a central message on the possibility of redemption.

To better understand what Tolkien is doing with his orcs, for a brief moment we need to turn aside and look at a far older text. The Old English *Beowulf* places the monstrous at the center: the dragon, Grendel, Grendel's mother. In 1936, Tolkien responded to those scholars who dismissed the poem for placing the important at the fringes and indulging in the frivolous struggles with monsters. Grendel and the rest, Tolkien maintains, are

> not an inexplicable blunder of taste [but] fundamentally allied to the underlying ideas of the poem... Most important to consider is how and why monsters became "adversaries of God," and so begin to symbolize (and ultimately become identified with) the powers of evil, even while they remain, as they do still remain in *Beowulf*, mortal denizens of the material world, in and of it.[3]

It is not sufficient to call a being evil; one must examine how it came to be so. In Tolkien's Legendarium, the orcs are a stand-in for evil. They are its physical representation, throughout doing the work of their dark masters. Yet dismissing them in the manner of the *Beowulf* critics would be to dismiss a basic element in Tolkien's story: the nature and place of Evil.

Tolkien criticism has long been invested in the question of good and evil within the Legendarium, and Tolkien did not fail to provide fertile ground. Examination of his texts, personal notes and letters demonstrates if not a preoccupation then a persistent working out of the question for himself. The framework he consistently utilizes emerges from the works of St. Augustine, Boethius, and St. Thomas Aquinas. In response to W. H. Auden's review of *The Return of the King*, Tolkien wrote: "In my story I do not deal with Absolute Evil. I do not think there is such a thing, since that is Zero,"[4] echoing the sentiments found in Boethius' *The Consolation of Philosophy* and Augustine's *Confessions*. The statement arises from the argument Augustine makes in Book 9: To exist is better than not to exist; to be incorruptible is better than to be corruptible. Corruption therefore is diminution of good within a thing. If the thing is infinitely good, the process merely continues without end. Otherwise, the goodness must at some point be utterly depleted. Yet if the thing continues to exist, lacking further goodness, it has attained incorruptibility—a philosophical impossibility. Therefore, it must cease to exist. In consequence, anything that does exist must be good to some extent. Therefore, evil cannot exist. If it does not exist, it cannot create. It can, however, corrupt and pervert that which already has being. The notion of perversion and evil has a significant impact on how we read Tolkien. Numerous critics such as Rose Zimbardo, John Wm. Houghton, Neal K. Keessee, Colin Gunton and Tom Shippey have all weighed in on how we read the Ring, Saruman and Sauron. It is equally invaluable for how we read the orcs.[5] If evil does not, as a Platonic idea, exist, then what is the nature of the evil beings roaming Middle-earth?

The Silmarillion, as the story of the First Age of Eä, is intimately bound to the concept of creating—through shaping, forming, orchestrating and ultimately giving life. Melkor begins as one of the highest and most powerful Ainur created by Ilúvatar. The Ainur in the beginning sing individually, and then with their maturation, "in unison and harmony."[6] Tolkien sets the tone for the highest order and greatest good in the opening paragraph. Throughout the text, these concepts remain the lodestone for goodness, righteousness, and beauty. Yet from the start Tolkien also introduces a counter-point, a wrong note that in its placement draws attention to the perfection surrounding it. Whereas all the other Ainur cooperate to weave together their interchanging melodies, Melkor attempts to dominate with his own thoughts, separate from his brethren and Ilúvatar. The moment he does so, discord follows. Corruption has entered the story. In attempting to create something of his own, in coveting the products of Ilúvatar, Melkor has introduced chaos to the governing order. Similar in this respect to Grendel, Melkor, "hates [the] music, a dynamic metaphor of [the] communal harmony; this enmity places him outside the realm of the social and aligns him with everything abjected from the warmth of Heorot [or the house of Ilúvatar] in order to render it a livable world."[7] Divorced from his own community by his own inability to render the self accountable to others, Melkor becomes a threat. The danger of Melkor, and therefore of the orcs, is that evil originates from what is good. Aquinas, in his *Summa Contra Gentiles*, takes great pains in his theory on evil (*malum*) to show how all evil acts and substances derive from an originating good.[8] Melkor was one of the Ainur; orcs were bred from elves and men.[9] Even men who have not been subject to Melkor's corruption do evil. The question of orcish evil is thus fundamental to that of humanity overall.

It is not necessary to expound at length on Melkor's evil. From the beginning, he seeks his own elevation and misuses the gifts he has gained from Ilúvatar. What is of greater consequence are the forms his evil takes. On the physical side, he pollutes the land with dark vapors and abuses nature to produce the dank and fetid. "Rank and poisonous" fens combine with "slime" covered rivers to mar the order imposed by the Valar.[10] While the dwarves delve into mountains and fell forests, no appellation of evil clings to their deeds. In Augustinian terms, while the dwarves are selfish, they do not carry malicious intent. They do not seek the diminution of good within the trees they fell or the stones they hew. From the standpoint of Aquinas, their vision of what is good is misguided because they apprehend a narrow, selfish good but their act of will is still in itself good.[11] Melkor, on the other hand, makes the rivers and fens imperfect and defective by removing the qualities they ought to have and which are natural to them.[12]

The distinction lies at the heart of why dwarves are not akin to the orcs. Aulë crafts the dwarves before the coming of the Children of Ilúvatar. That he performs his work in secret suggests an element of shame — knowledge that the thing done is wrong. Like Melkor, he labors in subterranean darkness. Both bear the fault of impatience and for neither is the vision of the Music complete. Yet there can be no doubt that Aulë's devisings are not wicked and without the disobedience of Melkor might even be unproblematic. Dwarves and orcs are both bound to the will of their masters, and "can live only by that being," guided by their masters' thoughts. Hence does the nature of those thoughts shape their own character. Aulë by his nature delights in craftsmanship and sharing his knowledge, whereas Melkor seeks dominion, envying the lordship of Manwë. Melkor desired to use the greatness Ilúvatar had bestowed upon him to subject others for his own glorification. In contrast, Aulë chiefly sought to share the bounty he had received. Within a Christian theology shaped by Augustine and Aquinas, this willing of disruption and dominance make all the difference.[13] Although Aulë is misguided, his intentions were to contribute to the wonders of Arda. Tolkien's judgment of the two becomes explicit through motivation. "Melkor spent his spirit in envy and hate, until at last he could make nothing save in mockery of the thought of others."[14] He is the usurper, aspiring to a position he does not deserve and cannot legitimately have. Aulë is the devotee, adoringly pantomiming what he does not understand "without thought of mockery."[15] Neither can create on their own, but both have the potential for sub-creation. Melkor's is bound by his own envy, but Aulë seeks to imitate out of a willful adoration. Unlike Melkor, he is willing to "submit all that he did to Ilúvatar's will."[16] As Aulë's internal nature holds no malice, so his external expression in the form of the dwarves exhibits no perversion, merely the propensity for folly found in the fashioner.

If corruption is defined in Augustinian terms as the diminishment of good within a thing and by Aquinas as lack of a substance's proper characteristics, then we can understand the perversion of Melkor and his servants not only as a function of will, but action: both how much they pollute and how they respond to those things that remain pure. Not only do the perverted orcs dislike the sun, but their natures are so deformed that they cannot withstand sunlight for long. And though fashioned from elves, the orcs avoid the water — the irresistible pull that lies in the heart of the Children has turned backward in the orcs. The mainstays of life, the connections to the sacred, become for the orcs dreadful. Where they ought to gain strength and hope, they find only weakness and fear. Perversion stems as much from what one shuns as what one embraces; its definition can only be complete through such negativity. Melkor has taken what is good and pure and actively twisted it, perverting the accident and marring the substance. In this fashion, he withdraws orcs from the perfection of Ilúvatar.

The orcs were not created. That is to say, they do not appear fully formed, as do elves and men, and even the dwarves. As Melkor's *creatures*, the language of the text holds them in linguistic contempt and ambiguity. T. A. Shippey argues that, "there can be little doubt that the orcs entered Middle-earth originally just because the story needed a continual supply of enemies over whom one need feel no compunction,"[17] and certainly their hideous mutating of the elven body in *The Silmarillion* encourages this attitude.

> [A]ll those of the Quendi who came into the hands of Melkor, ere Utumno was broken, were put there in prison, and by slow arts of cruelty were corrupted and enslaved; and thus did Melkor breed the hideous race of the Orcs in envy and mockery of the Elves, of whom they were afterwards the bitterest foes.[18]

If as readers we are meant to sympathize with the Children, both first-born and followers, the orcs invite our revulsion. Tolkien does more with his perverted elves, however, than inform his reader where right and goodness lie. He has carefully placed the monstrous within the center of his texts, and here we might remember his defense of the *Beowulf* poet. Extant in the text from beginning to end, from the First Age through the end of the Third, the orcs are more than literary devices. They do not appear merely to better define the goodness of the elves, to show that though the Noldor may have acted wrongly they have not lost so much of their purity as to become orcish. Rather, the orcs illuminate essential aspects of humanity. In *On Fairy-Stories*, Tolkien notes that it is post–Lapsarian man who "has stained the elves ... with his own stain."[19] Orc, man and elf are inseparable. In *The Silmarillion*, man and elf are the Children of Ilúvatar, while the orc is the mutated, corrupted product of the tortured elf. In *The Lord of the Rings*, the orc comes from both man and elf. Within the Legendarium, orcish origins periodically shift as Tolkien seeks a way to elucidate these three sides of humanity. He spent so much time puzzling out the orcs for just this reason. Indeed, Tolkien's notes indicate a continual struggle to understand the orcs, culminating in his conclusion that they were corruptions of men, bred from them[20]; humanity itself could become so corrupt and debased as to "be reduced almost to the Orc-level of mind and habits,"[21] able to "vie with them in cruelty and destruction,"[22] then mated with orcs to produce new half-breeds.[23] Tolkien's various revisions of the orc have little to do with aesthetics and far more with the theological implications of their existence.

Middle-earth redounds with postlapsarian themes, redemption not least among them. In the *Enchiridion*, Augustine foresees the emptied ranks of angels being filled by the redeemed of mankind. Tolkien strove to resolve for himself the tension between this ultimate assumption and the Augustinian problem of Free Will within a being bearing original sin.[24] In his letters and notes, he repeatedly mulls over the question, especially as it applies to the orcs. Because Evil is nothing, the orcs as mortal beings who eat, drink and breed have within them some element of good. And because they were shaped by Melkor, who through Ilúvatar had the sub-creative ability to make other rational creatures, they have some power to choose.[25] In his later essays on orc origins and nature, Tolkien posits them as beings of independent will who do possess the possibility of redemption, even if it cannot be at the hands of elves or men.[26] Fundamentally, the orcs have to be capable of moving toward the good, evincing pity. This is not only necessitated by a theology that dictated that all things intend good,[27] but by the fact that the orc is an ugly elf, a deformed human, and if humanity needs anything, it is the hope of salvation.

The body of the orc plays out these deeper problems, but because the orc is so hideous and ubiquitous a foe, he has been easily dismissed. Some have disputed the idea that the orcs are mortal in the same manner as the other races,[28] and the author himself struggled with this concept, both in terms of granting orcs *fëa* (a soul) and in their nature as either Maiar or fully mortal beings.[29] Yet as we will see, the orcs are soundly mortal — in fact, it is this mortality that makes the question of their redemption so vital. Other critics, like Nataša Tučev, read the orcs as, "deformed and mindless creatures ... embodying the suppressed and consequently demonized forces of Nature,"[30] equating them with the trolls who as mockeries of the ents fit the description. Yet the orcs do not embody any aspect of Nature in caricature, though they are natural in that their ultimate ancestors are the Quendi and men. Nor can we long maintain the fiction that the orcs are "mindless." Even if Tolkien himself had not directly refuted this,[31] the texts give the orcs language and social structure, comprehensible to themselves and identifiable by others. The arguments that take place among the orcs of Isengard and Mordor and those between Shagrat and Gorbag could scarcely be envisioned if the orcs had no more independent thought than a puppet. As Tolkien puts it when he ultimately concludes that orcs are independent creatures, proven by their continuing to act and be after Sauron's defeat: "'puppets,' with no independent life or will, would simply cease to move or do anything at all when the will of their maker was brought to nothing."[32]

The orc body is monstrous, but it is rational. It follows certain laws and is articulated in the texts in a consistent fashion. But rationality does not preclude fear. The orc embodies the medieval trope that internal nature finds expression in the external self, giving the character a "visible soul."[33] Thus, the elves appear strong and great and fair, filled with a beauty that has its center within their essence as the Children of Ilúvatar. All those whom Melkor perverts, however, become black, hideous and dark, the "distortion of [their] bodies" becoming "a physical signifier of their moral state."[34] The body is incapable of dissimulation,[35] reflecting without distortion the soul; therein lies the source of what makes Tolkien's orc so terrifying. Melkor's scheming makes the familiar unfamiliar. On his own, as he changes from one of the glorious Ainur into the terrible dark lord, he becomes an Other. He stands outside the society, but he retains the potential to be identified as one of its own, for the text never lets us forget that he had been the most powerful of the Ainur. Through his creatures, Melkor gives the newly born world its own set of Others. Craven and bent, the orcs are guided by what Melkor — and later Sauron and Saruman — wills, and his desires will never be in harmony with those of society. In terms of modern theory, we can understand the orcs as, "symbols or representatives of a disruptive power inimical to established order."[36] The disruption marks them as unable to conform, destines them to be perpetual strangers. A monster becomes truly horrifying and fearsome when it proceeds from the known. An abomination taken from the Void may frighten, but it is no part of us. Once it is vanquished the fear is dispelled. But the orcs were once elves and men. Defeat one orc or a legion; so long as there is the elf, or humanity itself, there is the *potential* for the orc: "Elves may turn into Orcs, and if this required the special perversive malice of Morgoth, still elves themselves could do evil deeds."[37] The orc is like Jeffrey Cohen's Intimate Stranger. "He is ... a monsterized version of what a member of society can become when [its] dictates are rejected, when the authority of leaders or mores disintegrates and the subordination of the individual to hierarchy is lost."[38] But where the medieval giant was a monstrous, hyper-aggrandized individuality, Tolkien's orc is the result of this process in Melkor. Melkor rejects the hierarchy of Ilúvatar, his creations are subordinate to him and his lieutenants, but only out of fear. *Athrabeth Finrod* tells a similar tale for men turning to Melkor and becoming enthralled, adhering to a wrong hierarchy, a perverted one. The orcs, like their progenitors, are dominated but not crushed: just as some men rebel against Melkor, so do some orcs rebel. Thus the individual orc is a perversion of individual man and a cruel reminder of the fetid depths of humanity. At the same time, orc society stands in contrast to human society, mocking its forms and turning away from a rightly ordered world to a governance built on fear and thralldom.[39] The orc is a disordered body — both as a corporal body as body social — whose very presence requires confrontation and resolution.

The orc body is powerful, and there are two of them. Just as he is man and not all at once, he must be simultaneously read as his physical self and his figurative self. *The Silmarillion* focuses on the discord the orc represents against the harmony of the Music of Ilúvatar. Akin to the "beasts [that] become monsters of horn and ivory" at Melkor's interference,[40] they "smell out," are "savage," and in their "lust for ruin and death" avidly engage in "butchery." These depictions do not disappear by the Third Age, but the emphasis changes. The orcs are not simply Other to Eä and the elves, but to all the major races. In their movement and their being they teeter between Intimate and Stranger. Hobbits and elves routinely receive comment as silent travelers, and dwarves and men can move skillfully with great stealth. In contrast, the orcs unfailingly mark their passage with unbridled noise. Their movement is as discordant as their bodies. Yet although one cannot come away from a reading of Tolkien without an image of the orc, the descriptions are segmented.

Glimpses of long arms, slanted eyes, clawed hands, hairy ears, crooked legs, stooped backs, yellow fangs and halitosis come frequently, but rarely more than two at a time. The text emphasizes the disorderliness of the orc by constantly dismembering him. Orc death continues the practice, chopping off heads and severing limbs, as though the unity of the deformed could not be long abided. The reader receives a body in pieces.

Yet at the same time as the text strengthens the revulsion, emphasizing the animality of the orc and denying identification, it undermines the process by humanizing the creature. Frodo reminds Sam as they sit in Cirith Ungol that orcs need to eat and drink like the rest of us (*RK*, VI, i, 190). Orcs not only must obey the demands of a mortal body, but disordered as they are they must obey mortal law as well.[41] They cannot take poison and find nourishment, nor is the rotten and fetid their desired fare. Like us, they eat of necessity those foods past their prime, but not of preference. Indeed, for all the horror the orc body holds, it has identifiable norms that elevate it above the level of insensate beast. It is easy to imagine the orcs as cannibals, that ultimate sign of social and physical aberration. Yet when cannibalism arises, it finds its place as an insult (*TT*, III, iii, 49). Two groups of orcs, pitted against one another on their march with Merry and Pippin, bicker and hurl out accusations of cannibalism and other insults familiar to any student of humanity. Although the orcs often display an incorrect reading of bodies generally, such as Grishnáck's threat to "untie every string in [Merry's and Pippin's] bodies" and search them "to the bones" (*TT*, III, iii, 59), they do draw a line. At the same time, they have an appreciation for the body that does not involve savagery. The mere fact the orcs possess medicine suggests that they have an active respect for health and the body's proper functioning. While the orc draught has specific practical purposes in terms of keeping an orc body on the move for days, it is not entirely dissimilar to *lembas* (except in taste) and is indicative that a segment of orcs have the knowledge and skill to produce the drug.

Tolkien's orc never emerges from this contradictory state. The dialogue of society takes place on the body. It is the site of society's regulations and the locus of individual resistance.[42] As society becomes more complex in *The Lord of the Rings*, the "messages" on the orc body deepen.[43] Orcs are leaders and chiefs of several orc tribes. For any society to function, division of labor and recognition of authority are necessary. The latter can be seen when orcs pull rank on one another with the expectation that they will be heeded, and even in the camaraderie and loyalty they express toward each other.[44] The former emerges from the various orc breeds. The Uruk-hai are the fighters, then there are the "snufflers," the tracking and scouting orcs, and finally the laboring "snaga" or slaves. True to the ethos of the "visible soul," each of these trades has a physical embodiment: the Uruk-hai are tall and broad shouldered; the trackers have wide, flat noses; the slaves are smaller and stooped. Everyone has their place, identifiable and unavoidable due to their bodies. The dictates of society involve more than the division of labor and behavioral rules, however. They also encapsulate the theoretical and metaphorical — the figurative body. Perhaps the single most important and prevalent in our understanding of the orc is the perversion of the body's natural order through blood.

Blood has a significant metaphorical role to play throughout the Legendarium. In its most basic form, it determines relationships and genealogies, along which the mighty feuds and friendships are carried and which can restore a king to his throne. It binds together commonalities, both within a group and across races. Therefore, as Tolkien explains in a letter to Milton Waldman, "in Men ... there is a strand of 'blood' and inheritance, derived from the Elves."[45] Blood in this capacity is wholesome. Physical and figurative in equal measure, its conception belongs to an interconnected, harmonious arrangement. The moment that blood becomes external, it loses this consonance. By its very nature, blood belongs within the body. That it should emerge indicates a disruption, an injury that has been incurred, compromising the unity of the *corpus*. Here the perversion manifests. Within *The Silmarillion* and largely throughout *The Lord of the Rings*, all mention of spilled blood remains staunchly metaphorical. When Fëanor's sons swear their oath and raise their swords, those implements of disunity, the metal gleams "red as blood."[46] The expected sight is denied through simile. In like vein, as the Valar pronounce the Doom of the Noldor, the land of Aman is said to have been stained with blood,[47] yet this is no more than metaphor and hyperbole. The text diverts us from the blood shed in the slaying. Thus, though the Noldor have done wrong, they maintain a respect for the proper placement of blood, and so find an oblique exoneration in the text. Yet when the focus shifts to the monstrous, the texts do not hesitate to embrace the full unnaturalness of the actions. Black orc blood smokes on the ground,[48] slicking the rocks[49] until all is wet with it. No metaphor softens the disgusting exsanguinations and no familial relationships appear to counter-balance the sheer physicality of the imagery. Indeed, unlike the elves and men from whom they derive, orcs lack the most fundamental aspect of figurative blood: family. Their only genealogy is their corrupt descent from elves and men; what the latter hold dear and repeatedly refer to with pride and veneration as the principle of their societies, orcs have perverted and denied a place in their own social structure. In taking the lofty, near-ethereal and misshaping it, Melkor and his creatures lose the spiritual nature of their identities.

The orcs are the height of disordered corporeality. Without direct speech in *The Silmarillion*, their illustrious progenitors are denied by their behavior. When their language is heard, it is harsh, guttural, and between orc tribes the dialects are mutually unintelligible, further corrupting the fairness of their forbearers. Blood is for them an external substance, at once unnatural and divorced from its sublime ability to bind through inheritance. Tolkien's language regarding the orcs is raw, visceral. Every action of theirs is physical and they are best characterized in relation to a disjointed assortment of limbs. As in medieval romances, Tolkien presents "a fantasy of the body in pieces [the orcs] coupled to a 'final' identification with a wholly imaginary form of the ideal self [the elves as 'a representation or an apprehension of a part of human nature' (*Letters* 149)]."[50] It is the monsters' corporeality without anything that might raise them above it that, in their Intimate Strangeness, make them so monstrous. It unnerves and becomes fundamental to the text. As Pascal wrote, "I can easily conceive of a man without hands, feet, head... But I cannot conceive of man without thought; that would be a stone or a brute." We have need of a self that transcends the corporeal — the metaphor of the blood as much as its circulatory presence. In other words, the interior must be more than what the exterior can show.

Simple will does not control this exteriority. Rather, an intimate interplay between inner and outer dictates form. The physical manifestation of character has value beyond serving as a marker for good and evil. The orcs, though deformed, have value in the texts. Though tremendously corrupted, moments of humor and pity show through. In their jocularity, though vulgar and inclined toward the sadistic,[51] they are humanized in their intellect just as their need for real food humanizes their bodies.[52] Their capacity for pity, meanwhile, negates the idea of some critics that the orc is the insatiable, uncontrollable id.[53] "Pity must restrain one from doing something immediately desirable and seemingly advantageous."[54] As the orcs abduct Merry and Pippin from the company, they do not act as mindless brutes or evil thugs. Suffering loss of limb at Merry's sword, they do nothing other than grab the two hobbits. And while their treatment of them may be rough during the march, they are not entirely neglectful of the hobbits' needs. Though the extent of this pity is severely limited, the fact that the orcs have the capability to act rationally bolsters the notion that they are not entirely irredeemable. Jeffery Cohen wrote of the giant in medieval literature as it "is at once a seemingly monolithic representation of otherness and a figure whose indomitable corporeality suggests the difficulty of being merely human in a world that demands the austere discipline of minute self-regulation."[55] A constant presence in the text, the orc and his body do more than provide us with a face to hate. He shows the danger of unrestrained individuality and willfulness and that of an intemperate society. It is not enough to simply defeat this monster. Evil has an interiority that none can escape. It is therefore imperative that even though elves and men may view orcs as irredeemable, in reality they are not so. Their unrealized potential for good encapsulates the hope of the end of the Third Age. Just as Finrod cautions Andreth that she must have *Estel* (trust) that the race of man would see the reunification of *fëa* and *hröa* after death, repairing the damage that the separation in death had caused, *Estel* must exist that the corruption caused by Melkor will not last. Augustine and Aquinas both wrote that all things strive for good, though they may be turned aside in their journey or misapprehend a selfish, personal good for a greater one.[56] So too do the orcs strive as they mirror, however distortedly, human form, speech, food, society and camaraderie. The lesson of the orcs is that if they can find redemption in all their perversity, than so too can the men who stooped to do evil hope to find the same.

The Silmarillion and *The Lord of the Rings* are stories about power. Voice has power. In the tones of music, it can fashion a world, but with that power comes risk. The wrong note and the meaning shifts, altering course and changing the end product. As the note spawns a chord, so can the disharmony multiply and threaten the entire orchestration. Yet the threat is an inalienable part of the composition, because its potential lies inside. So the texts are also stories about selfhood. The monster that shares our traits haunts us more viscerally, more hungrily than the one who bears us no resemblance. Forests are transformed into Wild Woods, Night becomes Void, Elves rendered into Orcs. These present a challenge all must face. It is against the propensity for impurity within the self that we fight, against the utterance of the wrong words. Cognizant of the threat, we order our societies, tailor our unique melodies into a single harmony in the belief that unity will hold at bay the Other within ourselves. Along the way, we watch the fallen for signs that the evil inside does not have to win and that our own failings may be forgiven.

Notes

1. Adapted from the conference paper "Blasphemy and the Creation of the Orcs" given at the 4th Annual Tolkien Conference at UVM, April 13–15, 2007.

2. Though published and partially written out of order, this paper will be regarding the two works according to their interior chronology. The purpose of this is to be able to retain the narrative coherence of Tolkien's vision.

3. J.R.R. Tolkien, *Beowulf: The Monsters and the Critics* (Folcroft, PA: Folcroft Press, 1936), 17–18.

4. Tolkien, *Letters*, 243.

5. As Tom Shippey began to do in "Orcs, Wraiths, Wights: Tolkien's Images of Evil," *J.R.R. Tolkien and His Literary Resonances: Views of Middle-earth*, ed. George Clark and Daniel Timmons (Westport, CT: Greenwood Press, 2000), 183–189.

6. *Sil*, 3.

7. Jeffrey Jerome Cohen, *Of Giants: Sex, Monsters, and the Middle Ages* (Minneapolis: University of Minnesota Press, 1999), 25.

8. Thomas Aquinas, *Summa Contra Gentiles*, III.10.1951. For a detailed examination of Aquinas' statement, see Norman Kretzmann, "III. Badness," *Medieval Philosophy and Theology* 9.2 (September 2000), 147.

9. Although Tolkien never explicitly rejected the idea that orcs were bred from elves, his final essays on the subject favor men as the origin of these creatures. Due to the fact that *The Silmarillion* retains elves as the origin, I refer to orcs as corruptions of both elves

and men. Within the context of *Athrabeth Finrod* in *Morgoth's Ring*, which discusses the close association of men and elves, the dual origins of the orcs makes sense and is in keeping with the Legendarium and Tolkien's notes.
  10. *Sil*, 29.
  11. Aquinas, III.10.1946a. Kretzmann, 151.
  12. Aquinas, III.5&6.1899. "A substance is bad ... in some respect and to some extent if and only if 'it lacks something that [1] is natural for it and that [2] it ought (*debet*) to have.'" Kretzmann, 136.
  13. For Aquinas, see Kretzmann, 152.
  14. *Sil*, 18.
  15. Ibid., 38.
  16. Ibid., 18.
  17. Tom Shippey, *The Road to Middle-earth* (Boston: Houghton Mifflin, 1983), 174.
  18. *Sil*, 47.
  19. "On Fairy-Stories," Google Scholar, http://www.doc.ic.ac.uk/~rac101/texts/tolkien.pdf, 11.
  20. *Morgoth's Ring*, 417.
  21. Ibid., 418.
  22. Ibid., 420.
  23. Ibid., 419.
  24. *Athrabeth Finroth* is an example of Tolkien trying to understand the Fall and humanity's yearning to return to a previous, perfect state.
  25. *Letters*, 195; *Morgoth's Ring*, 409–11.
  26. *Morgoth's Ring*, 419.
  27. Aquinas, III.4.1892. Kretzmann, 126.
  28. Anderson Rearick III, "Why Is the Only Good Orc a Dead Orc? The Dark Face of Racism Examined in Tolkien's World," *Modern Fiction Studies* 50.4 (Winter 2004), 870.
  29. *Morgoth's Ring*, 410, 417.
  30. Nataša Tučev, "The Knife, the Sting and the Tooth: Manifestations of the Shadow in The Lord of the Rings," *Linguistics and Literature* 3.1 (2004), 4.
  31. *Morgoth's Ring*, 417–418.
  32. Ibid., 421.
  33. J.S. Ryan, "German Mythology Applied. The Extension of the Literary Folk Memory," *Folklore* 77.1 (Spring 1966), 47; Cohen, *Of Giants*, xvii.
  34. Cohen, *Of Giants*, 35.
  35. Lisa Silverman, *Tortured Subjects: Pain, Truth, and the Body in Early Modern France* (Chicago: University of Chicago Press, 2001), 9.
  36. Randel Helms, *Tolkien's World* (Boston: Houghton Mifflin, 1974), 69.
  37. *Letters*, 286–87.
  38. Cohen, *Of Giants*, 26.
  39. Shippey, "Orcs, Wraiths, Wights," 188.
  40. *Sil*, 29.
  41. As Shippey points out, inability to find sustenance in poison extends to an inability to base behavior on a code of complete amorality. Shippey, "Orcs, Wraiths, Wights," 184.
  42. Barbara Creed, "Horror and the Carnivalesque: The Body Monstrous," *Fields of Vision: Essays in Film Studies, Visual Anthropology, and Photography*, ed. Leslie Devereaux and Roger Hillman (Berkeley: University of California Press, 1995), 127–28.
  43. Ibid., 127.
  44. Shippey, "Orcs, Wraiths, Wights," 186.
  45. *Letters*, 149.
  46. *Sil*, 90.
  47. *Sil*, 96.

48. *FR*, II, v, 339.
49. *RK*, VI, i, 179.
50. Cohen, *Of Giants*,163.
51. Jane Chance, "'In the Company of Orcs': Peter Jackson's Queer Tolkien," *Queer Movie Medievalisms*, ed. Kathleen Coyne Kelly and Tison Pugh (Farnnam, Surrey: Ashgate, 2009), 90.
52. Shippey, "Orcs, Wraiths, Wights," 185.
53. Chance, *Of Giants*, 91. Helms, *Tolkien's World*, 29.
54. *Letters*, 191.
55. Cohen, *Of Giants*, iv.
56. Aquinas, III.8&9.1928. Kretzmann, 146.

Works Consulted

Augustine. *Confessions*, trans. Henry Chadwick. Oxford World's Classics. Oxford: Oxford University Press, 1992.
_____. *Enchiridion*, trans. J. F. Shaw. *St. Augustin: On the Holy Trinity, Doctrinal Treatises, Moral Treatises*, Select Library of the Nicene and Post-Nicene Fathers, First Series, III, ed. Philip Schaff. Grand Rapids: Eerdmans, 1980.
Boethius. *Consolation of Philosophy*, trans. Richard Green. Indianapolis: Bobbs-Merrill, 1962.
Chance, Jane. "'In the Company of Orcs': Peter Jackson's Queer Tolkien." *Queer Movie Medievalisms*, ed. Kathleen Coyne Kelly and Tison Pugh, 79–96. Farnham, Surrey: Ashgate, 2009.
Cohen, Jeffrey Jerome. *Of Giants: Sex, Monsters, and the Middle Ages*. Minneapolis: University of Minnesota Press, 1999.
Creed, Barbara. "Horror and the Carnivalesque: The Body Monstrous." *Fields of Vision: Essays in Film Studies, Visual Anthropology, and Photography*, ed. Leslie Devereaux and Roger Hillman, 127–159. Berkeley: University of California Press, 1995.
Gunton, Colin. "'A Far-off Gleam of the Gospel': Salvation in Tolkien's *The Lord of the Rings*." *Tolkien: A Celebration*, ed. Joseph Pearce. London: HarperCollins, 1999.
Helms, Randel. *Tolkien's World*. Boston: Houghton Mifflin, 1974.
Houghton, John Wm., and Neal K. Keessee. "Tolkien, King Alfred, and Beothius: Platonist Views of Evil in *The Lord of the Rings*." *Tolkien Studies* 2.1 (2005): 131–159.
Kretzmann, Norman. "III. Badness." *Medieval Philosophy and Theology* 9.2 (September 2000): 126–156.
Rearick III, Anderson. "Why Is the Only Good Orc a Dead Orc? The Dark Face of Racism Examined in Tolkien's World." *Modern Fiction Studies* 50.4 (Winter 2004): 861–874.
Ryan, J. S. "German Mythology Applied. The Extension of the Literary Folk Memory." *Folklore* 77.1 (Spring 1966): 45–59.
Shippey, T. A. *J.R.R. Tolkien: Author of the Century*. New York: Houghton Mifflin, 2001.
_____. "Light-elves, Dark-elves, and Others: Tolkien's Elvish Problem." *Tolkien Studies* 1.1 (2004): 1–15.
_____. "Orcs, Wraiths, Wights: Tolkien's Images of Evil." *J.R.R. Tolkien and His Literary Resonances: Views of Middle-earth*, ed. George Clark and Daniel Timmons, 183–196. Westport, CT: Greenwood Press, 2000.
_____. *The Road to Middle-earth*. Boston: Houghton Mifflin, 1983.
Silverman, Lisa. *Tortured Subjects: Pain, Truth, and the Body in Early Modern France*. Chicago: University of Chicago Press, 2001.
Tolkien, J.R.R. *Beowulf: The Monsters and the Critics*. Folcroft, PA: Folcroft Press, 1936.
_____. "On Fairy-Stories." Google Scholar. 18 April 2011. http://www.doc.ic.ac.uk/-rac101/texts/tolkien.pdf.

Tučev, Nataša. "The Knife, the Sting and the Tooth: Manifestations of the Shadow in *The Lord of the Rings.*" *Linguistics and Literature* 3.1 (2004): 111–121.

Zimbardo, Rose A. "Moral Vision in *The Lord of the Rings.*" *Understanding* The Lord of the Rings: *The Best of Tolkien Criticism*, ed. Rose A. Zimbardo and Neil D. Isaacs, 68–75. Boston: Houghton Mifflin, 2004.

PART III

The Discursive Body

Light (noun, 1) or Light (adjective, 14b)?
Female Bodies and Femininities in The Lord of the Rings

ROBIN ANNE REID

Previous scholarship on the female characters in Tolkien's *Legendarium* tends to focus on such questions as the medieval sources and influences, their narrative functions, their tendencies toward spiritual rather than material power, and their relationships with the male characters. Only a few scholars (notably, Brenda Partridge, Edith Crowe, Leslie Donovan, and David Pretorius) use feminist approaches and methodologies in their analysis of female characters. However, little scholarship analyzing the narrative's construction of female bodies in *The Lord of the Rings* from contemporary queer studies exists; gender and queer approaches have been more utilized in scholarship on Peter Jackson's film, but that lies outside the scope of this paper. This project draws from queer studies and applied linguistics (stylistics) to develop an analysis of the grammatical construction of female characters' bodies in *The Lord of the Rings*.

Critical response in periodicals and academic journals on the question of women in Tolkien's work has been mixed. Early publications criticized the scarcity of major female characters and the stereotypical nature of the existing ones; rebuttals argued that the female characters possessed strength and thematic importance that cannot be easily dismissed. Critical disagreement over whether Tolkien was personally misogynistic or simply an average man of his time and place underlies much of the gender debate. To consider Tolkien's attitudes, instead of his text, is to move toward trying to analyze authorial intentionality, which is problematic. Debates over gender and gender roles applying to female characters in Tolkien's work exist within the historical context of the twentieth century, particularly the changes in women's lives and in the social expectations for women and men during that time. The changes were taking place during Tolkien's professional life, as Oxford allowed women to take degrees rather than simply enroll in classes, after World War I, and continued after his death as a growing number of women began to engage in graduate work and academic scholarship. "Gender" is certainly not a modern or contemporary ideology that does not apply to older texts. Nevertheless, contemporary constructions of gender differ from those existing in earlier historical periods and other cultures. The earliest scholarship on *The Lord of the Rings* tended largely to ignore the question of women in the text even as a significant number of women began producing scholarship on the text.[1] To observe that most anthologies and major monographs of Tolkien scholarship make little or no mention of female characters and that what mention exists is slight compared to the male characters is not to claim the early work is misogynistic any more than Tolkien's work can be declared misogynistic based on the narrative space given female characters. However, it is possible to claim that the body of scholarship is gendered primarily male and primarily hetero-normative due to historical circumstances, including the access of women to post-graduate programs, the extent to which access has primarily benefited white and straight middle-class women, and to cultural norms which affect disciplinary standards, methodologies, epistemologies, and ideologies.

As a queer woman, and as a feminist, I am not concerned to make a larger argument about the questions of relative misogyny or feminism in Tolkien since the extent to which a reader sees "sexism" or "feminism" in Tolkien's novel is related in part to that individual reader's own world-view and belief system, not to mention individual definitions of "sexism" and "feminism." Instead, in this essay I consider the question of how female bodies are constructed, given the traditional binaries of gender that have been identified in *The Lord of the Rings* (male/female and virgin/whore). My analysis is informed by queer theory, namely Judith Halberstam's *Female Masculinity*. Queer theory builds upon earlier work by feminist and gender theorists that argues that gender roles are socially constructed; queer theory moves to argue that a socially constructed gender can be separated from the body, complicating the extent to which some earlier gay/lesbian theory tended to essentialize a homosexual, then a homo-normative theory of identity. Blending queer theory with stylistic evidence acknowledges the extent to which gender, as constructed socially, is constructed in part through language, and as not contingent upon the body. Thus, my project is not interested in traditional literary assumptions which have denied critics/scholars their bodies and histories in a demand for a fictional objectivity which situates the white male as falsely universal and either ignores gender or reduces it to hetero-normativity, all assumptions which are increasingly dubious in the twenty-first century.[2]

My project is situated in a contrarian reading of *The Lord of the Rings*;

as a white woman and a feminist, I know I am, and have been since the age of ten, reading against the grain of Tolkien's novel and his stated intentions (within his *Letters* and as embodied in earlier drafts of his work) about the nature of "women." What I am concerned with in this paper is presenting an interdisciplinary model of methodologies. My method draws upon functional linguistics, or stylistics, and queer theory. Michael D.C. Drout's "Tolkien's Prose Style and its Literary and Rhetorical Effects" (2004), is the only publication I'm aware of using functional grammar. Queer readings of Tolkien's novel have been done by David M. Craig ("'Queer Lodgings': Gender and Sexuality in *The Lord of the Rings*"). *The Modern Fiction Studies* (Winter 2004) Tolkien special issue has a unit on "Queering *The Lord of the Rings*," but only one of the three essays focuses primarily upon Tolkien's novel: Jes Battis, "Gazing Upon Sauron: Hobbits, Elves, and the Queering of the Postcolonial Optic." I find the correlation of queer readings being done by male scholars and feminist readings being done primarily by female scholars to be noteworthy but not surprising. David Pretorius' "Binary Issues and Feminist Issues in *The Lord of the Rings*" has three sections, one of which develops a limited feminist reading, but he ignores the extent to which gender is a binary in Tolkien's work.[3]

My stylistic reading focuses on selected passages dealing with five major female characters in the novel: Goldberry, Arwen, Galadriel, Éowyn, and Shelob.[4] My analysis begins with a stylistic analysis of women's bodies in the novel, considering agency and light imageries, then concludes with a queer reading of Éowyn, which complicates the types of femininities and possible responses by female readers of *The Lord of the Rings*.[5]

Critical consensus exists on the spiritual and thematic importance of light imagery in *The Lord of the Rings* although no quantitative study has been done. I would also note that few scholars consider the double meanings of "light" in English. The first definition of "light," the noun, in the *Oxford English Dictionary* (*OED*) is the emanations of the sun, the medium of sight, set in opposition to darkness; the fourteenth definition of "light," the adjective, in the *OED*, is defined as "Of persons (chiefly of women) and their behaviour: Wanton, unchaste." That the same sign can contain two disparate meanings is not unusual. That one meaning is gender neutral and relates to an aspect of the natural world, albeit having many positive symbolic associations in human cultures, and that the other is largely gender specific (all the quotes specify "light" women, in one case paired with "lewd" men; no usage in the dictionary refers to "light" men) and negative shows the extent to which meaning is arbitrary and, as scholars have argued, the extent to which arbitrary meanings are part of gender roles created through the social medium of language. Light, in the first meaning of the word, plays an important thematic role in Tolkien's Legendarium in both its physical manifestations on Middle-earth and in its symbolic associations with Tolkien's creation myth, the Valar, major characters, and the structuring of conflicts in the First and later Ages. Light, in the second meaning of the word, plays no role in Tolkien's world unless one chooses to consider the monstrous spirit in spider form, Shelob, who mates with her offspring to produce bastard children which she also kills and devours as an example of a wanton female.[6] This layering of meanings, in which the positive symbolic term co-exists with the negative and sexually oriented term applied solely to women, provides a key to the construction of female bodies and femininities in *The Lord of the Rings*.[7] The construction of bodies and type of agency associated with the good female characters are non-sexual and operate primarily in non-material realms (spiritual rather than material) with one exception (Éowyn) while the evil non-human character is constructed as greedy, malicious and perverse in her malice and much more embodied because of her appetites, in all meanings of the word.[8]

As Leslie A. Donovan argues persuasively in "The Valkyrie Reflex in J.R.R. Tolkien's *The Lord of the Rings*" (2003) one characteristic shared by Tolkien's primary female characters is their association with light, whether that association is that of power from (Galadriel, Arwen, Éowyn)[9] or vulnerability to light (Shelob) (121). The dominant patterns of imagery in passages relating to Galadriel and Arwen connect them to light (physical and spiritual). Éowyn's connection with light imagery is less important than that of the elves, but her white dress and the light falling upon her at the climactic moment when she kills the Ringwraith supports her association with light and power, and Donovan notes that she is the most directly connected to the Germanic valkyrie figures. In contrast, the narrative description of Shelob is of darkness, with her faceted eyes shown as first reflecting the light of the star-glass, then having their own kindled light which can be quenched by the power of Galadriel's phial. Donovan argues not only that the female characters have their origin in the valkyrie tradition but that Tolkien adapted the tradition, as he adapted other medieval models, to serve his "Christian, post–World War II, prefeminist vision of modern epic." His adaptation includes deleting the concept of valkyrie as inciter of vengeance and emphasizing it as "reflective of moral good, heroic ideals, noble behavior, and responsible leadership by means of female identity concordant with contemporary perceptions of women as significant forces within society and the world."[10] Donovan's reading of the association with light and power is an exemplary one; my analysis adds only more specific details in examining how "light" is embodied (or not) in the text, and how bodies are described (or not) in the text. Stylistic methodology rarely uncovers interpretations at odds with critical consensus; the strength of the method is that specific and quantitative data can be produced to support critical conclusions by using a system that was developed outside of and for other purposes than literary studies.

My stylistic methodology draws upon M.A.K. Halliday's functional grammar, which provides a systemic model and a way of understanding language by describing how it is used. The method is generative rather than structuralist. Halliday's system allows me to describe how meaning is constructed on the clause and word level in excerpts from my selected text. While Halliday's system includes some traditional prescriptive grammatical terms, he developed his own extensive terminology. My analysis of Agency will be familiar to those who can identify grammatical subjects, but my discussion of processes (verbs) necessarily draws on Halliday's categories. His system identifies six categories of processes: relational (verbs relating to the world of abstract relations, generalizations); verbal (verbs relating to speech); mental (verbs relating to thinking and other processes in the world of consciousness); behavioral (verbs that show the acting out of mental states); material (relating to actions in the physical world); and existential (the marking of how all things are seen as existing, "being"). Appendix A contains the book, chapter, page, and line numbers of each of the clauses within excerpts selected based on the first appearance of the character in the novel and complete data on the stylistic analysis of those excerpts. Those excerpts are fairly brief, consisting of first descriptions of the characters and major plot events or climactic moments.[11]

Agency

Agency, in Halliday's system, is based on identification of the grammatical subject of clauses; when the process of the clause is a material one, the subject is the one doing the action. Halliday's terminology for what traditional grammar calls subjects is complex, and I do not go into detail here (distinguishing between Actor or Agent, Senser, etc.). Subjects need not be human or other animate beings, but in regard to my excerpts for this analysis, I considered how often the female character was the subject of the clauses in sections focusing on her (as opposed to other characters).

Table 1. Subject of Clauses

Arwen	*Galadriel*	*Goldberry*	*Éowyn*	*Shelob*
40%	44%	51%	58%	54%

The majority of subjects of the clauses are in the form of the character's name or the form of a pronoun referring to the character, or a title or some other reference. On occasion, there are subjects that reference the character, but not fully: for example, nouns referencing a part of the character's body (the most popular choice being, with the exception of Shelob, eyes and hair; for Shelob, her belly) or the character's clothing. In fact, Shelob is the character most often described in bodily terms (64 percent) more often than by name/

pronoun. Galadriel is most often described with regard to her name, title (the Lady), or pronoun (81 percent). Some of the disparity in the use of names could well be due to the point of view issue: Sam and Frodo have no way of knowing Shelob's name. Goldberry is the single character whose clothing (including accessories) is most often described; four mentions, or 10 percent of the subjects in her excerpts focus on clothing. Éowyn is next, with two subjects, but those items are weapons and armor associated with the male, Dernhelm.

Table 2: Subjects (types)

	Arwen	Galadriel	Goldberry	Shelob	Éowyn
name-or-pronoun	72%	81%	56%	36%	70%
part-of-body	22%	19%	34%	64%	25%
Clothes	6%	0%	11%	0%	5%

As a character, Goldberry is physically contained within the text in a way that may be argued is unique. Tom Bombadil will not leave his boundary of his lands, but Goldberry seems even more limited to the house and the hill immediately next to it. However, the grammar of her sections constructs her as the primary Agent in more than half the clauses (independent and dependent). The verbal processes in the clauses are primarily behavioral (often vocal: singing, laughing, rustling). These are processes used by the characters or narrator, not her direct dialogue. She is in movement throughout most of her section, except for the hobbits first view of her. However, her power extends beyond the house and hill. She meets the hobbits first through the medium of her song, compared to the sound of water (*FR*, I, vi, 133). As the Daughter of the River, her description and images combine light and water, both the sound of it and its actual presence in the rain of her washing day. She is embodied first as voice, song and water, and then seen sitting among flowers, compared to a young elf queen. Her movements are light and quick, ethereal, and, like Tom's, connected to nature. The hobbits in her presence are described and seeing, knowing, and feeling, without necessarily thinking or analyzing; they react the same way to Tom's stories.

My analysis in this paper cannot do justice to Arwen since a full discussion of her grammatical construction must include "The Tale of Aragorn and Arwen" in Appendix A and should include a comparative analysis with Aragorn, and I lack the space. The lack of text in the body of the novel (as opposed to the book as a whole) reflects Tolkien's writing process; Arwen appeared late in the process of drafting the story (as did Rose Cotton).[12] My analysis of Arwen's two main scenes in the novel show a focus on her function as Aragorn's reward and queen, but she is also present for Frodo, and her actions affect him greatly. We see her through his eyes at Rivendell and again at Minas Tirith. In terms of grammatical agency, she has the least of the characters discussed in this project: she is the subject of only 40 percent of the clauses in the excerpts. Most of the text in the first scene is dedicated to her appearance as she sits in the hall. However, that number considered in isolation may well be misleading. The most complex syntax and clause structures are found in the excerpts dealing with Arwen, with some startling variations to the rule which, in standard modern English, describes the fact that most clauses have the same word or phrase serving as the theme (the words that begin the clause) and the grammatical subject. In Tolkien's prose, consciously archaic at points, that pattern is not always used. His narrative voice consciously reverses the standard order of SVO (Subject, Verb, Object), at times for emphasis, and to varying degrees. Subjects may be embedded after introductory phrases, conjunctions, or dependent clauses, and are often followed by a series of dependent clauses. One of the best examples of extreme variation in word order is found in the sentence describing the procession of elves arriving at Minas Tirith for Aragorn and Arwen's wedding. In this case, the syntax of the sentence mirrors the order of the procession. I've broken the sentence into the six constituent clauses:

1. First rode Elrohir and Elladan with a banner of silver,
2. and then came Glorfindel and Erestor and all the household of Rivendell,
3. and after them came the Lady Galadriel and Celeborn, Lord of Lothlórien, riding upon white steeds
4. and with them [came] many fair folk of their land, grey-cloaked with white gems in their hair;
5. and last came Master Elrond, mighty among Elves and Men, bearing the sceptre of Annúminas,
6. and beside him upon a grey palfrey rode Arwen his daughter, Evenstar of her people.

Each of the six clauses is independent; all have a theme that is not the subject. In all cases, the themes indicate their order in the procession (plus, in 2–6, the conjunction "and"). But the purpose of the procession is to bring Arwen to her marriage with Aragorn. Each clause indicates the devices or escort accompanying the characters, but all accompany Arwen. She is the focus of the sentence although her name is not mentioned until word 83 of a 90-word sentence.

Arwen's body, like Goldberry's, is constructed in terms of her hair, eyes, and clothing. In contrast to Goldberry, Arwen is given a genealogy that leads back to the First Age through Elrond, her father and through her likeness to Lúthien. Her significance in the text comes not from any action, any behavior or effect upon the material world; it is in her being, embodying the characteristics of both elves and men, bringing the sundered lines together again in her marriage. She does act in one material way at the end, gifting Frodo with a white gem, as Galadriel gave him the star-glass, to help him heal.

Galadriel's agency is complex because in many of the clauses, she is paired with Celeborn (either through a complex subject formation, or through the plural pronoun). She is the subject of only 46 percent of the clauses in the excerpts. Like Arwen, she is presented as beautiful, but she is described in more masculine terms: she is the partner and equal (or superior) to her husband, not a daughter of a powerful father. Galadriel is as tall as Lord Celeborn. Her voice is deeper than other women's. She speaks more than Celeborn does although early drafts show that a number of her lines were originally spoken by Keleborn.[13] While Galadriel's body is described in ways similar to Goldberry's and Arwen's (clothing, hair), so too is Lord Celeborn's. The main difference in the construction of Galadriel's body compared to the other humanoid females is in how much of the text is devoted to her eyes: she acts through looking at the Fellowship, seeing more than their bodies.

Éowyn is the only human female character (save for Ioreth). While, as Donovan notes, she is associated with light as are Goldberry, Arwen, and Galadriel, the associations seem more natural than supernatural. She is lit by the sun; she does not shine through her own agency. However, her agency is clearly established: she is the grammatical subject of nearly 60 percent of the clauses in the excerpts, and she acts more in the material world, destroying the supernatural figure of the Ringwraith with the help of a hobbit, his blade, and her sword. More of her verbal processes are behavioral than any of the other characters, save for Shelob, who also is described as fighting. But even before her fight, she is described in movement; like Goldberry, she welcomes guests and serves them. She is described in terms of her dress and hair, but she disguises herself in the garb of a man, including a helm to hide her hair. She bears a cup, but she also bears a sword.

Shelob is a powerful spirit in the form of a female spider, but she lacks much of the sentience and all of the language of the others discussed above. She has the greatest agency, in 66 percent of her clauses, but she is defeated, killed at the end. She can hear and see, and be seen, but her actions are described as instinctive, driven by a lust for blood and life. Her body is described in simple terms, the focus primarily on her belly (never mentioned for any other character) and glowing eyes which are the first things that Sam and Frodo see in the dark. The extent to which her power is embodied in her eyes seems to mirror Galadriel's opposing power.

Imagery

Tolkien's use of imagery does not fall into a Manichean binary: dark=bad, light=good. Good characters, including Arwen, have dark hair; Shelob's eyes have a pale, glowing (evil) light. The elves are associated with the stars of night, and the lights in the Dead Marshes are evil traps. However, natural light and symbolic white light are most often associated with characters opposing the domination of Middle-earth by Sauron and others. My analysis of light imagery associated with the bodies of the female characters focused more on the word level than the clause level; I analyzed the patterns in nouns, adjectives, and processes.

	Goldberry	Arwen	Galadriel	Éowyn	Shelob
Nouns					
light	90%	18%	100%	8%	0%
dark	10%	3%	0%	3%	100%
neutral	0%	79%	0%	89%	0%
Adjectives					
light	45%	57%	34%	14%	15%
dark	0%	7%	6%	3%	39%
neutral	55%	36%	60%	83%	46%
Processes					
shining/light	9%	9%	7%	5%	10%
dimming/Dark	2%	0%	4%	1%	5%
neutral	89%	91%	89%	94%	85%

I identified words that were associated with light and the processes of shining, lightening, with dark and the processes of dimming, and neutral terms. The nouns provided the most detail, with clear differences between Shelob (100 percent dark) and the others, although nouns associated with Arwen and Éowyn were primarily neutral. Adjectives were the second most useful, and the processes (verbs) least useful. The data supports Donovan's argument that Éowyn is least associated with light, with only 5 percent of the nouns and 14 percent of the adjectives in her passages being related to light. I read this amount as relating to light being part of the natural setting, not her being associated with darkness; in most cases, the data shows the largest percent of "neutral" terms being found in her excerpts as well (from 83 percent to 94 percent). Shelob, not surprisingly, has the most associations with darkness. Goldberry and Galadriel are nearly equal in the light imagery associated with them in all categories, with Arwen's totals falling between them and the mortal, Éowyn.

Although Tolkien's work is often denigrated as an "action" novel, my linguistic analysis supports what a number of other scholars have argued: that the important actions are not always the martial actions in the material world. While as an adult, I can see the ways in which Tolkien's style constructs Goldberry, Arwen, and Galadriel as having a range of spiritual and moral powers, as argued by Craig and Donovan, I also would argue that the reason Éowyn appealed, and appeals, the most to me can be supported in part by the grammar of the text: she acts. My analysis of the processes in the excerpts show that 63 percent of Éowyn's verbs are material (Shelob, with 49 percent, comes second; Galadriel, with only 29 percent, has the fewest material processes).

	Goldberry	Arwen	Galadriel	Éowyn	Shelob
Verbal	10%	6%	8%	2%	2%
Relational	11%	9%	22%	16%	18%
Mental	17%	15%	8%	11%	23%
Behavioral	5%	7%	18%	7%	2%
Material	42%	39%	29%	63%	49%
Existential	8%	15%	0%	1%	2%
meteorological	7%	9%	15%	0%	4%

If, as Donovan argues, Éowyn is most strongly affected by the valkyrie tradition, her agency and behavior can be connected to those figures. However, Tolkien himself criticized the idea of a "strong Amazon," mythic figures in classical Greece, and the valkyrie are also mythic creatures, linking the material and spiritual worlds. What many may enjoy as a myth or story would not necessarily be considered a model for human behaviors; such behavior might well be considered queer, unwomanly, and so condemned.

Engaged in constructing a queer reading, I would not join in that condemnation although Tolkien expresses some measure of it. Instead, I draw upon queer theory, specifically Judith Halberstam's *Female Masculinity*, a second-generation queer theory text, building upon the early work in gender done by Eve Kosofsky Sedgwick. Earlier feminist theorists argued that gender roles are socially constructed, but tended to focus on heterosexuality as the norm. Gay and lesbian theory in the earlier years tended toward a homo-normative construction, with the "gay" or "lesbian" an essential, if privileged, category in opposition to heterosexuality. Contemporary queer theorists can complicate both social essentialism (the idea that all female bodies, all women, are socialized toward femininity) and homo-normativity (the idea of an essential gay or lesbian self). Halberstam argues the need to consider gender as being constructed socially, in part through language, and as not contingent upon the body, allowing for female participation in the construction and performance of masculinity.

Moving from arguing that gender is socially constructed to analyzing how a socially constructed gender can be separated from the body complicates theoretical reliance on binary assumptions, such as the idea that there are only two genders, femininity and masculinity, or two sexualities, heterosexual and homosexual. Halberstam argues that culture has ways of signifying masculine females and feminine males but that (as is true in a patriarchal system), much more attention is paid to feminine males than masculine women. Because she does not ignore class and ethnicity, she can argue for the existence of multiple masculinities. The range of masculinities includes the dominant one (of white middle class men) as well as a range of alternative ones created by the intersections of class, ethnicity, and sexual identity with masculinity. Halberstam focuses on queer female masculinities because she sees heterosexual female masculinity as more hetero-normative and less challenging (although worthy of study by others). Halberstam's work intervenes in a range of discourses and subjects: historical, performative, literary, autobiographical, etc., and I find many of her rhetorical moves useful, particularly the claim that mainstream culture has acted to suppress female masculinities but that those masculinities have existed, both historically and in contemporary sub-cultures. To suppress something means that, culturally, people are aware of its existence. Alternative female masculinities exist even when women who are ambiguous in gender presentation are suppressed or marginalized. The result of suppressing female masculinities is that "male masculinity [stands] unchallenged as the bearer of gender stability and gender deviance." Examples of female masculinities are: "the tomboy, the masculine woman, and the racialized masculine subject."[14] Halberstam does not argue that creating new language will change heteropatriarchal attitudes; instead, she moves to claim that a breakdown of gender difference as a signifying system is already taking place in some parts of contemporary society and that such local breakdowns can be used to cause change in other areas.

Even the tomboy I was as a child understood on some level that Tolkien probably intended Éowyn's powers and actions to be read as a breakdown in the social order that would need to be condemned or cured, unlike the spiritual and moral powers of the mythic figures of the elves and Goldberry. Éowyn is "saved" from traveling down a road that, in Tolkien's text, may have led to an existence similar to Shelob's. I base this limited statement of his intention upon three pieces of evidence: a scene in the novel, revisions made during his writing process, as described by Christopher Tolkien, and language in his letters. When Éowyn lies injured and ill in the Houses of Healing, she does not respond immediately to Aragorn's powers and the athelas. Instead, Aragorn confesses to a limit on his power; he is able to heal only her body not her spirit. The scene shows a group of men standing around her in the Houses of Healing trying to analyze when she first was made unhappy, stricken with Aragorn calls a malady and which her brother thinks may be her feelings for Aragorn. Gandalf provides a slightly different view of her queerness (a reflection of the idea of a woman warrior): saying that she her courage is the equal of her brother's even though she is a woman. As a masculine woman, her earlier anger at a traditional woman's role, especially when told to wait and die, is cast in a negative light as illness or despair by men around her; the narrator seems to share this sense of her anger since he described her, after Aragorn's rejection, as stricken and stumbling after begging him to let her ride with him. This sort of diagnosis sounds all too familiar to contemporary feminists who have been told that they and the feminists preceding them are too angry, are going too far, that feminism is an illness of the body or mind or perhaps both, that they are "unnaturally" trying to act as men, against their nature as "women." The patriarchal solution to such problems is, of course, marriage, as the narrator happily provides for her instead of the originally planned death in an earlier draft.

The changes Tolkien instituted during his long and complex revision process are one reason that David Craig characterizes Éowyn as the most complex character in the novel. A comparison of the different drafts in *The Treason of Isengard* shows that the first draft had two women standing behind the king. The two are Idis and Éowyn; the first is Théoden's daughter, the second and younger, is Éowyn.[15] Idis soon disappears, and the meeting of Aragorn and Éowyn is significant because they look at each other and fall in love. Notes in the text indicate several different plans for her after Arwen is created, including her death on the battlefield. The possibility of Aragorn's mourning Éowyn's death and never marrying was also considered.[16] In the final draft, Éowyn's final destiny is to marry Faramir, changing to become a Healer and rule by his side in Ithilien. A letter Tolkien drafted discussed his sense of the (final) character, disowning any sense of her as an Amazon and explaining that her feelings for Aragorn were not really romantic, and that she was not really a soldier, just a woman acting in a crisis.[17]

In another letter to his son, Michael, Tolkien clearly sets forth his ideas of essential differences between men and women which can be summarized as heterosexist and as correlating to his religious philosophy of a fallen and imperfect world, allowing that women can be corrupted but stating that they are naturally and "instinctively" monogamous, naturally and instinctively happiest when married, unlike men.[18] I know Tolkien would have perceived homosexuality as a corruption; but I do not feel I must accept his perceptions. As a number of critics note, he grew up in the homosocial culture of late Victorian and early twentieth-century England. There is no evidence of female same-sex relationships or love in *The Lord of the Rings*; simple friendship between women is hardly shown except perhaps in Ioreth's companionship with her kinswoman at the Coronation. A brief reference to a close friendship between Melian and Galadriel is given in *The Silmarillion*.[19] Generally, women are isolated from all other women, a feature not at all uncommon in works by male authors who would have had little or no access information about female friendship, female love, female bonding. The lack of such relationships described in the text does not preclude a female reader from connecting to a female character or characters.

The author Tolkien constructed Éowyn to serve his purpose in his narrative, but her development through multiple revisions is complex. His very obvious dislike of the concept of a woman picking up arms to fight as men do is clear; yet he is the sub-creator who showed her voicing that impassioned statement to Aragorn criticizing his, and the Rohirrim, attitudes about women who are denied the chance for battle but can still be killed after the battle is lost. "[20] She fears a cage—bars that keep her from doing great deeds. She expresses herself in the language of the heroic epic because that is the language she has; that is the language of her people and culture. Tolkien's own work revises the epic heroic model by embedding later, Christian, elements, but it is equally possible for a reader of Tolkien's work to read in sympathy with Éowyn and against the grain of her sub-creator who once planned for her death because of her masculine qualities. Such a reader can imagine much more in the character than the author could show directly. There are gaps in every text, and the gaps in this text are large enough to allow for a queer reading.

My favorite characters as a child and adolescent were Frodo and Éowyn. Both were considered to act "queerly" by the norms of their culture. Craig notes the extensive use of the word "queer" to describe Bilbo and then Frodo by the hobbits around them.[21] The behaviors that set the two hobbits apart were not only their reading, interest in elvish history and culture and languages, but also their choice not to marry. While the word "queer" is not applied to Éowyn in part because the diction would not be appropriate for the Rohirrim, I believe that the concept would have been applied by many of her people in reference to her choices during much of the time of the story.[22]

Frodo's storyline and characterization are clear since he is the primary point of view character; in contrast, Éowyn tantalizes. She has more story time than other female characters, moving through the text and through Middle-earth in contrast to the others who seem confined to one location and playing a climactic role in the final battle in a way that hinges on her cross-dressing (being taken for a man before being revealed as a woman). While she was always more present for me than other female characters, I was confused about the sense of doom that seemed to surround her in the text, the expressed fears of Gandalf and Aragorn to Éomer that she is likely to die if she cannot regain hope. One could argue those fears are part of the larger story—certainly her individual despair exists within a conflict that threatens the entire world and might bring about the death of all that is good and true, but even as a child, I had the sense that she was suffering from problems other than the Dark Lord's attacks on Middle-earth and all its inhabitants. I had no language to express either my sense of her problems (and my attendant disgust at the healing/marriage resolution to her plot) or to express my attraction to her during my first decades of reading the novel; that language would come only years later, in a doctoral program during the 1990s as I began to study gender and queer theory. Ironically, by that time, I had not read Tolkien's work for some years, choosing to read more feminist work and to read the women writers not assigned in my earlier college programs. I came back to the novel by way of Peter Jackson's live-action film, as well as coming to scholarship on Tolkien, the film, and fan fiction. As an adult reader, I can bring a number of contemporary theories and methods, specifically, stylistics and queer theory, to my reading of the texts, finally voicing the reading that began when I was a child.

Appendix A:
LOTR Excerpts & Stylistic Analysis

Goldberry

1. FR, I, vi, 133, ll. 23–25.
2. FR, I, vii, 134, ll. 6–7.
3. l. 7.
4. ll. 7–8.
5. ll. 9–10.
6. ll. 10–11.
7. ll. 11–12.
8. ll. 14–16.
9. ll. 16–18.
10. l. 18.
11. ll. 18–20.
12. ll. 20–21.
13. ll. 23–24.
14. l. 24.
15. ll. 24–25.
16. l. 29.
17. ll. 29–30.
18. FR, I, vii, 135, l. 6.
19. l. 12.
20. ll. 12–13.
21. l. 13.
22. l. 14.
23. FR, I, vii, 136, l. 30.
24. ll. 30–32.
25. ll. 32–33.
26. ll. 33–34.
27. ll. 37–38.
28. ll. 38–40.
29. FR, I, vii, 140, l. 15.
30. l. 15.
31. ll. 15–17.
32. l. 17.
33. ll. 17–18.
34. ll. 18–19.
35. ll. 19–20.
36. FR, I, vii, 142, l. 37.
37. ll. 37–38.
38. l. 38.
39. ll. 38–39.
40. ll. 39–40.

41. ll. 40–41.
42. FR, I, vii, 143, l. 7–8.
43. ll. 8–9.
44. l. 9.
45. ll. 9–10.
46. l. 10.
47. ll. 10–12.
48. ll. 12–13.
49. ll. 13–14.
50. l. 14.
51. l. 15.
52. ll. 15–16.
53. l. 16.
54. ll. 16 17.
55. l. 17–18.
56. l. 25.
57. ll. 25–26.
58. ll. 26–27.
59. ll. 27–28.
60. ll. 28–29.
61. ll. 29–30.
62. FR, I, viii, 146, l. 24.
63. l. 24.
64. ll. 24–25.
65. ll. 25–26.
66. l. 26.
67. l. 26.
68. ll. 26–27.
69. l. 27.
70. l. 28.
71. l. 29.
72. l. 30.
73. l. 30.
74. l. 30.
75. FR, I, viii, 147, l. 26.
76. ll. 26–27.
77. ll. 27–28.
78. ll. 28–29.
79. l. 29.
80. ll. 29–30.
81. l. 30.
82. ll. 30–31.

Arwen

1. FR, II, i, 239, ll. 21–22.
2. ll. 22–23.
3. l. 23.
4. ll. 23–24.
5. l. 24.
6. ll. 24–25.
7. ll. 25–26.
8. l. 26.
9. l. 27.
10. l. 28.
11. ll. 28–29.
12. l. 29.
13. l. 29.
14. ll. 30–31.
15. ll. 31–32.
16. l. 33.
17. l. 33.
18. l. 33.
19. l. 34.
20. ll. 33–34.
21. l. 34.
22. l. 35.
23. ll. 35–37.
24. FR, II, i, 242, ll. 17–18.
25. l. 18.
26. FR, II, i, 250, l. 27.
27. l. 27.
28. l. 28.
29. ll. 28–29.
30. l. 29.
31. ll. 29–30.
32. l. 30.
33. ll. 30–31.
34. l. 31.
35. ll. 31–32.
36. l. 32.
37. ll. 32–33.
38. ll. 33–34.
39. RK, VI, v, 250, l. 36.
40. l. 36.

41. ll. 36–37.
42. l. 37.
43. ll. 37–38.
44. ll. 38–39.
45. ll. 39–40.
46. ll. 40–41.
47. *RK*, VI, v, 251, ll. 1–2.
48. ll. 2–3.
49. ll. 3–4.
50. l. 5.
51. ll. 5–6.
52. ll. 6–7.
53. *RK*, VI, vi, 253, ll. 5–6.
54. l. 6.

Galadriel

1. *FR*, II, vii, 369, ll. 32–34.
2. ll. 34–36.
3. l. 36.
4. ll. 36–37.
5. l. 37.
6. ll. 37–38.
7. l. 38.
8. l. 39.
9. ll. 39–40.
10. ll. 40–41
11. ll. 41–42.
12. *FR*, II, vii, 370, l. 1.
13. ll. 1–2.
14. ll. 2–3.
15. ll. 24–25.
16. *FR*, II, vii, 371, ll. 31–32.
17. l. 32.
18. ll. 32–34.
19. l. 34.
20. ll. 34–36.
21. l. 36.
22. l. 36.
23. *FR*, II, vii, 372, ll. 21–22.
24. ll. 22–23.
25. ll. 23–24.
26. l. 25.
27. ll. 25–26.
28. l. 27.
29. ll. 28–29.
30. *FR*, II, vii, 376, l. 32.
31. l. 32.
32. ll. 32–33.
33. ll. 33–34.
34. l. 34.
35. ll. 35–36.
36. ll. 36–37.
37. l. 37.
38. ll. 37–38
39. ll. 38–39.

40. ll. 39–41.
41. ll. 41–43.
42. l. 43.
43. *FR*, II, vii, 377, ll. 1–2.
44. l. 2.
45. l. 2.
46. *FR*, II, vii, 380, ll. 15–16.
47. ll. 16–17.
48. l. 17.
49. l. 18.
50. l. 19.
51. ll. 19–20.
52. l. 20.
53. ll. 20–21.
54. *FR*, II, vii, 381, l. 20.
55. ll. 20–21.
56. l. 21.
57. ll. 21–23.
58. l. 23.
59. l. 24.
60. l. 24.
61. ll. 24–25.
62. ll. 25–26.

Éowyn

1. *TT*, III, vi, 117, l. 1.
2. *TT*, III, vi, 119, l. 20.
3. ll. 20–21.
4. ll. 21–22.
5. l. 31.
6. l. 31.
7. ll. 31–32.
8. l. 32.
9. l. 32.
10. ll. 32–33.
11. l. 33.
12. l. 34.
13. l. 34.
14. l. 35.
15. ll. 35–36.
16. ll. 36–37.
17. ll. 38–39.
18. ll. 39–41.
19. l. 41.
20. ll. 41–42.
21. l. 42.
22. *TT*, III, vi, 127, l. 25.
23. l. 25.
24. l. 28.
25. ll. 28–29.
26. l. 29.
27. l. 29–30.
28. l. 30.
29. ll. 30–31.
30. l. 31.

31. l. 31.
32. l. 32.
33. *RK*, V, vi, 116, ll. 25–26.
34. l. 26.
35. ll. 26–27.
36. ll. 27–28.
37. l. 28.
38. ll. 28–29.
39. ll. 29–30.
40. ll. 30–31.
41. ll. 31–32.
42. l. 32.
43. ll. 32–33.
44. l. 34.
45. *RK*, V, vi, 117, ll. 6–7.
46. ll. 7–8.
47. l. 8.
48. l. 9.
49. l. 9.
50. ll. 9–11.
51. l. 11.
52. ll. 11–12.
53. l. 12.
54. ll. 13–14.
55. ll. 14–15.
56. ll. 15–16.
57. l. 16.
58. l. 16.
59. ll. 16–17.
60. l. 17.
61. l. 17.
62. l. 18.
63. l. 19.
64. ll. 19–21.
65. ll. 21–22.
66. ll. 23–25.
67. l. 25.

Shelob

1. *TT*, IV, ix, 329, l. 31.
2. l. 32.
3. ll. 32–33.
4. ll. 33–34.
5. l. 34.
6. ll. 34–35.
7. ll. 35–36.
8. ll. 36–37.
9. ll. 37–38.
10. ll. 38–39.
11. ll. 39–40.
12. ll. 40–41.
13. ll. 41–42.
14. l. 42–*TT*, IV, ix, 330, l. 1.
15. ll. 1–2.
16. l. 23.

Light (noun, 1) or Light (adjective, 14b)? (Reid) 113

17. l. 23.	37. ll. 26-27.	57. ll. 23-24.
18. l. 24.	38. l. 27.	58. ll. 24-25.
19. l. 24.	39. ll. 28-29.	59. ll. 25-26.
20. ll. 24-25.	40. l. 29.	60. l. 26.
21. ll. 25-26.	41. ll. 29-30.	61. ll. 26-28.
22. ll. 26-27.	42. ll. 30-31.	62. ll. 28-29.
23. l. 27.	43. l. 31.	63. *TT,* IV, x, 339, l. 10.
24. l. 27.	44. l. 32.	64. ll. 10-11.
25. l. 28.	45. ll. 32-33.	65 l. 11.
26. l. 28.	46. l. 33.	66. ll. 12-13.
27. ll. 28-29.	47. ll. 33-34.	67. ll. 13-14.
28. ll. 29-30.	48. ll. 34-35.	68. l. 14.
29. *TT,* IV, ix, 334, l. 21.	49. *TT,* IV, x, 337, ll. 16-17.	69. ll. 14-15.
30. l. 21.	50. ll. 17-18.	70. ll. 15-16.
31. l. 22.	51. ll. 18-19.	71. ll. 16-17.
32. ll. 22-23.	52. ll. 19-20.	72. l. 17.
33. ll. 23-24.	53. ll. 20-21.	73. l. 17.
34. ll. 24-25.	54. ll. 21-22.	74. l. 18.
35. l. 25.	55. ll. 22-23.	75. l. 18.
36. l. 26.	56. l. 23.	76. ll. 18-19.

Stylistic Results
Light Imagery

Feature	Goldberry N=20	Arwen N=78	Galadriel N=2	Éowyn N=106	Shelob N=1
Nouns	% (#)	% (#)	% (#)	% (#)	% (#)
Light	90% (18)	17.9% (14)	100% (2)	8.49% (9)	0
Dark	10% (2)	2.56% (2)	0	2.83% (3)	100% (1)
neutral	0	79.4% (62)	0	88.6% (94)	0
Adjectives	N=42	N=30	N=53	N=36	N=61
Light	45% (19)	57% (17)	34% (18)	14% (5)	15% (9)
Dark	0	7% (2)	6% (3)	3% (1)	39% (24)
neutral	55% (23)	36% (11)	60% (32)	83% (30)	46% (28)
Colors	N=21	N=22	N=14	N=10	N=20
Light	100% (2)	91% (20)	93% (13)	80% (8)	60% (12)
Dark	0	9% (2)	7% (1)	20% (2)	40% (8)
Processes	N=91	N=55	N=84	N=81	N=83
shining/light related	9% (8)	9% (5)	7% (6)	5% (4)	10% (8)
dimming or darkening	2% (2)	0	4% (3)	1% (1)	5% (4)
neutral	89% (81)	91% (50)	89% (75)	94% (76)	85% (71)
	N=91	N=55	N=84	N=81	N=83
verbal	10% (9)	6% (3)	8% (7)	2% (2)	2% (2)
relational	11% (10)	9% (5)	22% (18)	16% (13)	18% (15)
mental	17% (16)	15% (8)	8% (7)	11% (9)	23% (19)
behavioural	5% (5)	7% (4)	18% (15)	7% (6)	2% (2)
material	42% (38)	39% (21)	29% (24)	63% (53)	49% (41)
existential	8% (7)	15% (8)	0.00%	1% (1)	2% (92)
meterological	7% (6)	9% (5)	15% (13)	0	4% (3)

114 Part III: The Discursive Body

Feature	Arwen Mean	N	Galadriel Mean	N	Goldberry Mean	N	Shelob Mean	N	Éowyn Mean	N
Physical-elements	46.67%	7	33.33%	6	39.47%	15	98.15%	53	37.93%	11
Hair	14.29%	1	16.67%	1	20.00%	3	0.00%	0	27.27%	3
Face	14.29%	1	0.00%	0	0.00%	0	1.89%	1	18.18%	2
Arms	14.29%	1	16.67%	1	6.67%	1	0.00%	0	0.00%	0
Eyes	14.29%	1	33.33%	2	0.00%	0	45.28%	24	36.36%	4
Other	0.00%	0	0.00%	0	20.00%	3	24.53%	13	18.18%	2
Head	14.29%	1	0.00%	0	0.00%	0	7.55%	4	0.00%	0
Brow	28.57%	2	0.00%	0	0.00%	0	0.00%	0	0.00%	0
Hands	0.00%	0	16.67%	1	20.00%	3	0.00%	0	0.00%	0
Voice	0.00%	0	16.67%	1	26.67%	4	0.00%	0	0.00%	0
Feet	0.00%	0	0.00%	0	6.67%	1	1.89%	1	0.00%	0
Neck	0.00%	0	0.00%	0	0.00%	0	1.89%	1	0.00%	0
Body	0.00%	0	0.00%	0	0.00%	0	7.55%	4	0.00%	0
Legs	0.00%	0	0.00%	0	0.00%	0	9.43%	5	0.00%	0

Feature	Arwen Mean	N	Galadriel Mean	N	Goldberry Mean	N	Shelob Mean	N	Éowyn Mean	N
Accessories	46.67%	7	27.78%	5	15.79%	6	0.00%	0	10.34%	3
Clothing	14.29%	1	40.00%	2	50.00%	3	0.00%	0	66.67%	2
Gems	28.57%	2	20.00%	1	0.00%	0	0.00%	0	0.00%	0
Cap-helm-crown	14.29%	1	0.00%	0	0.00%	0	0.00%	0	0.00%	0
Girdle	14.29%	1	0.00%	0	33.33%	2	0.00%	0	33.33%	1
Armor	0.00%	0	0.00%	0	0.00%	0	0.00%	0	0.00%	0
Chain-ring	28.57%	2	40.00%	2	0.00%	0	0.00%	0	0.00%	0
Shoes	0.00%	0	0.00%	0	16.67%	1	0.00%	0	0.00%	0

Feature	Arwen Mean	N	Galadriel Mean	N	Goldberry Mean	N	Shelob Mean	N	Éowyn Mean	N
Processses	6.67%	1	38.89%	7	44.74%	17	1.85%	1	51.72%	15
Verbal	0.00%	0	28.57%	2	41.18%	7	0.00%	0	0.00%	0
Material	100.00%	1	14.29%	1	52.94%	9	0.00%	0	80.00%	12
Mental	0.00%	0	57.14%	4	5.88%	1	100.00%	1	20.00%	3
Singing	0.00%	0	0.00%	0	57.14%	4	0.00%	0	0.00%	0
Laughing	0.00%	0	50.00%	1	14.29%	1	0.00%	0	0.00%	0
Speaking	0.00%	0	50.00%	1	0.00%	0	0.00%	0	0.00%	0
Blessing-Prophesying	0.00%	0	0.00%	0	28.57%	2	0.00%	0	0.00%	0
Sitting	100.00%	1	0.00%	0	11.11%	1	0.00%	0	0.00%	0
Standing	0.00%	0	0.00%	0	44.44%	4	0.00%	0	25.00%	3
Fighting	0.00%	0	0.00%	0	0.00%	0	0.00%	0	41.67%	5
Smiles	0.00%	0	100.00%	1	11.11%	1	0.00%	0	0.00%	0
Running	0.00%	0	0.00%	0	22.22%	2	0.00%	0	0.00%	0
Dancing	0.00%	0	0.00%	0	11.11%	1	0.00%	0	0.00%	0
Turning-and-Moving	0.00%	0	0.00%	0	0.00%	0	0.00%	0	33.33%	4

Light (noun, 1) or Light (adjective, 14b)? (Reid)   115

	Arwen		Galadriel		Goldberry		Shelob		Éowyn	
Feature	Mean	N	Mean	N	Mean	N	Mean	N	Mean	N
Seeing	0.00%	0	0.00%	0	100.00%	1	0.00%	0	100.00%	3
Looking/ Piercing	0.00%	0	100.00%	4	0.00%	0	100.00%	1	0.00%	0

	Arwen		Galadriel		Goldberry		Shelob		Éowyn	
Feature	Mean	N	Mean	N	Mean	N	Mean	N	Mean	N
Female-character	39.13%	18	44.26%	27	50.65%	39	54.10%	33	58.06%	36
Other	56.52%	26	50.82%	31	44.16%	34	42.62%	26	40.32%	25
Dummy	4.35%	2	4.92%	3	5.19%	4	3.28%	2	1.61%	1
Name-or-pronoun	72.22%	13	81.48%	22	56.41%	22	36.36%	12	69.44%	25
Part-of-body	22.22%	4	18.52%	5	33.33%	13	63.64%	21	25.00%	9
Clothes	5.56%	1	0.00%	0	10.26%	4	0.00%	0	5.56%	2

Notes

1. Two of the three most well-known scholars of Tolkien are women: Verlyn Flieger and Jane Chance. The three anthologies edited by Neil Isaacs and Rose Zimbardo, are as follows, in chronological order. First, *Tolkien and the Critics* (1968) with fifteen essays, four by women (27 percent): one by Patricia Meyer Spacks on power (only male characters), one by Zimbardo (on morality, mostly among the male characters), one by Mary Quella Kelly (on the poetry), and one by Marion Zimmer Bradley (on the love and hero-worship between men). Second, *Tolkien: New Critical Perspectives* (1981) with twelve essays, three by women (one by a contributor identified only by initials): 23–35 percent. The women are Verlyn Flieger (on Frodo and Aragorn and the concept of the hero), Zimbardo (on the Medieval and Renaissance concept of harmony through the male characters), Lois R. Kuznets (on Tolkien's rhetoric of childhood in *The Hobbit*), and J.S. Ryan (on Tolkien's' use of folklore and myth). Third, *Understanding The Lord of the Rings: The Best of Tolkien Criticism* (Isaacs and Zimbardo, eds., 2004) included essays from both the first two and some newly printed ones. Of the fourteen essays, five (35 percent) are by women (reprints of Spacks, Zimbardo, Bradley, and Flieger), and an essay by Jane Chance (on Tolkien's use of Germanic and Christian epic elements and moral systems). The gender neutral J.S. Ryan's essay is reprinted; in the introduction to this essay, unlike the introduction to an essay by R.J. Reilly, no pronoun is used.

This Far Land (Robert Giddings, ed., 1983), the first British anthology, contains ten essays. Three are by women (30 percent): Janet Menzies' argument for the adolescent nature of Tolkien's work, Diana Wynne Jones' analysis of the narrative pattern, and Brenda Partridge's feminist psychoanalytic argument about Tolkien, sex, and the nature of Shelob. Harold Bloom's anthology on Tolkien (2000) in the "Modern Critical Interpretations" series contains nine essays, three by women (33 percent): the Chance and Zimbardo essays are reprints of the ones from the Isaacs and Zimbardo anthologies described above; an essay by Kathryn W. Crabbe deals with differences between *The Hobbit* and *The Lord of the Rings*. *J.R.R. Tolkien and His Literary Resonances* (George Clark and Daniel Timmons, eds., 2000) contains fourteen essays, four by women (approximately 30 percent): Tanya Caroline Wood (on the influence of Sidney's *Defense of Poesy* on Tolkien's "On Fairy Stories"), Debbie Sly (on Milton's and Tolkien's use of darkness, gender, sexuality, and religion), Verlyn Flieger (on Tolkien's environmentalism, on his use of trees), and Faye Ringel (on the focus from Tolkien to his influence on the next generation of women fantasists, many of whom define themselves as writing against Tolkien).

Tolkien the Medievalist (Jane Chance, ed., 2003), has sixteen essays and the greatest percentage of women contributors (50 percent) with eight essays by seven writers: Chance (the introductory essay) Flieger (on folklore, and on Tolkien's Wild Men), Mary Faraci (on the *Beowulf* essay), Christine Chism (on the use of medieval myth in World War II rhetoric), Margaret A. Sinex (on oath-breaking in Tolkien and a twelfth-century text), and Miranda Wilcox (on "The Seafarer" and *The Lord of the Rings*). Only one focuses on the female characters: Leslie A. Donovan (on the "valkyrie reflex" in the major female characters in the novel).

Tolkien's Modern Middle Ages (Jane Chance and Alfred K. Siewers, eds., 2005) is part of The New Middle Ages series which states, as its purpose, a focus on "transdisciplinary studies of medieval cultures, with particular emphasis on recuperating women's history and on feminist and gender analysis." This anthology contains fourteen essays with four and a half by women (Chance is the co-writer of the introductory essay, and writer of one essay). Flieger analyzes modern and postmodern elements existing alongside medieval elements in Tolkien's work. Deidre Dawson discusses Tolkien's languages in the context of twentieth-century language theory on multilingualism, and Rebekah Long compares Tolkien's work with the post war poetry of David Jones' poetry in terms of their common references to Chaucer. Chance analyzes race and gender in Tolkien's world.

The works discussed above are all anthologies, but monographs (by such scholars as Curry, Flieger, Shippey, and others) are much the same: they do not have "gender" as an analytical category, and their attention is on other, commonly perceived "universal" elements of the novel which tend to require more attention paid to the male heroes and literary influences focusing entirely on men. Feminist and gender scholarship on Tolkien tends to appear in the journal articles: David Craig, Edith L. Crowe, and Melanie Rawls all published their work in *Mythlore* or *Mallorn*. The majority of anthology editors are male, with the exception of Chance and Zimbardo.

Outside of the major anthologies, women scholars have produced articles and monographs on Tolkien's. Sarah Beach, Rhona Beare, Lynn Brice, Jane Chance, Dmitra Fimi, Verlyn Flieger, Margaret Hiley, Allegra Johnson, Ruth Noel, Anne C. Petty, and Elizabeth Whittingham have produced important work on the mythic elements of Tolkien's work. Christina Scull (in collaboration with Wayne G. Hammond) has produced ground-breaking publications on Tolkien's art. Dmitra Fimi has produced the only monograph on race in Tolkien's work. Recent work on gender and sexuality includes essays by Jennifer Neville, Holly A. Crocker, and Esther Saxey (in *Reading* The Lord of the Rings*: New Writings on Tolkien's Trilogy*, edited by Robert Eaglestone.)

I do not present this overview of the body of Tolkien scholarship to blame earlier scholars, male or female, for their work. Individual scholars, like individual writers, choose to pursue questions and ideas that most interest them. What is of interest to me is the pattern of scholarship which, driven by individual choice, still, I argue, reflects contemporary as well as past cultural valorization of the male as universal and worthy of greater attention. Such attitudes shape fictional, critical, theoretical narratives and arguments as well as social institutions' choices and values, including access to resources and degrees. That a greater percentage of women appear in the medieval anthology rather than the modern anthologies probably indicates more women in that field than in other literary fields, quite possibly women influenced by Tolkien's work.

2. Ethnicity and class as well as gender and sexuality are identities excluded from the falsely objective analysis. More intersectional work, especially drawing upon critical race theories, is needed in Tolkien Studies, but that lies outside the scope of this project.

3. Jane Chance likewise addresses the issue of queerness as difference in "Power and Knowledge in Tolkien: The Problem of Difference in 'The Birthday Party,'" (1995).

4. I began my data analysis transcribing passages about/concerning Lobelia Sackville-Baggins and Rosie Cotton as well, but so little text exists that directly deals with their actions (as opposed to the reporting of those actions by another character, most notably in the case of Farmer Cotton reporting Lobelia's attack upon Sharkey's men) that I did not think any conclusions could be supported. Ioreth is primarily represented in the text through dialogue, which removed her from much effective consideration for this project. My stylistic analysis covers fairly brief narrative excerpts (ranging from 520 to 720 words) involving introductory and climactic scenes for each character.

5. I am in debt to David Craig's excellent discussion of the psychological complexity of Éowyn relating to the various versions of her that Tolkien created over time. While that issue is not a major part of his essay, which focuses primarily on Frodo and Sam's relationship, I am building on that portion in this essay.

6. Just such an argument is made by Brenda Partridge, "No Sex Please — We're Hobbits," 1983.

7. Further work needs to be done analyzing the bodies of women characters in *The Silmarillion* and, perhaps, the analysis of light imagery and male bodies in both works.

8. Time does not allow me to analyze the construction of male bodies in regard to this binary, but I believe that such an analysis would show that the male characters are not described or defined in terms of physical sexuality; Tolkien's emphasis is much more on the spiritual, and his sense of relationships between men and women is much more romantic and chivalric. Bodily sins and physical lust and sexuality are simply not Tolkien's subject, one reason why many modern critics considered his work "adolescent." This comparison will be one of the topics in my planned Tolkien Corpus study.

9. Leslie A. Donovan, "The Valkyrie Reflex in J.R.R. Tolkien's *The Lord of the Rings*: Galadriel, Shelob, Éowyn, and Arwen," *Tolkien the Medievalist*, ed. Jane Chance (New York: Routledge, 2003), 111.

10. Donovan, "The Valkyrie Reflex," 109. I differ from Donovan in regard to how much we can "read" Tolkien himself as positively inclined to value the greater contemporary freedoms of women — as in many things, he expressed contradictory ideas a different times, shown in letters as well as fictional texts. I agree with her on his tendency to idealize women and see that idealization as well as the hetero-normativity as more restrictive, perhaps, than she states in this article. This minor disagreement in no way is meant to undercut the strength of her reading of his work.

11. A note about point of view: in all cases, the women (like many of the male characters) are not the major point of view characters; they are primarily perceived through another's view (Frodo's, Merry's, the third person narrative persona's), all male. A detailed stylistic analysis of the narrative persona(e) in *The Lord of the Rings* would be an immense project, needing not only time but collaborative efforts in a corpus project (a statistical, computer-assisted analysis, of the complete text).

12. Christopher Tolkien, ed., *Sauron Defeated* (Boston: Houghton Mifflin, 1992), 52, 66. The original name given the Queen was Finduilas; later that name was transferred to Boromir and Faramir's mother. Sam and Rosie (Ibid., 108).

13. Christopher Tolkien, ed., *Treason of Isengard* (Boston: Houghton Mifflin, 1989), 247–50.

14. Judith Halberstam, *Female Masculinity* (Durham: Duke University Press, 1998), 41.

15. *Treason*, 445.

16. *Treason*, 448. Christopher explains the item of Galadriel's message as relating to the Elfstone message which originally referred to a green stone Théoden was wearing, and told Aragorn to "look in the shadow of the dark throne" where Éowyn was standing.

17. *Letters*, 323.

18. *Letters*, 48–51.

19. *Sil*, 115, 126.

20. *RK*, V, ii, 58.
21. Craig, "Queer Lodgings," 16.
22. Here, I draw upon Shippey's argument about the essentially modern culture and diction of the Shire in contrast to the medieval and Anglo-Saxon culture and language of the Mark (*Author of the Century*, 47–49, 90–92). The earliest date of a citation in the *OED* for "Queer" is 1508. It is not a word that would have appeared in the language of the Rohirrim. *OED Online*, s.v. "queer, v.[1]" *The Oxford English Dictionary*, 2d ed. (Oxford University Press, 1989), accessed April 12, 2011, http://oed.com/view/Entry/156298.

Works Consulted

Battis, Jes. "Gazing Upon Sauron: Hobbits, Elves, and the Queering of the Postcolonial Optic." *Modern Fiction Studies* 50.4 (Winter 2004): 908–926.
Bloom, Harold, ed. *J.R.R. Tolkien*. Philadelphia: Chelsea House, 2000.
Chance, Jane. "Power and Knowledge in Tolkien: The Problem of Difference in 'The Birthday Party.'" *Proceedings of the J.R.R. Tolkien Centenary Conference 1992: Mythlore 80 and Mallorn 33*, ed. Patricia Reynolds and Glen H. Goodknight, 115–120. Milton Keynes, Buckinghamshire and Altadena, CA: The Tolkien Society and The Mythopoeic Press, 1995.
_____, ed. *Tolkien the Medievalist*. New York: Routledge, 20003.
_____, and Alfred K. Sievers, eds. *Tolkien's Modern Middle Ages*. New York: Palgrave, 2005.
Clark, George, and Daniel Timmons, eds. *J.R.R. Tolkien and His Literary Resonances*. Westport, CT: Greenwood Press, 2000.
Craig, David M. "'Queer Lodgings': Gender and Sexuality in *The Lord of the Rings*." *Mallorn* 38 (2001): 11–18.
Donovan, Leslie A. "The Valkyrie Reflex in J.R.R. Tolkien's *The Lord of the Rings:* Galadriel, Shelob, Éowyn, and Arwen." *Tolkien the Medievalist*, ed. Chance, 106–32. New York: Routledge, 2002.
Drout, Michael D.C. "Tolkien's Prose Style and its Literary and Rhetorical Effects." *Tolkien Studies* 1 (2004): 137–62.
Eagleston, Robert. *Reading* The Lord of the Rings: *New Writings on Tolkien's Trilogy*. London: Continuum, 2006.
Giddings, Robert, ed. *This Far Land*. London: Vision, 1983.
Halberstam, Judith. *Female Masculinity*. Durham: Duke University Press, 1998.
Isaacs, Neil, and Rose Zimbardo, eds. *Tolkien: New Critical Perspectives*. Lexington: University Press of Kentucky, 1981.
_____, and _____, eds. *Tolkien and the Critics*. Notre Dame: Notre Dame University Press, 1968.
_____, and _____, eds. *Understanding* The Lord of the Rings: *The Best of Tolkien Criticism*. Boston: Houghton Mifflin, 2004.
Partridge, Brenda. "No Sex Please — We're Hobbits: The Construction of Female Sexuality in *The Lord of the Rings*." In *This Far Land*, ed. Robert Giddings, 179–197. London: Vision, 1983.
Pretorius, David. "Binary Issues and Feminist Issues in *The Lord of the Rings*." *Mallorn* 40 (2002): 32–38.
Tolkien, Christopher, ed. *Sauron Defeated*. Boston: Houghton Mifflin, 1992.
_____, ed. *The Treason of Isengard*. Boston: Houghton Mifflin, 1989.

A Body of Myth
Representing Sauron in The Lord of the Rings

GERGELY NAGY

J.R.R. Tolkien's work is today more and more widely recognized as fully relevant in a postmodern literary context as well. This is because his breathtakingly detailed fictional world consistently highlights some aspects and concepts that are decidedly interesting for such approaches. His stress on textuality is of course deeply informed by his own profession as a philologist, and the same spirit permeates the attitude to language and culture that appears in his stories. But while always bearing in mind the individual text, the individual account, the single individual's use of language as embedded in its various larger contexts, Tolkien produces a complex representation of culture, with many cardinal points uniquely applicable to the concerns of the twenty-first century.

Changing approaches to Tolkien's central concepts have surprisingly shown them as not the least obsolete and outdated. In theoretical discussions as much as in more recent views of the philological practice, his work seems surprisingly fresh and contemporary. Even his emphasis on *The Lord of the Rings* being a "fundamentally religious and Catholic work,"[1] the appearance of religion in his work (one of the "Grand Narratives" postmodernism no longer believes in[2]) can be seen as relevant and meaningful today: the theologically grounded ontology of Middle-earth, when looked at with an eye to Yuri Lotman's typology of cultures,[3] yields insights into Tolkien's specifically *medieval(ist)* way of seeing and creating his work.[4] Middle-earth has a theological center, Ilúvatar, from whom everything that exists "emanates"[5]: a spiritual counterpoint and grounding for the physical reality of the world. Ilúvatar functions not only as the Creator in the style of the Christian Godhead in medieval culture; he also takes on the role of Jacques Derrida's "metaphysical center,"[6] the signified that is not at the same time a signifier and that thus guarantees the meaning of all other signifiers in the world. Tolkien's medieval-style fictional world easily accommodates contemporary concepts and approaches.

This appearance of religion, the stress on the "sacred" element of the world (which Tolkien shares with very few fellow fantasists, at least in this depth and philosophical detail), his insistence on the curiously "doubled" textuality of his works and the counterpoint of the physical world evolve a very special representation of cultures and their elements. Tolkien's texts are always conceived to be texts in the fictional world, by fictional authors, translators, compilers; therefore, what they illustrate for the theoretician is how those fictional subjects in fictional cultures write their own world, not only in cosmologies, but also as a palpable, corporeal setting for everyday stories. What are their most important, recurring motifs? What frameworks do they imagine to contextualize their writings? To what stories do they refer and how? What discourses do they use? What language? In nearly all Tolkien's texts and works, these questions are relevant and meaningful: one level higher, they all come together in the question "how does Tolkien imagine/write his fictional subjects doing all those things?" But if we connect these queries specifically to the representation of the "sacred," even more intriguing questions arise about some of Tolkien's most interesting characters: his mythological subjects.

Elsewhere I have pointed out that for Tolkien, the individual subject producing language and meaning is always one of the focal points[7]; but these writing subjects are always individuals, and always "earthly" (even when they are elves, termed by Tolkien as "super-natural" in "On Fairy-Stories"[8]). These characters are at the same time "subjects" in the more theoretical sense of producing language and meaning (in the form of stories and texts), and also in the sense of being "subjects" of a world order (Lotman's pansemiotic, medieval world order) or of some political power (a more Foucauldian use of the term). They are individuals in a world imagined to be just as real and corporeal as our own. The way Faramir tells his story to Frodo is obviously grounded in the fact that he is a man of Gondor (political affiliation, integration into a culture that conceives of its own subjects in a certain way); the way Gollum fragmentarily refers to Sauron reflects his having been subjected to his dreadful power (not exclusively, not even primarily political). The way our "ordinary," storytelling subjects talk about the sacred is therefore a very special case: since this is not merely metaphysics, but rather theology, the sacred is represented by persons, characters, who themselves become the *subjects of stories*. Ilúvatar, Morgoth, Sauron and the rest of them are mainly narrated through others.

Tolkien treats the theological not only as an option but as the center, and the discourse describing it as a central aspect of representation. Its foci are connected with the concern for subjects and their meaning producing activity, and appear in the story as definite characters, themselves as subjects. Most such characters are shown to enter the human world from a supernatural sphere (like those Ainur who enter Eä in the "Ainulindalë," thus becoming the Valar); and they can be termed mythological not simply because of their prevailing representation as "above (physical) nature," but also because they function as metaphysical centers and generators of both subjects and the subject matter of stories. They create a frame for stories with their own story, open a space where mythology can operate; they assign (stories about) themselves special cultural functions.

Creating such mythological subjects involves traditional conventions of representation on the one hand, and techniques special to Tolkien on the other. As the signifying system of Middle-earth, the system inside the fiction in which meanings and stories are produced is a theologically grounded one; these mythological beings are a "natural" part of it. But the only one of these whose representation can be said to be entirely out of the text's otherwise largely realistic logic is Sauron. Sauron's depiction is linked to the subject role he fulfils, to his relation to other subjects, and to discourses that determine subjects. In this paper, I will look at the layers of Sauron's representation in *The Lord of the Rings*, and show how his mythological status is mediated and captured in language — primarily that of the fictional authors. I will pay special attention to the concept of the body, since (as I have shown elsewhere, in Gollum's case[9]) this is essentially connected to the integrity and the ontology of the subject (whether "ordinary" or "mythological"). In the course of this inquiry, I will survey how the body functions in the representation of such a subject, then go on to show how the body focuses Sauron's personal history, and finally look at how (the disembodied) Sauron's activities still leave the body as the key point of his power and action, supplying a surrogate body for him in the representation of the text. The figure of Sauron is generally seen in criticism in the context of Tolkien's representation of morality and evil, but an emphasis on Tolkien's use of fictional authors to layer the representation necessarily places him in a web of more embedded discourses. Since one of Tolkien's ever-present epithets is that he is a "mythopoeic" author, the examination of his specifically mythological subjects is very much central to a meaningful interpretation of what that epithet really means.

Mythological Subjects and the Body

Tolkien never questioned the traditional soul/body dichotomy of Western Christianity. In his fiction, the body is always an essential aspect of the individual's existence. It is a resource of meaning and a drawback at the same time, and means limitations, narrowing, and controlled readings, but it also signals the individual's (at least potential) integrity. Corporeality is thus also an aspect of the representation of the mythological figures. Their mythological status is associated with images of that corporeality, represented in terms of the physical/spiritual divide, and their activities involve not only the influencing of others, but also playing out their power on their own body.

Mythological subjects are center and context at the same time. Theologically, they are surrogates of the metaphysical center, descending guarantees of meaning; in the story, their figure and their power surrounds, context-like, the activities of all the other subjects. Their problem is that they only *want to* (actually) *be* the metaphysical center: Morgoth disobeys Ilúvatar's authority and does not accept that only the Godhead is a real center, the totality of existence and meaning. Both Morgoth and Sauron desire to produce their own meaning, not just interpretations of Ilúvatar's, but since "no theme may be played that hath not its uttermost source in me"[10] (as the Creator says), this is an impossibility. You cannot create a meaning that is not found in the *totality* of meaning. Morgoth and Sauron, therefore, attempt to go pragmatic from being theoretical: in a material, corporeal, even political world they become involved *corporeally*, and intend to affect the *bodies* of others. They try to become the metaphysical central signified, controlling not only physical realities in their various modes (the fictional worlds' political or military scenes), but also to establish a system inside which other, more ordinary subjects are situated, and where the everyday meaning production activity of subjects becomes controlled along with (again) their physical, bodily realities. The body for Tolkien is a reserve, a sort of guarantee, for all sorts of meaning-producing subjects: so it is (at least initially) for Sauron too.

The fictional narrators and the theology-conscious author need various representative conventions to figure Sauron as a subject. In real world mythologies, such personages have conventional ways of being represented, as Tolkien knew very well: naturally he employs such methods here as the positioning of Sauron in a theological hierarchy (like Homer, solidifying the relationships of the Olympian gods), the problematization of the connection between name and thing (as in traditions of the "true name," used by other fantasists, most notably Ursula K. LeGuin in her Earthsea novels), and the complex of attributes and functions ascribed to this figure (there in any more or less systematic pantheon). He gives Sauron a history, through which his relationship to his body and its transformation can be followed to its ultimate end. But he also represents Sauron in terms of other subjects, in their operation and their very constitution, in their language and their relation to his influence and power. Sauron appears as context and (attempted) center, sign and subject, a key signifier and signified, the centre of a whole discourse. The fact that he is not a genuine center, and his discourse of power is not "theologically approved" is responsible for his eventual fall. But even until then, he has to be shown while there still is something to show, and talked about when there isn't.

Sauron and the Body: A Short Biography of a Dark Lord

In the theological structure of Middle-earth, Sauron holds a status comparable nearly to no one else. He is a being prior to the world and above it, essentially different by its nature: a Maia of Morgoth, the prime Dark Lord.[11] If we look at the whole of Tolkien's *oeuvre*, this situatedness is very clear. But since *The Lord of the Rings* is generally very implicit in theological matters, indication of this status appears there only in hints, mentions and in the Appendices.[12] In *The Lord of the Rings*, Sauron has to be represented in palpable and still distinctive terms in a text that does not have recourse to the explicitly theological.

Gods *per se* may not have bodily forms, but then gods who do not have bodily forms perceived or imagined by their worshippers may not be gods after all.[13] Sauron strictly speaking *does not have a physical body*: creatures of his order take "shape[s which] come [...] of their knowledge of the visible World, rather than of the World itself; and they need it not, save only as we use raiment."[14] Since their forms are determined by their knowledge of the creator's intention (the "master meaning"), they are the result of *interpretation*, a representation (of what they understand of Ilúvatar's totality). Melkor's impatience with the creator's plans[15] in the end causes him to revert to the form of "a dark Lord, tall and terrible. In that form he remained ever after."[16] This fixation of physical form (uncharacteristic of the Valar) clearly underlines his loss of some of his native power, but also his moral failure: he becomes more and more "of the world," and cannot (or will not) change his form. Sauron suffers the same fate. Instead of the completely controlled and intentional representation, after the destruction of Númenor he "could never again appear fair to the eyes of Men," having been "robbed [...] of that shape in which he had wrought so great an evil,"[17] even though earlier, going by the name Annatar, he could still take up a shape "of one both fair and wise."[18] Appendix A of *The Lord of the Rings* adds that he "became black and hideous," and ruled only "through terror" (317).

These changes of Sauron's body are referred to several times in the text of *The Silmarillion*.[19] At the end of the "Akallabêth," it is said that he "took up again his great Ring in Barad-dûr, and dwelt there, dark and silent, until he wrought himself a new guise, an image of malice and hatred made visible; and the Eye of Sauron the Terrible few could endure."[20] This passage importantly fails to elaborate what that "new guise" actually was; it only says that one result of the process was the emergence of the "Eye of Sauron"—a body part most associated with him and his power in *The Lord of the Rings*. This shape is also connected to the One Ring, which Sauron made himself, and "let a great part of his own former power pass into it" (*FR*, I, ii, 61)—indeed, the Ring itself becomes not only a symbol for Sauron but something nearly identical with him. In *The Lord of the Rings*, Sauron is never figured in his bodily reality, and therefore our examination of what discourse, what language steps in to substitute for that leads us on to the other aspects of Sauron's representation in this book.

In *The Lord of the Rings*, as in *The Silmarillion* too, Sauron is always associated with the concept of the "Shadow,"[21] and in the "Akallabêth," the text introduces Barad-dûr, the Dark Tower that seems to be both his home and emblem.[22] In every instance when Sauron is temporarily set back, his strengthening is always figured as a "return" to his tower and its "rebuilding"[23]: the tower and the shadow offer complementary visualities and corporealities for the fictional authors of the text to represent Sauron.

From the Physical to the Theoretical: Somebody Without a Body

But neither Sauron's personal history nor his position in the theological hierarchy are used extensively in representing him in *The Lord of the Rings*. He appears in the text of fictitious authors who do not know much about these, but who are deeply involved in fighting him and his minions. And since they never actually meet him, other ways need to be found. One of these is naming him and describing his attributes, spheres of action; another is the description of what he does and how he affects others (the authors included).

The question of Sauron's name as a sign for him of course has close links with his attributes and functions. The word "Sauron" is an Elvish word (meaning "abominable"), unlikely to be his real name (or even one he particularly likes); and he does not "use his right name, nor permit it to be spelt or spoken" (*TT*, III, i, 18). This thematizes the perception of Sauron by different cultures: representing Sauron generally depends on who is doing that representation. He is more customarily named in terms of his attributes and his antagonism with cultures: the "Dark Lord," the "Enemy," often simply substituted by a pronoun ("He") or refused to be given a name: "Unnamed," "Nameless," "the Nameless One" (ironically becoming names themselves). The elusive nature of the name as a sign for a thing of this order highlights that mythological beings are always represented in terms of the cultures and languages to which they are known, and that their names as signs always refer to functions and attributes, sensed (collectively) as persons.

The attributes most frequently employed for Sauron suspend the representation between physical and spiritual. Never appearing in person in *The Lord of the Rings*, Sauron (as Joe Abbot writes) "is consistently described in nebulous terms."[24] Darkness, blackness, fear and despair are associated with him, and his effects are described in terms that draw heavily on the representation of the Gorgon and the Basilisk in primary source material.[25] Sauron's distinct effects and definable sphere of action appear in the representation as attributes, metaphorized into physical traits (such as blackness, darkness), or presented as consequences of his influence (as despair[26]). His figure is thus circumscribed by these traditional modes of the representation of mythological beings, a point where a variety of representations come together.

But at the end of the "Akallabêth," we saw Sauron's "new guise" connected to the image of the "Eye." This image also serves as a marker on his people's gear (the Red Eye) and a name for him ("the Eye of Mordor," "the Eye in Barad-dûr," "the Lidless Eye"). The Eye represents Sauron in visual terms, physically, linking his power and his actual representation. In iconographical tradition, the eye is only relatively recently associated with God and His Providence or the Trinity; before that, it nearly invariably stood for the Evil Eye, the power to harm by the gaze[27] (which ties up with Sauron's mythological connections with the Basilisk and the Gorgon). The "shining Eye" in a triangle as representing "the Trinity in his omnipresence and omnipotence" (a Humanist allegory)[28] is a further adapted layer of conventional representation. Sauron's power is always said to rest in his gaze, his capacity for discernment and apprehension, and thereby knowledge, of subjects (both Gollum and Denethor are explicitly afraid that Sauron "sees," as Denethor says, their "very thoughts," [*RK*, V, iv, 97; *TT*, IV, ii, 241 for Gollum][29]). Sauron's pictorial representation thus underscores the account of his powers as seen in Gollum (and indeed partly in Frodo), and shows that his concrete physical representation is very closely linked with something else: the Ring. Indeed, the Ring is identified with the Eye in no uncertain terms when Bilbo says that he associated it with an "eye looking at me" (*FR*, I, i, 43).

But in fact the compression of representations in Sauron's figure is discernible even in the sign of the Eye; for the Eye is a sign for Sauron in more than one way. It compresses all significations of Sauron, and functions as several types of sign at the same time, showing that in any way of signification, its meaning is fixed. It is an *iconic* sign in the first place: the Eye is *physically like* Sauron, at least like all that is knowable of him for subjects in the signifying system of Middle-earth.[30] Frodo actually sees it in the mirror of Galadriel (*FR*, II, vii, 379), and Galadriel too claims to have seen it (*FR*, II, vii, 380). It is also an *indexical* sign, since it is the source and cause of Sauron's most poignantly felt effect, his *gaze*, the horizon of his operation, knowledge and presence. The Eye (and Sauron) is a "horrible growing sense of a hostile will that strove with great power to pierce all shadows of cloud, and earth, and flesh, and to see you" (*TT*, IV, ii, 238) — as Frodo feels in Mordor. Finally, the Eye is undoubtedly a *symbolic* sign for Sauron, as in his being called the "Great Eye," "Lidless Eye," "Eye of Barad-dûr," words to signify a supposedly non-linguistic reality; also as an emblem on banners and war-gear. It anchors this being, this meeting point of discourses and effects in language and "normal" signification. Sauron *is* the Eye: because in *The Lord of the Rings* it is all that is accessible of him for the signifying system in which meanings and representations are possible to be produced at all.[31] And even his own people seem to participate in this system: thus we have the only pun ever recorded to be made by an orc, calling the Nazgûl "the apple of the Great Eye" (*TT*, III, iii, 55).

As we saw, in Tolkien's world the body is always an interpretation; but it is not always the interpretation of the subject whose body it is. Sauron's (loss of) bodily form signals aspects of his personal history and morals, but also his unwillingness and later inability to relate to the Creator's meanings in the "right" way. But the way he is represented by the other fictional authors is of course also an interpretation, and it is *theirs*, not Sauron's, based on the fictional traditions of representing this being, and the experience they themselves have with his power and effects. Sauron's "new guise" has something to do with the image of the Eye (with a pun, we might say he fashions himself a "new I," a new self); for the others writing (about) him, the Eye is, however, only an image and a metaphor, and all that is "real" of it is channeled through the one piece of physical reality they actually see about him: the Ring. Through looking at Sauron's activities as represented in the text and connected to the Ring, we can thus gain some insight into his corporeality in *The Lord of the Rings*.

The Power and the Body: Sauron and the Ring

Being a mythological subject, Sauron functions as the center of a discourse that assigns meanings instead of being assigned meanings by something else. Another system, another discourse gives him his meanings, but that is largely retrospective: the accounts of (fictional) others write Sauron and his transformed/erased body for us. The texts' ways of representing, narrating this as a theologically contextualized, "othered" (since it has become particular and isolated from the fullness of meaning from which it derives) and "othering" (since its *modus operandi* is to lump everyone and everything else into the category of its own "subjects," *his* others) center of discourse effectively lifts Sauron above anyone else (anyone else's speech, narration, interpretation) in the fiction. Only apparently, however: he is merely usurping the place of the center (this is why he can be overcome), and despite being a character to be signified in a special way in a text about this story, he does not triumph exactly because of the body and the exclusivity with which his power treats this grounding aspect of subjectivity. A non-corporeal center is something of a paradox in a system where all items are simply its "others," "subjected" to it and interchangeable with each other — but still grounded as (independent) "subjects" by their body. On the one hand, this is so because Sauron's activities are always sensed as corporeal, his power as a power over the body; and on the other hand because such subjects would have problems understanding what a "metaphysical center" is. He would gain nothing but dominance over mindless, erased subjects.[32]

In *The Lord of the Rings*, characters handle Sauron in two different ways. Pragmatically, he is a dangerous enemy, and his danger lies in his military strategy and supremacy — like a particularly strong but wholly "earthly" opponent. Metaphysically, however, he always has an extra advantage: his strategy and supremacy are overwhelming exactly because of his status as a mythological subject. The difference is seen well in all strategy meetings in *The Lord of the Rings*, especially in the Council of Elrond: while Boromir sticks to the first view of their enemy, Elrond and Gandalf (who are aware of Sauron's theological position) constantly warn that this is not the whole picture. Sauron's own activities tend to muddy this, for example when he stages his most symbolic act of overpowering others by the giving of rings, a ritual that in the Old English tradition is associated with the political ruler's assuming of responsibility for his retainers.

This last literary historical connection also highlights for us that Sauron's actions are always represented on two levels. Firstly, we have how the *text's* fictional speakers and authors talk about him, showing the two ways described above. This already holds a further differentiation, since fictional authors of course write in retrospect, aware of the truth of the differences speakers like Boromir might overlook or not understand at the time. But secondly, we also see how *Tolkien* talks about the text's fictional speakers and authors talking about Sauron; and this is how the several conventions of representation, the horizons of Sauron's activities become very much elaborated. We have the signifying system of Middle-earth on the one hand; we have our own on the other, which includes familiar modes of representing gods, of theorizing mythologies and reflecting upon subject positions and metaphysical centers. Middle-earth might not have had its postmodern turn; we have. The text's largely realistic logic thus means that Tolkien's medievalized framework allows us to use much of our real-world theoretical presuppositions within the signifying system of Middle-earth; but it also means we necessarily see meanings in the text that its fictional authors do not, and should not confuse our meanings with theirs.

In both signifying systems, the body is posed as the opposite pole to Sauron, as the essential constituent of normal subjectivity — and this is important since his activities can be seen in other subjects under his sway. While Sauron is a spiritual being, his influence is primarily bodily: it changes the body of its subjects, and is sensed basically as physical, symbolized in the Eye, which serves to represent Sauron in visual terms, physically, linking his power and his actual representation. Sauron's power grabs Gollum through his bodily desires, as Tom Shippey's interpretation of Gollum as an addict amply illustrates,[33] and changes the physical object of this desire, the Ring, into a complex and many-layered signifier which operates Gollum's subjectivity (demolishing it because defining Gollum simply as Sauron's meaningless "other") and determines his language to the point where it becomes something entirely bodily, an *action*, instead of being symbolic, meaningful.[34] Through affecting the body, Sauron erases the subject, but ironically while the body lasts cannot do so totally (his most perfect servants are the Nazgûl, whose bodies have been erased as well).

What Sauron does with other subjects comes back to him with a vengeance. His transformed body still remains, of course, the ground of subjectivity, and text appears as the representation of this modified, "othered," theologically contextualized body. Apparently emerging as center, becoming a central, metaphysical signified for a reflective reader, he nevertheless also remains a character in the representation of the world, not simply a function but a person for the fictional authors. Even though his power is overwhelmingly physical, his purpose is to become the ultimate meaning simply by erasing all other meanings or subjects able to produce them: his discourse of power is very materially focused, and is mirrored well in the image of the blasted Mordor landscape. In his signifying system, there are only two elements: himself as center, and everything else as "other," periphery, non-meaning. Subjects here only become meaningful by losing meaning. Such a system is not even properly symbolic, since it is built on one difference only; consequently Sauron himself is not even participating in a signifying system that would enable language. On the one hand, he thus appears to be represented not *in language* but rather in *determining language* and thus subjects, knowledge, and action: he functions as the focus of linguistic and non-linguistic signs, a center defining its own system of signification. Sauron is a discourse of power, represented along rather Foucauldian lines in the imagery of the eye and of vision — Jane Chance identifies it with "the power of hegemonic authority."[35] But on the other hand, he is clearly represented *in the language of* the fictional narrators: the medium of representation in Tolkien is emphatically textual, linguistic, and thus the "normal" symbolic system into which Sauron has to be integrated to be signified and battled is given by the text. In Sauron's figure, the mythological status as a palpable, physical presence and backing is set against the elusive non-explicit theological discourse. The fact that he is represented not as a(n allegory for) "discourse" but as a subject with some physical aspects of the representation points out the problematic nature of imagining such a subject: it is fully "other," but still a subject.

The fact that Sauron not only functions in the system of representations but has aims and purposes of his own further underscores his status as a subject. His goal is to immerse everything in his crude binary system. He is represented in terms of discourses he operates, constituting the frames (or limits) of other subjects' meaning producing activities. We see the Nazgûl and Gollum (nearly) erased in Sauron; we constantly see him tempting, corrupting, destroying others (all actions of reduction, all taking away the individual's autonomous meanings and interpretations and replacing it with something prefabricated: Sauron is not only a discourse, he is ideology). He is represented by these actions to be still for some extent a part of the normal symbolic system, still capable of being affected, involved in stratagems and political intrigue; and for some extent still material, or at least associated with material images (the Eye, the Ring, Barad-dûr). Sauron's loss of body and its replacement by the immaterial "shadow" on the one hand, and the multi-layered but certainly material Ring on the other highlight the fact that to control symbolic systems, mythological subjects have to be (represented as) a part of those systems.

It is through the Ring that Sauron can do this, or that the fictional authors can manage him. Without the Ring, Sauron cannot take physical shape again.[36] Without a way of referring to him, representing him, he cannot be written. Without a body, he cannot function as a subject in the created world of Middle-earth, however mythological; but his corporeality, along with much of his innate power, is transferred to the Ring. In effect, the Ring functions as Sauron's body in *The Lord of the Rings* (this is also consonant with the way it becomes a signifier, both a linguistic and a pictorial representation for Sauron in the text). The process of transformation is described in terms of enclosing (of Sauron's power in the Ring) and loss (Sauron loses power and the freedom of choosing his shape). But these are exactly the effects Sauron has on other subjects: a mythological subject trying to usurp the place of the metaphysical center runs into the paradox of being the alternative to totality, and therefore of being empty, erased. As parts of the represented world of fiction, of the story, and of normal, subject-grounding corporeality, he is finally defeated, and even the dissolution of his controlling discourse (as superior, as in control) involves the body and its final changes. When the Ring is destroyed and Barad-dûr falls, "a huge shape of shadow" (*RK*, VI, iv, 227) rises threatening but is blown away by the wind.[37] Sauron at his fall appears both as a shadow and a body (at least in shape). The destruction of this shape is an effective way of representing its absence from the center, which Sauron never really occupied, the failure of his control of meaning.

Conclusions

Three important conclusions emerge from this survey of how Tolkien represents the mythological subject of Sauron and how its representation is connected to the concept of the body. The first concerns the representation of the theological in a text whose logic is by and large realistic, and that does not make its theology explicit. The second is about the role of representation as connected to the creation and maintaining of culture, whether in fact or in fiction. The third is an addition to the definition of "mythopoeic."

Tolkien takes the theological seriously, and separates it sharply from other discourses of culture. He does not, however, assert its independence, but handles it as one discourse of representation. Subjects of this order are, however, still represented largely as real-world cultures represent them, with a stress on corporeality and its connection to the individual subject's integrity. In this context, to be able to carry his experiment of representing how fictional authors represent subjects not of a realistic order, Tolkien shows them making use of real-world conventions (in terms of language) and body substitutes (in terms of theory). Sauron's figure is much more realistically mythological for its deep and complex connection to the Ring, the Shadow, and Barad-dûr, than it would be without these. His special subjectivity is inscribed in a body that is not there, but the text, the representation, always makes up one.

As his fiction deals with language, cultural representation, and the power over meanings and subjects that certain positions in the system offer (or the positions we ourselves, as subjects doing the representation, construct for our fictions), Tolkien here shows these positions to fall partly outside the system, as mythological subjects elude anyone's speech, narration, representation. Still, they remain just as represented as anything else: this stress on subjects and their positions, both centers and contexts, might be seen as a special kind of metafiction, *meta-representation*, and constitutes a uniquely interesting way fantastic literature can be aware of the complexity of discourses in which the world or a fiction can be represented and in which it itself is contextualized. But this metafictional/meta-representational stance in fact replays the dissolution of the center imagined in the story or the fiction: it reveals and liberates; when talking about and creating culture it reaches an unparalleled level of *representing cultural representation*. In this context, the emphasis placed on the body of exceptional mythological subjects adds to the variety in which cultural discourses are used in fiction.

Finally, the "mythopoeic" qualities of Tolkien's texts emerge as at least partly constituted by this specific way of using mythological subjects to contextualize the uses of stories in culture. When the theological gains such an important part in the representation and creation of culture, we cannot escape the conclusion that stories about such beings and their defeat are ultimately less "factual" than functional, and by creating a fictitious culture where these stories about such beings can really happen, Tolkien is telling us something about the specific cultural uses that make a story a myth. It is not gods who make myths but people; ultimately, it is of course the people who make the gods, body and power and all.

Notes

1. *Letters*, 172 (letter no. 142).
2. For more about "Grand Narratives," see Jean-Francois Lyotard, *The Post-Modern Condition: A Report on Knowledge* (Minneapolis: University of Minnesota, 1979), where he introduced the term.
3. See Yuri Lotman, "Problems in the Typology of Culture," *Soviet Semiotics: An Anthology*, ed. Daniel P. Lucid (Baltimore: Johns Hopkins University Press, 1977), 213–21.
4. See my "The Medievalist('s) Fiction," 2005.
5. For the Neoplatonic connection, see Verlyn Flieger, "Naming the Unnameable," 1986.
6. See Jacques Derrida, "Structure, Sign, and Play in the Discourse of the Human Sciences," 1972. Derrida starts by defining the center as "a point of presence, a fixed origin" (247).
7. See my "The 'Lost' Subject of Middle-earth," 2006, passim.
8. Tolkien, "On Fairy-Stories," *The Tolkien Reader* (New York: Ballantine, 1966), 34.
9. See "The 'Lost' Subject," 63–65.
10. *Sil*, 17.
11. *Sil*, 31–32.
12. Gandalf's reference to being "sent back" (*TT*, III, v, 106) and Faramir's allusion to "beyond Elvenhome" in the West (*TT*, IV, v, 285) are perhaps the only "clear" references to the theological. In Appendix B of *The Lord of the Rings*, Sauron is explicitly called a "servant of Morgoth" (363).
13. See Tolkien's short argument about Thórr and the thunder in "On Fairy-Stories," 50–51.
14. *Sil*, 21.
15. Ibid., 16.
16. Ibid., 73.
17. Ibid., 280.
18. Ibid., 287.
19. Most notably when he "took upon himself the form of a werewolf," then "shifted shape, from wolf to serpent and from monster to his own accustomed form" (*Sil*, 175) when fighting with Lúthien and Huan.
20. Ibid., 280–81.
21. This is something he shares with Morgoth from the beginning; but in view of how *The Lord of the Rings* speaks of the ominous "shadow of Sauron," this is perhaps a telling point.
22. *Sil*, 267.
23. Ibid., 302.
24. Joe Abbott, "Tolkien's Monsters: Concept and Function in *The Lord of the Rings*. Part III: Sauron," *Mythlore* 16.3 (1990), 54.
25. As Gwenyth Hood showed in "Sauron as Gorgon and Basilisk," *Seven* 8 (1987), 59–71.
26. See Hood, "Sauron," 64.
27. Engelbert Kirschbaum, *Lexicon der christlichen Ikonographie*, vol.1 (Rome: Herder, 1968–69), 222.
28. Ibid., 224.
29. This is also in *The Silmarillion* as well, where exactly the same qualities are emphasized, sometimes explicitly "mirroring" (even ironically) the situation in *The Lord of the Rings*: "No living creature could pass through that vale that Sauron did not espy from the tower [of all towers, one named Minas Tirith] where he sat" (*Sil*, 156).

30. See Hood, "Sauron," 59.

31. Cf. Ibid. The "Shadow" is also such a sign, but since it is immaterial, or rather expresses the influence of something immaterial, I consider the Eye and the Ring more important.

32. There are, of course, indications that this is exactly what he wants. His best servants, the Nazgûl, are precisely like this; and Morgoth's traditional claim for the Kingdom of Arda as his own (*Sil,* 20–21) hints that he already thought only of the physical reality of the world to be conquered and nothing more. A parallel can be seen in Aulë's creation of the Dwarves, who initially are similarly "empty" subjects: but whereas Aulë does not desire such mastery, and pleads with Ilúvatar to "bless [his] work and amend it" (*Sil,* 44), we have the feeling that Morgoth and Sauron would be very happy with unamended, "remote-controlled" subjects.

33. Tom Shippey, *The Road to Middle-earth,* 3d ed. (Boston: Houghton Mifflin, 2003), 139–40.

34. See "The 'Lost' Subject," 59–63.

35. Jane Chance, The Lord of the Rings: *The Mythology of Power,* rev. ed. (Lexington: University Press of Kentucky, 2001), 57; cf. 21–2.

36. Gandalf explains that without the Ring, Sauron will be reduced to "a mere spirit of malice" who cannot create a body for himself any more (*RK,* V, ix, 155).

37. Cf. the description of Saruman's death, evidencing that even when the physical body was intact, the destruction of one of the Maiar involves this shadow-form (*RK,* VI, viii, 300).

Works Consulted

Abbott, Joe. "Tolkien's Monsters: Concept and Function in *The Lord of the Rings.* Part III: Sauron." *Mythlore* 16.3 (1990): 51–59.

Chance, Jane. The Lord of the Rings: *The Mythology of Power,* rev. ed. Lexington: University Press of Kentucky, 2001.

Derrida, Jacques. "Structure, Sign, and Play in the Discourse of the Human Sciences." *The Structuralist Controversy,* ed. Richard Macksey and Eugenio Donato, 247– 265. Baltimore: Johns Hopkins University Press, 1972.

Flieger, Verlyn. "Naming the Unnameable: the Neoplatonic 'One' in Tolkien's *Silmarillion.*" *Diakonia: Studies in Honor of Robert T. Meyer,* ed. Thomas Halton and Joseph P. Williman, 127–132. Washington, D.C.: Catholic University of America Press, 1986.

Hood, Gwenyth. "Sauron as Gorgon and Basilisk." *Seven* 8 (1987): 59–71.

Kirschbaum, Engelbert. *Lexicon der christlichen Ikonographie,* 8 vols. Rome: Herder, 1968–69.

Lotman, Yuri. "Problems in the Typology of Culture." *Soviet Semiotics: An Anthology,* ed. Daniel P. Lucid, 213–221. Baltimore: Johns Hopkins University Press, 1977.

Lyotard, Jean-Francois. *The Post-modern Condition: A Report on Knowledge.* Minneapolis: University of Minnesota, 1979.

Nagy, Gergely. "The 'Lost' Subject of Middle-earth." *Tolkien Studies* 3 (2006): 57–79.

_____. "The Medievalist('s) Fiction: Textuality and Historicity as Aspects of Tolkien's Medievalist Cultural Theory in a Postmodernist Context." *Tolkien's Modern Middle Ages,* ed. Jane Chance and Alfred K. Siewers, 29–41. New York: Palgrave Macmillan, 2005.

Shippey, Tom. *The Road to Middle-earth.* 3d ed. Boston: Houghton Mifflin, 2003.

Tolkien, J.R.R. "On Fairy-Stories." *The Tolkien Reader,* 31–99. New York: Ballantine, 1966.

PART IV

The Body and the Source Material

Emblematic Bodies
Tolkien and the Depiction of Female Physical Presence

JAMES T. WILLIAMSON

> *Her feet were light as bird on wing,*
> *her laughter lighter than the spring;*
> *the slender willow, the bowing reed,*
> *the fragrance of a flowering mead,*
> *the light upon the leaves of trees,*
> *the voice of water, more than these*
> *her beauty was and blissfulness,*
> *her glory and her loveliness.*[1]

My purpose here is to look at the physical depiction of the four major female characters in *The Lord of the Rings*: Goldberry, Arwen, Galadriel, and Éowyn. My chief argument is that Tolkien's depiction of the female body is conventional and figural, tied to thematic associations with the physical creation — earth, plants, and waters, as well as with the heavens — and with cyclic time, the rhythms of which permeate the physical creation. In short, the female body in *The Lord of the Rings* is emblematic rather than biological.

I suggest that the thematic significance of these depictions of "emblematic bodies" extends beyond *The Lord of the Rings* itself, that Tolkien's method of presenting the female body was evident in writings preceding *The Lord of the Rings*, and that this represents a notable stylistic continuity between the material constituting the Legendarium and *The Lord of the Rings*, in many respects notable for their divergences of style and narrative approach. In turn, this approach to the body can be seen in the earlier traditional literatures of northern Europe and the British Isles which preoccupied Tolkien professionally and which provided models for the narrative forms in which the material of the Legendarium is manifest. I will expand on this connection briefly at the end of my discussion.

The passage which heads this essay is from the earlier fragment of "The Lay of Leithian," composed between 1925 and 1930, and included in *The Lays of Beleriand*, the third volume of *The History of Middle Earth*. In terms of specific description of Lúthien as an autonomous biological being we have very little to go on, and even that is thoroughly conventional: She has "lissom limbs," grey eyes, hair "dark as shadow," and light feet, and her laughter is also light. On the other hand, the description is awash with images drawn from the natural world, into which the physical depiction of Lúthien is effectively subsumed. More notable than her limbs' "lissomness" is the fact that they "run/on the green earth beneath the sun"[2]; her robe and eyes are seen as "summer skies" and "grey as evening"[3]; the sequence of images in lines 31–36, with little alteration, become a description of the surrounding woodland.

The description of Lúthien is, of course, a composite, and is not tied to a particular dramatic incident. But the approach is evident later when the narrative is under way: when Beren first sees Lúthien she is, again, described in terms that reflect the natural world around her:

> He gazed, and as he gazed her hair
> within its cloudy web did snare
> the silver moon beams sifting white
> between the leaves, and glinting bright
> the tremulous starlight of the skies
> was caught and mirrored in her eyes.[4]

Beren sees, not a biological woman, but a conduit for moonlight and a mirror for starlight. Upon her departure, Beren laments:

> "'Where art thou gone? The day is bare,
> the sunlight dark, and cold the air!
> Tinúviel, where went thy feet?
> O wayward star! O maiden sweet!
> O flower of Elfland all too fair
> for mortal heart! The woods are bare!
> The woods are bare!' he rose and cried.
> 'Ere spring was born, the spring hath died!"[5]

For Beren, the absence of Lúthien is equated with barren woods, cold air, failed sunlight, and failed spring: the negation of the associations in the preceding passages.

The depiction of Lúthien's body, then, circles around vegetation, water (which nourishes vegetation), and the light of heavenly bodies (which merges with water through the "cloudy web" of her hair). Additionally, her association with spring and moon can be seen to suggest an association with the cyclic time of nature. This is consolidated in Tolkien's locating her "from dawn to dusk, from sun to sea," in a place where cyclic time ("dawn to dusk") is conflated with the natural world ("sun to sea").

This depiction of Lúthien is a good jumping off point for a couple of reasons. First, in a broad sense, we can see quite clearly Tolkien's tendency to develop female physical presence in terms of nature-based poetic figure rather than in terms of flesh, in a context where the tendency is less muted and less impeded by the rich representational detail which characterizes *The Lord of the Rings*. Seen in such a context, it is perhaps easier to spot where it is less obvious. Second, more narrowly, there is the direct relation between Lúthien and Arwen, who is physically represented as the "likeness" of Lúthien (*FR*, II, i, 239), and the key images attached here to Lúthien are attached themselves to Arwen in the pages of *The Lord of the Rings*.

While it is true that, of the four key female figures of *The Lord of the Rings*, only Goldberry is depicted with a similar denseness of imagery, nevertheless the increasingly spare imagery which attends the physical presence of Galadriel, Arwen, and Éowyn is of like kind with like thematic resonances, and a close reading suggests that it was chosen carefully and deliberately. It is also far more notable than the terse, conventional references to yellow hair and slenderness. I will now turn to the four in sequence.

Goldberry

Goldberry is identified simply as the daughter of the otherwise unnamed River God, and Tolkien does not seem to have further glossed this except to note, in a letter to Forrest Ackerman in 1958 on a prospective film adaptation of *The Lord of the Rings*, that she inhabits "real river-lands in autumn" and "represents the actual seasonal changes in such lands."[6] This is suggestive in terms of thematic significance, but not much help when considering Tolkien's general shying away from allegory in favor of history. It would not seem unreasonable to speculate that since "Godhead" is associated with the Valar and Maiar, the River God, and hence Goldberry, are Maiar.[7] However, there is no evidence that Tolkien intended such a connection, or even that it had occurred to him, and Goldberry, like Tom Bombadil, stands as something of an enigma.

As with Lúthien in "The Lay of Leithian," the introduction of Goldberry in Book One of *The Lord of the Rings* moves quickly from very brief, conventional observations of her individual physical appearance (here equally emphasizing her apparel) to a dense fabric of natural images, with particular emphasis on water and water based vegetation. This strain of imagery continues as the hobbits hesitate before her approach (see full passage in *FR*, I, vii, 134). Upon hearing her name, Frodo responds with a rhyme that embodies similar imagery (see *FR*, I, vii, 135).

While all this is in fact physical imagery, tied specifically to the physical presence of Goldberry, we nevertheless know nothing of Goldberry's appearance as a discrete biological entity except that she has yellow hair — which, invoking water, "rippled" (*FR*, I, vii, 134) — and that she is slender. Rather, Goldberry's physical being, her body, is seen as indivisible from forget-me-nots, water-lilies, and reeds, from beads of dew, living pools, and waterfalls. It is these that form our image of her.

Like images attend Goldberry's presence through the hobbits' stay at the House of Tom Bombadil. When she leaves the hobbits safely in bed, her identification with water extends to the audible, when the departing tread of her feet is likened to running water (see *FR*, I, vii, 136). When she appears to give her farewell to the hobbits, her voice is described as "rippling," and her hair like a "glint of water" (*FR*, I, viii, 146). In their last sight of her, she is seen as a "sunlit flower" (*FR*, I, viii, 147).

That this welter of imagery underscores Goldberry's association with fertility is obvious. It serves to situate her, not in a timeless world, but in the cyclic time of the world of nature, where rippling streams and living pools beget and nourish reeds and lilies according to the rhythm of the seasons. Her body is emblematic of the natural world independent of "those that go on two legs," within yet separate from the historical world in which the chief events of *The Lord of the Rings* occur.

Galadriel

Galadriel is one of those Noldori (a branch of the Eldar, or Elves) who returned across the Ocean to Middle Earth in the First Age with Feanor, to regain the Silmarils stolen by Morgoth. Refusing the command of the Valar to return after the kin-slaying of the ship-building Teleri, she was among those subsequently banished to Middle-earth. Her aid in the struggle against Sauron at the end of the Third Age forms a sort of penance, the ban is lifted, and she is, at the end of *The Lord of the Rings*, permitted to return to the West. She has, therefore, been a part of the major chronological events of all three ages of Middle-earth, which clearly distinguishes her from Goldberry, whose world is bound entirely by the endlessly repeating cycles of the seasons.

Nevertheless Galadriel is clearly associated with the cyclic time of nature, and with fertility, though with less immediate familiarity and intimacy. Her physical presence is in fact evident in the woods of Lothlórien before she actually enters the story as a character. In a pause on the journey through the forest to Caras Galadhon, the dwelling place of Galadriel, Frodo reflects on what he sees around him, perceiving it as both ancient and newly made and named, without "blemish or sickness or deformity" (see *FR*, II, vi, 365).

Frodo's puzzling about his perceptions elicits Sam's observation that he feels as if he was "inside a song." The elf Haldir remarks that Frodo feels "the power of the Lady of the Galadrim" (*FR*, II, vi, 365).

There is a dual current evident here absent in Tolkien's depiction of Goldberry. The vivid life that surrounds Frodo here is clearly bound up with the physical presence of Galadriel, but it also exists without her, at a remove. The fertility of Lothlórien precedes Galadriel, while that of the little land of Tom Bombadil accompanies Goldberry. The "ancientness" that emerges in Frodo's perception is itself an implicit confirmation of chronological, historical time: what he sees is present, but it is also an echo of the past. The pervasive present of Goldberry's world does not allow "ancientness," and even the idea of "blemish or sickness or deformity" as contrast is alien to her world. Sam's observation, that he feels as if "inside a song," underscores this: song is perhaps the chief mode in which the "ancient" is passed on, through which the past is made present. It is in song that the tales of Beren and Lúthien, of Eärendil, and of Nimrodel, have appeared in the text of *The Lord of the Rings*. Indeed, it was with song that Ilúvatar began time and creation in the "Ainulindalë."

The opening words of Galadriel's song at the beginning of the scene where she parts from the Fellowship are suggestive in this regard: she sings of leaves and wind, and leaves and wind manifest (see *FR*, II, viii, 388) Where Goldberry is a present, active participant in the cycles of nature, Galadriel initiates through song, echoing Sam's earlier observation. It is significant that the song is cast in the past tense: the fertility of Galadriel's Lothlórien is the result of a past act, while that of Goldberry's world seems to move with her in a very immediate, intimate way, and her involvement is ongoing.

The element of fertility is therefore more removed here: the fluid immediacy of running water and blooming lilies are replaced by more static images of shape and color, the sense not of a present, but of a "vanished world," and the element of fertility is primarily tied to the association of the images with beginnings, birth, coming into being, and naming, rather than to an ongoing cyclic process. More significant in terms of an explicit connection to fertility is Galadriel's gift to Sam at the company's parting from Lothlórien: the soil, which aids and quickens the recovery of the Shire after the depredations of Saruman's ruffians and the seed of the *mallorn* tree, which enables Lothlórien to be re-born in muted form after the end of the Third Age and to remain after Galadriel herself has left Middle-earth.

But all of this occurs in the absence of Galadriel as a physical dramatic character, though in the present context it would not be amiss to say that the life of Lothlórien is in fact an extension of Galadriel's physical being. In a specifically biological sense, however, we have no more to go on than we did with Goldberry. When the Fellowship first encounters her, she is described as being equally tall as Celeborn, her consort, and her hair is "deep gold" (*FR*,

II, vii, 369). The denseness of natural images that accompanies both Lúthien and Goldberry is almost entirely absent from her initial appearance, extant only in an image that moves from the earth to the heavens: her eyes are "keen as lances in ... starlight ... yet profound, the wells of deep memory" (*FR*, II, vii, 369).

While brief, this image is significant: it follows Frodo's ruminations, situating Galadriel in the time of beginnings, for at the first awakening of the elves Middle-earth was lit only by starlight. It also situates Galadriel in broader cycles of time than simply the changing of the seasons. She is the living reflection of beginnings and of the ancient world, tied to its renewal in the succession of seasons through chronological time, bearing the power of renewal, albeit in gradually diminishing form: the ancient world at this point remains only in the circumscribed, beleaguered land of Lothlórien; later, it remains only in the *mallorn* tree planted by Sam. And it remains in song.

The well reflecting starlight, which constitutes Galadriel's chief bodily emblem, can also be seen to imply perspective and wisdom. Wedded to starlight, the element water functions distinctly from the simple nourishing capacity suggested in its relation to Goldberry. Notably, the water of a well is still. It serves as a tool reflecting what is unchangeable, "deep memory." It is a necessary adjunct to perspective and wisdom. The water of the aptly named Mirror of Galadriel is an extension, even an externalization, of this emblem: Sam first sees the stars in its depths; Frodo sees broad vistas of distant parts of Middle-earth and Valinor, and of Middle-earth's past. Galadriel's parting gift to Frodo also embodies both the emblem and its significance: in the Phial of Galadriel the light from the star of Eärendil is set into the water of the Mirror (See *FR*, II, viii, 393).

This emblematic significance extends to Galadriel's body quite literally. At the end of the scene when the Fellowship first meets her, she tells them that there is hope for the quest while all the members of the company remain true, and then looks deeply at each of them in turn, a gaze only Legolas and Aragorn can hold (see *FR*, II, vii, 372). Later, when the Company reflects back on this moment, they realize that they each felt as if they were being offered something desirable if they abandoned the quest (*FR*, II, vii, 373) Galadriel's eyes here have served quite clearly as a mirror, giving a form to desires of the individual members of the Fellowship that had not been fully defined or fully conscious. In Galadriel's eyes, the members of the Fellowship see themselves. While not memory in a strict sense, it is like, in that where memory stores what is past and unalterable, this glimpse of unconscious desire made conscious also reveals what is unalterable, with its seeds both in the individual's past and the individual's nature.

In this sense, the "mirror" of Galadriel's body, centered in the wells of deep memory that are her eyes, make clear the ethical and moral dilemmas which confront the individual characters. I have said that memory is a necessary adjunct to perspective and wisdom. But the reverse is also true here: perspective and a certain wisdom are necessary for memory (or an unambiguous vision of one's desires) to be understood and to serve a constructive purpose. For example, Sam's desire to return to a pleasant hobbit hole with a garden in the Shire (*FR*, II, vii, 373) reflects a certain, unalterable component of Sam's nature. But Sam has the wisdom and perspective to recognize (as is implicitly evident) that such a desire, put into action, would be ethically and morally unconscionable, that commitment to the Quest must come before pursuit of his own self-centered desires. In contrast, Boromir, by implication tempted to seek to possess the Ring, dissembles his desire and directs suspicion toward Galadriel (*FR*, II, vii, 373). There is little doubt that Aragorn's stern rejoinder, that the only evil in Lothlórien is that brought by visitors (*FR*, II, vii, 373), falls on fundamentally deaf ears.

These thematic extrapolations (and one could pursue Boromir a good bit further) emerge quite naturally from the image of the wells of memory reflecting starlight, which are Galadriel's eyes. Galadriel's physical presence, the focal point of which is those eyes, is a mirror: the members of the Fellowship see true things with regard to themselves in that mirror. What Boromir sees is at odds with his conscious, pride-distorted image of himself, and he locates the "evil" he perceives in the mirror rather than in himself, and is hence defenseless against that evil. The readiness to ascribe evil to the mirror is itself attached to the broader failing of collective human memory (in this case, memory of Elven kind), a "blemish or sickness or deformity" in the perception of chronological time, in which "unscathed" replaces "unchanged" (as Aragorn corrects Boromir's terminology regarding the effects of Lothlórien), danger becomes evil, evil is projected onto external objects when it is unwittingly carried within. That Galadriel herself has a clear understanding both of her personal motivations and of historical time is evident when she declines Frodo's offer of the Ring. Her gaze has the capacity to make clear things necessary to an understanding of oneself and the world: it cannot, as we see with Boromir, guarantee that the perception will be used to facilitate understanding.

As the foregoing suggests, the implications of the emblems attached to Galadriel's physical presence are of some complexity — considerably more complex than those attached to Goldberry, or, as we shall see, to Arwen or Éowyn. The implicit connection of her physical presence to the vivid life of Lothlórien, the suggestion that her song brought Lothlórien into being and that being in Lothlórien is like being "inside a song," as Sam says, connects her in a way to fertility. In a sense, Lothlórien itself is her body. But as we have seen, this is a connection that exists independent of her presence as a dramatic character. The lone image attached to her physical being suggesting fertility occurs in the scene where the Fellowship is taking leave of Lothlórien.

Here the narrator observes on her head a "circlet of golden flowers" (*FR*, II, viii, 388), a clear reflection of her association with the fertility of golden-leaved Lothlórien.

But the chief emblem attached to her physical being, her body, is her eyes, the "wells of deep memory" reflecting starlight. This places the cyclic time of nature and fertility as a repeating pattern within the context of chronological time, underscoring Frodo's perception of the natural world of Lothlórien as a "vanished world." The still water of these "pools of memory" represents the fixed, immutable nature of the past. But chronological time leads out of the fixed and immutable past into the future, which can be shaped by present action. Galadriel is last seen by the Fellowship as they depart from *Lothlórien* to the barren world without, on the moving waters of the Great River. The onward rush of the stream, sweeping the Fellowship away, leaves her shrinking form behind, and can be seen as an emblem of chronological, historical time. Galadriel and Lothlórien are moving away from them, "slipping backward," not only into the distance, but into the vanished world of a disappearing past (*FR*, II, viii, 393). The English rendering of the elvish song which follows the company over the water situates Lothlórien in relation to chronological time: "Like gold fall the leaves ... long years numberless ..." it begins, and then turns to "...the Queen of the Stars" (*FR*, II, viii, 394).

While Goldberry is defined, through the images that constitute her physical presence, by her association with the cyclic time of nature, Galadriel represents the cross-bonding of cyclic time with chronological historical time.[8] She is immanent in Lothlórien, her physical presence tied to its vivid growth, but only with the circlet of golden flowers she wears as the Fellowship departs is that integrated into an image associated with her physical being. Ultimately the fertility of her world passes out of her hands, remaining in the seed she gives to Sam. Her key physical emblem, starlight reflected in water, the still water of a well, reflects distance and perspective, and functions as a mirror in her interaction with the Fellowship, a sort of barometer of their individual motivations and dedication to the Quest. The water that flows out of Lothlórien, the world whose natural cycles she is tied to, is clearly suggestive of chronological time in its depiction. But it is the wisdom that emerges from the starry perspective of chronological time that facilitates, through the gifts of the *mallorn* seed and the Phial, completion of the historical cycle, and rebirth and renewal in a broader sense in Middle-earth.

Arwen

Arwen's makeup is the most complex of the four. Daughter of Elrond half-elven, son of Eärendil and Elwing, she carries both elven and human blood in her. Her mother is Celebrian, daughter of Celeborn and Galadriel, so in the elven part of her make-up she is connected to the Eldar, the elves who went into the West, and the Sindar, the elves who never left Middle-earth. In addition, from Elwing her geneology stretches back through Dior to Beren and Lúthien, and from Lúthien to Melian, and hence she also carries the blood of the Maiar. In her first brief appearances at the beginning of Book Two, the elven strain is dominant. But as an elf, she is considerably younger than Galadriel, born in the early years of the Third Age, and hence has been witness to the history of Middle-earth only during the period of the elves' decline. However, by marrying Aragorn she chooses human destiny, and hence in her brief appearance in Gondor after the fall of Sauron in Book Six, the human strain has become dominant.

Unlike Goldberry and Galadriel, she is not connected with the natural cycles of her home. Her power does not pervade Rivendell, which is the "House of Elrond," and her two brief appearances in the first chapter of Book Two, "Many Meetings," are restricted to two paragraphs before the meal at Elrond's table, and one as Frodo leaves the Hall of Fire. She is seen at a distance and her voice does not enter the narrative. In the first of the two brief passages (see *FR* II, I, 239), she is described with slightly more detail concerning her personal appearance than was granted Goldberry or Galadriel, but not much, and it is thoroughly conventional: she has dark braided hair, white arms and clear face, and grey eyes. More notable are the images that attach themselves to her physical presence: like Galadriel, the light of stars is in her eyes, and the wisdom visible in them suggests a similar thematic connection. In the even more brief later passage, this is echoed when she turns her gaze to Frodo, and that light, starlight, strikes Frodo (*FR*, II, i, 250). The image is reflected in the starry quality of her laced cap "netted with small gems." The sole image suggesting a connection to the life and growth associated with nature is her girdle of wrought silver leaves.

The thematic implications of these emblematic extensions of Arwen's physical being are not difficult to follow. Galadriel, with her immanent bond to the cyclical growth of golden-leaved Lothlórien, finally encapsulated in her circlet of golden flowers, is associated with beginnings, coming into being — with Spring, with the Morning. Her starry eyes can be seen to echo the "first time" for elves, before the Sun and Moon. In contrast, the colors associated with Arwen (white, silver, grey) suggest "end time," late fall and winter, Evening. While the image of starlight may suggest the "first time" of the elves as well, it is a "first time" which, unlike Galadriel, she did not see, though she carries it in her veins. More pertinent in this regard is the suggestion in the following paragraph, which situates her in relation to elvish history: she is known as Undómiel, identifying her as "the Evenstar of her people" (*FR*, II, I, 239). Galadriel is emblematic of the fading "first time" in the time of endings; Arwen is emblematic of the time of endings. The lone image suggesting fertility is the collection of leaves of her girdle, which is nevertheless silver. It is no accident that, after the fall of Sauron, when Éomer declares Arwen more beautiful than Galadriel, Gimli reflects: "You have chosen the Evening; but my love is given to the Morning" (*RK*, VI, vi, 253).

But, in a different way, Arwen is in fact associated with rebirth and renewal. The cycles of time that she represents, however, are the broader cycles embedded in the chronological history of Middle-earth. The starlight of her eyes can also be seen to connect to the Star of Eärendil, her grandfather, compassing the light of one of the Silmarils, set in the sky by the Valar at the end of the First Age as a sign of hope for those laboring against the evil initiated by Morgoth. This is the star that brings hope to Sam later during his struggle with Frodo through the land of Mordor. But the Evenstar is also the Morning Star: in Bilbo's version of the tale of Eärendil — recited, significantly, between Arwen's two appearances in the "Many Meetings" chapter—, it is described as "a wonder ere the waking dawn" (*FR*, II, i, 248); it appears to Sam in the evening. The "end time" brings with it the seeds of renewal and rebirth.

In the unfolding of the history of Middle-earth, Arwen represents a figure of her (and Aragorn's) ancestor, Lúthien. She is regarded as Lúthien returned (*FR*, II, i, 239), the narrator notes in the second paragraph attached to her first appearance in "Many Meetings." If we turn back to the first passage referred to from the "Lay of Leithian," we find Lúthien described with almost exactly the same spread of images (see ll. 28, 30, 560–2 in *Lays*).

But Tolkien is not simply concerned with a resemblance of the flesh — which is, needless to say, thoroughly conventional in both instances. The story of Arwen itself resembles the story of Lúthien. In the account of the tale of Aragorn and Arwen which appears in Appendix A, Aragorn first meets Arwen unintentionally in the woods, and the entire encounter is likened to the meeting of Beren and Lúthien, including Aragorn addressing Arwen as Tinúviel (see *RK*, Appendix A, 338).

Of course the most significant resemblance of the story is that, in marrying Aragorn, Arwen must become human and mortal: "'mine is the choice of Lúthien'" (*RK*, VI, vi, 252), she says to Frodo as she offers him her place on the voyage to the West. While Arwen is Evenstar to her people, the elves, representing their diminishment and ultimate departure from Middle-earth, it is ironically by her embracing of mortality through "the choice of Lúthien" that she comes to represent renewal and fertility in Middle-earth. Aragorn's discovery of the "sapling of Nimloth the fair," which will replace the barren tree in the Court of Minas Tirith (*RK*, VI, v, 249) as a symbol of the renewal of Gondor, is in the text followed by its consummation in fact: "when the sky was blue as sapphire and white stars opened in the east," Arwen, "Evenstar of her people," arrives in Minas Tirith on a grey palfrey and weds Aragorn

(*RK*, VI, v, 250). In embracing mortality she becomes fertile, and it is the resulting offspring of her body that signals renewal and continuance in Middle-earth. The Evenstar is also the Morning Star.

Éowyn

Éowyn is the only fully human female to receive sufficient development in *The Lord of the Rings* to discuss here. She is the niece of Théoden the King of Rohan, representing the non–Numenorean humans of Middle-earth. At her first appearance, when Gandalf enters the Hall of Meduseld with Aragorn, Legolas, and Gimli, Éowyn blends into the background: the narrator simply mentions in passing a "woman clad in white" (*TT*, III, vi, 117). It is only when she leaves the hall at Gandalf's behest that she receives some development (see *TT*, III, vi, 119). As with Goldberry, Galadriel, and Arwen, there is very little physical detail here, and it is thoroughly conventional: Éowyn is golden haired, she is tall, she is slender. The figural dimension of the description is more telling, and we can follow it in two directions. On the one hand, she is "strong" and "stern as steel," extended from her "white robe girt with silver." The suggestion is clearly martial, connecting her to the heroic, and male, world of the Rohirrim. On the other hand, we see her hair likened to a "river of gold," a natural image suggesting motion and life, partly extended and partly restrained by Aragorn's likening her to a "morning of pale spring ... not yet come to womanhood." She is associated with life and renewal, but the association is only latent at this point.

These two clusters of imagery anticipate Éowyn's development through the story. On the one hand, she is in fact a capable warrior: when Théoden leaves Meduseld a few pages later, she is set to rule in his absence, and as the army rides away, Aragorn again sees her with her hands set on the hilt of a sword before her, in shining sliver mail (*TT*, III, vi, 128). But the sword, its hilt, and the warrior's mail in which she has clad herself, are emblematic of the male warrior world of the Rohirrim: on a certain level, it is, for Éowyn, a disguise and a denial, however capable she might be. She is possessed of a certain maturity, but it is, in the context of Rohan, a masculine maturity.

But her womanhood, as Aragorn notes, is a latency, not yet fully formed. And this yet to be fully formed womanhood, an understandable lack of feminine maturity emerging out of a profound sense of frustration and inability to determine her own fate—in many ways, simply due to the fact that she is a woman—manifests in an impossible and obsessive romantic infatuation with Aragorn. When Aragorn, as he prepares to assay the Paths of the Dead after the defeat of Saruman, has declined Éowyn, she withdraws further into her masculine disguise. The thoughtfulness of her glance as initially depicted, has become eyes "on fire," wisdom has become madness, and she is last depicted in this scene standing still like a "figure carved in stone" (*RK*, V, ii, 59). The "morning of pale spring" has become frozen, running the danger of becoming barren. She leaves off being a warrior woman, a woman with masculine qualities, and simply takes on the guise of a man, in the form of Dernhelm.

Ironically, it is this disguise bred by her madness, a desperate evasion, psychologically, of what she is, which permits her to engage in battle with the chief of the Nazgûl at the Battle of the Pelennor Fields. That confrontation, the culmination of her male disguise and denial of her womanhood, is, again ironically, the turning point at which her womanhood begins to re-emerge (see *RK*, V, vi, 116). The imagery used by Tolkien to depict Éowyn at this point is interesting. The masculine and feminine images which were more carefully distinguished from, even opposed to, each other when she was first depicted at Meduseld, are mixed. The helm, the sword and shield, and the warrior eyes, the emblems of her assumed masculinity, are present. But the helm has been cast aside, revealing her "bright hair" that "gleamed with pale gold": she has cast aside her disguise and, ironically at the moment of her culminating masculine act, declared herself a woman. Her warrior eyes are softened by moving water/tears, signifying rebirth.

But it is later, in the Houses of Healing, where this rebirth comes full circle in her acceptance of herself, and in the subsequent growth of her love for Faramir. Significantly, at the moment when she accepts Faramir as her partner in waiting, relinquishing her essentially suicidal urge to bury her sorrows in martial action, we return again to the figure of spring (see *RK*, VI, v, 238). When her acceptance of Faramir as a partner in waiting matures to love, she rejects her role as shield-maiden and pledges to become a healer, and to "'love all things that grow and are not barren'" (*RK*, VI, v, 243). There is a psychological dimension, obviously, to the development of these images attached to Éowyn: they are bound up with her struggle to mature, to become what she is. In a sense, we might say that her battle with the Chief Nazgûl is a battle with her own demons, beginning a process of psychological healing which reaches its culmination in the self-acceptance and recognition that accompanies the flowering of her love for Faramir.

But there is also a broader significance echoing in more muted form the thematic essence of Arwen and her marriage to Aragorn. The consummation of the love of Aragorn and Arwen signals hope and renewal for Gondor by the mingling of Eldar and Edain. Likewise, the consummation of the love of Éowyn and Faramir signals hope and renewal by the mingling of the Numenorean with the wholly human. The offspring of Éowyn's body is/are the growth of a new spring in the relations between Rohan and Gondor, a spring in which the two have been brought together as one.

Some general observations concerning Tolkien's approach to the female body can be extrapolated from the preceding. One is a striking lack of interest in the body as a strictly biological entity. As dramatic characters, his female characters are primarily voices: what they say is far more developed than what they look like in an individual sense. Indeed, of the female characters not discussed here, the only visual image attached to Lobelia Sackville-Baggins occurs *when* Gandalf, observing her immediately after her departure in a huff from Bag End, describes her as sporting "a face that would have curdled new milk" (*FR*, I, i, 48) — a potent image given Lobelia's personality, but it is couched as Gandalf's observation and given no further development. Ioreth the Healer and Rosie Cotton are present entirely in speech, and there is no physical representation of them at all. In the instances of the four female characters discussed at length here, the only four who are represented physically by the narrator of *The Lord of the Rings*, representation of the body as a biological entity is conventional and lacking in individualized detail: they have golden or yellow or dark (black? brown?) hair, they are tall or slender, they have unblemished skin. Of course, they are beautiful.

But when the narrator's lens zooms in on their bodily presence, rather than biological detail we meet poetic image. And this is not merely aestheticized metaphor intended to underscore the sense of their beauty (though it does do that), but an emblematic language, which links their bodies to broader thematic significances. It is a dynamic language, in which the significance of similar images, or various images born of the same element, changes to reflect the situation and the identity of the individual character. Water is tied to fertility and rebirth with Goldberry and in Éowyn's tears; with Galadriel it is alternately a mirror in which the characters see their own unconscious motivations, or the river of historical time. With Goldberry, and more indirectly with Galadriel, the theme of renewal is conveyed by the suggestion of a magical association between their physical beings and growth in the natural world; for Arwen and Éowyn, renewal is tied, implicitly, to giving birth.

The preceding discussion has necessarily extended far beyond "bodily" issues in a narrowly representational sense. At the same time, the thematic issues I have explored emerge directly out of what the reader sees when the narrator's lens zooms in on the female body: body becomes poetic image, poetic image becomes thematic emblem, the emblem is the body. I will close by briefly reflecting on two possible directions the preceding might lead. It is tempting to link these "emblematic bodies" to Tolkien as a late Victorian (in his upbringing) Roman Catholic, reflecting stereotypically Victorian sexual repression coupled with the Roman Catholic notion of the flesh as sinful. That the sole female presence in *The Lord of the Rings* treated with vivid biological and sensory detail is Shelob, non-human (or "non-two-footed") in form, and concerned primarily with glutting herself with victims who she stings, binds, sucks the life out of, and consumes, might be cited as further evidence of this. At a Freudian extreme, the lack of attention to the physicality of the bodies of his most important female characters in favor of emblematic metaphor could be read as a classic case of repression/evasion and sublimation. Indeed, the precursor and original impetus behind my writing this essay arose while teaching *The Lord of the Rings*, and addressing the question of Tolkien's depiction of women. My initial observation was that Tolkien, faced with female presence, invariably sidestepped the body itself in favor of nature imagery. Over and over, I exclaimed to myself, "This *again*!" This kind of reading no doubt contains some amount of truth, and the critical apparatus associated with such an approach may, on one level, function as a sort of Galadriel's Mirror in bringing out some unconscious issues embedded in the text of *The Lord of the Rings*.

Nevertheless, the consistency and apparent deliberateness with which the imagery is deployed suggest that there is also something quite conscious going on here. For example, the figural description of Lúthien I cite from "The Lay of Leithian" is little different in approach, though, at least in the cases of Galadriel, Arwen, and Éowyn, less developed in degree, from what we have seen in *The Lord of the Rings*. However, in the context of a more distanced, less naturalistic narrative, more unabashedly replicating the style and approach of the heroic, saga, and romance literatures which inspired Tolkien, it fails to call the same kind of attention to itself. The likeness suggests that Tolkien was, in *The Lord of the Rings*, deliberately introducing a stylistic approach less common to a more "novelistic" context.

I would like to conclude here by looking at Tolkien's approach to the female body in relation to the traditional literatures of the British Isles and Northern Europe, not in terms of direct borrowing from "sources" so much as appropriation of techniques which, through long absorption in the texts, did much to shape Tolkien's vocabulary as a literary artist. The examples cited below could be multiplied far beyond what is pertinent to my suggestive intentions, and the areas I have drawn from are restricted to (a) the areas in which Tolkien was involved in a professional, scholarly capacity, on a day-to-day, year-to-year basis, and (b) the genres of secular narrative within those areas which may be said to have provided Tolkien with his most important formal models. With regard to the first instance, sources such as the Finnish *Kalevala* or fairy tales derived directly from oral sources, transcribed and/or adapted by more modern, antiquarian minded collectors such as the Grimms, have been omitted, as well as some sources noted below. The second consideration has led to my not including, for example, material connected to medieval legends of the Virgin and the lives of female saints— an area which would be well worth pursuing in its own right, but which would open up thematic issues beyond my present scope and intentions, and is outside the secular narrative genres of saga and romance.⁹ Lastly, my focus is simply on literary technique in the most contained sense, and I have made no attempt to explore the symbolic significance of my examples in their original contexts.

The importance of Germanic tradition, particularly in its Anglo-Saxon and Norse branches, to Tolkien and his Middle-earth corpus, and the ways it informs certain crucial aspects of that corpus, has been provocatively explored by Tom Shippey, Michael Drout, Jane Chance, and others. In the present context, however, it provides little. Female characters in the surviving Anglo-Saxon heroic literature, and most significantly *Beowulf*, the only complete Anglo-Saxon heroic narrative, are virtually non-existent. The surviving Icelandic material includes more, though the extremely sparse style of both the Eddaic poems and the heroic prose sagas provides little actual description of them (or anything else), either representational or figural. Some fleeting nods in the direction I have been discussing do appear, however. For example, the description of Brynhild in her first meeting with Sigurd in *Volsunga Saga* reads: "Therewith he [Sigurd] takes the helm from off the head of him, and sees that it is no man, but a woman; and she was clad in a byrny as closely set on her as though it had grown to her flesh."¹⁰ The warrior emblem, the "byrny" (or mail), merges with Brynhild's flesh here, conveying the sense that Brynhild's identity as a warrior woman has become an appurtenance of her body. This is, perhaps, tantalizing with regard to the passages concerning Éowyn noted above. At the same time, it is rather fleeting, and the heroic literature of Iceland provides us with little more of substance relevant in the present context.¹¹

The world of medieval Arthurian romance provides more fertile soil with regard to Tolkien's approach to the female body. At the same time, there are some limitations. The great proliferation of Arthurian romance in the twelfth and thirteenth centuries found its center in France, not England, and Tolkien's explicit distaste for the French language and its effects on the development of the English language and literature serve as a guard against seeing too much of a connection in this regard. Though, at the same time, distaste for something does not mean that Tolkien did not read it, and often quite closely, I nevertheless will omit continental Arthurian romance, though often French works (such as those of Chretien de Troyes) contain examples of the kind of technique Tolkien used.

On the other hand, some of the Middle English Arthurian romances of the fourteenth century did elicit, despite their debt to the earlier French works, enthusiasm and close attention from Tolkien. Of these, *Sir Gawain and the Green Knight*, written in the West Midlands dialect in which he specialized, is the most significant. The description of the Green Knight's Lady is noteworthy here:

> She was fairer in face, in her flesh and her skin,
> Her proportions, her complexion, and her port than all others...
> with rose-hue [her] ... face was richly mantled...
> on the kerchiefs ... many clear pearls were
> her breast and bright throat were bare displayed,
> fairer than white snow that falls on the hills.[12]

There is, perhaps, a little more flesh here than with Tolkien's characters, but it is conventionally rendered. It is the rose-hue, pearls, and "white snow that falls on the hills," not only underscoring the Lady's beauty per se, but also suggesting her connection to the natural world, that provide the most vivid elements of the description.

Other, perhaps more compacted, examples occur in the literature of fourteenth-century Middle English Arthurian romance. Though I have found no specific evidence that Tolkien read it, it seems likely that, given its Faerie content (if nothing else), Tolkien would have been familiar with Thomas Chestre's "Sir Launfal," a Middle English version of an Arthurian story that also survives in a Breton lay by Marie de France from nearly two centuries earlier. Here the hero, Launfal, straying into Faerie territory, encounters a pair of maidens and then the Lady Triamour, daughter of the King of Faerie. The maidens are described thus:

> Hare manteles were of grene felvett,
> Y-bordured with gold, right well ysett,
> Y-pelured with gris and gro.
>
> Hare heddis were dight well withalle:
> Everich hadde on a jolif coronall
> With sixty gemmes and mo.
>
> Hare faces were whit as snow on downe;
> Har rode was red, here eyen were browne.
> I sawe nevir non swiche!
>
> That on bare of gold a basin
> That other a towail white and fin
> Of selk that was good and riche.[13]

Though the natural images are restricted to the faces "whit as snowe on downe," the elaborate delineation of garb is akin to what we have seen with Arwen and Goldberry. In the description of Triamoure herself, the natural imagery predominates:

> She was as whit as lilie in May
> Or now that sneweth in winteris day —
> He seigh nevere non so pert.
>
> The rede rose, whan she is newe,
> Agens here rode nes naught of hewe,
> I dar well say in cert.[14]

As with the Green Knight's Lady, the natural images suggest a connection to the natural world, a pervasive connection with female Faerie characters. The "rede rose, when she is newe" in addition, carries an erotic overtone, appropriate in that she is about to begin a sexual relationship with Launfal.

These passages from *Sir Gawain and the Green Knight* and "Sir Launfal," without being posited as specific "sources" for Tolkien's descriptions of female characters, certainly evince a similarity in approach in their focus on nature imagery and ornament. They are not alone, either in Arthurian romance specifically, or in Middle English poetry generally. But medieval Arthurian literature points to the third, earlier, complex of literature I wish to touch on here, the Celtic. Scholars from Roger Sherman Loomis to John Matthews have probed the Celtic "roots" of medieval Arthurian romance exhaustively in many studies. In reference to the two poems cited here, for example, the beheading game which opens *Sir Gawain and the Green Knight* finds an earlier corollary, albeit with different dramatic and thematic significance, in the old Irish tale of Cuchulainn, "Bricriu's Feast." The Faerie encounter of "Sir Launfal" is little different in kind from many Faerie encounters which populate both Welsh and Irish traditional tales, and Marie de France's earlier Breton lay, though in French, was certainly rooted in the traditions of Celtic Brittainy (as, most likely, were the longer verse romances of Chretien de Troyes). That the echoes were substantially downwind and in most cases probably unwitting does not contradict this. Tolkien would certainly have been aware of this continuity.

Of course, there is ample evidence that the Arthurian *milieu* had an abundant presence in earlier Welsh tradition. Many of the Welsh Triads, a body of allusive poems which most modern readers, understandably, find cryptic, date to the sixth century and focus on Arthurian characters. Allusions to Arthurian subject matter in later Welsh material are deployed in a sufficiently familiar manner to suggest that the original audience would have understood them. Unfortunately, only one extended Arthurian narrative reflecting Welsh Arthurian tradition preceding French influence has survived: the tale of "Kilhwch and Olwen" from the medieval Welsh collection now known as the *Mabinogion*, probably composed in the tenth century. Here we find, more florid and developed than the Middle English examples, another description evincing the same kind of approach to depicting female presence as we find in Tolkien. Olwen, when first encountered by the hero Kilhwch, is described thus:

> More yellow was her head than the flower of the broom, and her skin was whiter than the foam of the wave, and fairer were her hands and her fingers than the blossoms of the wood anemone amidst the spray of the meadow fountain.... Her bosom was more snowy than the breast of the white swan, her cheek was redder than the reddest roses... Four white trefoils sprung up wherever she trod. And therefore she was called Olwen.[15]

Like Tolkien's description of Goldberry, this passage is positively awash with nature imagery, which effectively subsumes Olwen's actual physical being. Her hair is yellow, her skin white, her cheek red—all vague and conventional details on a representational level—, but it is the images of "the flower of the broom," "the foam of the wave," and "the reddest roses" which the reader envisions.

Like descriptions appear liberally in Old Irish tradition as well. In "The Exile of the Sons of Usnech," the tale of Deirdre, the cry of Deirdre from the womb elicits the following description from the druid Cathbad:

> Fair and curling locks shall flow round her,
> Blue-centered and stately her eyes;
> And her cheeks shall glow like the foxglove.
> For the tint of her skin, we commend her
> In its whiteness, newly fallen like snow;
> And her teeth are faultless in splendor;
> And her lips are red like coral[16]

Again the body—though here the body that is going to be—is subsumed in images of foxglove, newly fallen snow, and coral, and Deirdre is seen in terms of the natural world rather than as a biological being.

A note on the Celtic material is perhaps in order here, since, unlike Anglo-Saxon, Icelandic, and fourteenth-century Middle English, Tolkien's relation to it may be seen as somewhat ambiguous. In late 1937, Tolkien passed on his latest version of "Quenta Silmarillion" and the "Lay of Leithian" (discussed at the beginning of this essay) to Stanley Unwin, one of the readers of whose publishing firm read it and responded, according to Humphrey Carpenter, that he "disliked its 'eye-splitting Celtic names. It has something of that mad, bright-eyed beauty that perplexes all Anglo-Saxons in the face of Celtic art.'"[17] To this Tolkien responded to Unwin:

> Needless to say they [the names] are not Celtic! Neither are the tales. I do know Celtic things (many in their original languages Irish and Welsh), and feel for them a certain distaste: largely for their fundamental unreason.[18]

This may seem to argue against the significance of the Old Welsh and Irish material—like medieval French Arthurian romance—to Tolkien. But, on one count, Tolkien's distinction of his work from the Celtic is quite specific: nomenclature, an element about which he was virtually obsessive. In a broader sense, one might also suspect that the inconsistencies that mark even individual tales (particularly in the case of the Irish), and a general disregard for the kind of sober "historicity" far more evident in Anglo-Saxon and Icelandic material (as well as in *The Silmarillion* itself), would have been alien to Tolkien. Lastly, coming in 1937, he may well have objected to the possibility of his work being seen as a late offshoot of the "Celtic Twilight" sensibility.

On the other hand, Tolkien does assert that he knows "Celtic things" in their original languages, and his "distaste" for them does not elsewhere seem to extend to all their aspects. For example, the Welsh language had an enormous shaping effect on Elvish. And nearly two decades later, in a lecture on "English and Welsh," he stated that *The Lord of the Rings* "contains, in the way of presentation that I find most natural, much of what I personally have received from the study of things Celtic."[19] Taken together, it would seem that the earlier "anti–Celtic" statements do in fact point to things which Tolkien genuinely found distasteful in much old Celtic literature, but that specific factors attached to the occasion of his writing them led to some exaggeration which shouldn't be taken at face value. Of course, in the latter statement, precisely what is meant by "in the way of presentation" is left unelaborated. Here, I would at least float the possibility that his approach to the depiction of his female characters might be included by "presentation."

I will break off this discussion of earlier material relating to Tolkien's approach to the depiction of the female body by repeating a couple of qualifying points. One, my aim in the passages cited is to be suggestive rather than exhaustive, either with regard to the passages' significances within the contexts of the works they come from, or with regard to representation of the traditions from which they come, or, ultimately, with regard to representation of traditions which Tolkien had himself encountered. In the first case, close analysis would be a subject in itself—and a speculative one at that—and take us unduly far from my main focus. In the second, the passages were chosen with a degree of randomness, though culled, for obvious reasons, from heroic saga and romance narrative, and from works with which Tolkien was known to be pre-occupied, or which it seems highly unlikely that he would not have been familiar. In the last case, though these three general areas—Anglo-Saxon/Norse, Middle English, Celtic—may be said to represent to core foci of Tolkien's scholarly and imaginative interests, they do not stand alone. I have not touched on Finnish tradition and the *Kalevala*, though it had a profound effect on Tolkien; as noted, because Tolkien did not like French does not mean he did not read any French medieval Arthurian romances—closely; he was familiar, of course, with the literature of classical antiquity. All of these areas could have yielded examples relevant to my focus here.

This leads to my second qualifying point: the purpose here was not to go on a "source" hunt, that is: to suggest that, say, the description of Goldberry is "taken" from the description of Olwen. A close reading of the two suggests that this is clearly *not* the case. However, the two do share a similar approach to depicting female physical presence, and it is not amiss to suggest that Tolkien picked up certain ideas on technique from such sources, which became part of his artistic vocabulary, and which were very much adapted to his own purposes.[20]

In closing, then, the analysis of Tolkien's representation of the female body, or, perhaps more appropriately, his representation of female physical presence, suggests a notable lack of interest in the body as a strictly biological entity. His depictions of his female characters in-variably function in terms of nature imagery and emblem rather than individualized representation of the flesh. As far as the latter goes, depiction is invariably vague and conventional. The actual depictions as rendered tend mainly to reinforce the broader thematic significances of the individuals in relation to *The Lord of the Rings* as a whole, sometimes even to the entire conceptual design of the Middle-earth corpus. This, in turn, can also be seen to relate to the fact that Tolkien is simply not interested in romantic or sexual love, or, at any rate, that romantic or sexual love are not in themselves thematically significant to *The Lord of the Rings* or generally to the Middle-earth corpus. The love story of Aragorn and Arwen does not form a part of *The Lord of the Rings* proper, and is only narrated in the Appendix A, in a distanced style more akin to that of *The Silmarillion*. Though we know Celeborn and Galadriel are "married," there is no exploration of the dynamics of their relationship as characters. The relationship of Sam and Rosie Cotton does not extend much further than the "Aw shucks" blushes of Sam. The only romantic relationship in *The Lord of the Rings* to receive any attention per se is that of Éowyn and Faramir, but even here the treatment is conventionalized, to the point that it runs perilously close to Prince Valiant. Ultimately, it is its thematic significance rather than representational nuance that is important.

Taken together, both of these things can be seen as an evasion of something that Tolkien was uncomfortable with. Some readers may see the representational shortcomings of the Éowyn-Faramir passages, and lack of attention otherwise to anything having to do with romantic and sexual love, as a blemish. The diversion of attention away from the body as an individualized physical entity in favor of thematic emblem may be seen as an aspect of this blemish. On the other hand, this criticism can be seen to carry the underlying assumption that Tolkien *should* have explored the dynamics of romantic and sexual love more closely, *should* have paid more attention to the physical beings of his female, and, for that matter, male, characters. Other readers (including myself) may contend that, evasion or not, these "blemishes" are tangential to Tolkien's core conceptual pre-occupations and thematic intentions, and that the "blemish" question is ultimately a subjective one.

My analysis of the particular passages from *The Lord of the Rings* does suggest that Tolkien was, at least on stylistic and thematic levels, quite conscious of what he was doing. The imagery and emblematic significances are developed in a highly sophisticated manner and meld seamlessly into the thematic texture of the work as a whole. In addition, the latter discussion of examples deploying a similar technique culled from medieval and pre-medieval heroic and romance narrative from the Northern and Northwestern European traditions, which Tolkien immersed himself in, suggest that he was also extending and adapting to his own purposes a stylistic approach with a long history.[21]

Notes

1. J.R.R. Tolkien, *The Lays of Beleriand. The History of Middle Earth*, 3d ed., ed. Christopher Tolkien (Boston: Houghton Mifflin, 1985), 155. See ll. 23–38 for full passage.
2. Ibid., ll. 23–4.
3. Ibid., ll. 27–8.
4. Ibid., 1, 175, ll. 557–62.
5. Ibid., 1, 183–4, ll. 774–81.
6. *Letters*, 5, 272.
7. While I, as this suggests, would not argue for any conclusive identification of Goldberry as Maiar, I think that the possibility can be a little too glibly dismissed. Taryne Jade Taylor, in "Investigating the Role and Origin of Goldberry in Tolkien's Mythology" *Mythlore* 27: 1–2 (Fall/Winter 2008), states, "A Maia would not be called the River's daughter; instead a Maia would be the River's mother" (152). But, as I note, if it is possible the River God is Maia, we are left with the question of, who is the other parent? If Goldberry comes of Maia parentage, what then? I do not see this as ample evidence to support an argument that Goldberry "is" Maia, but I also do not see ample evidence to glibly dismiss the notion.
8. Ann McCauley Basso, in "Fair Lady Goldberry, Daughter of the River" *Mythlore* 27: 1–2, (Fall/Winter 2008), suggests a structural parallel between the two characters in the context of *The Lord of the Rings*, which can be seen as underscoring my suggestion that Galadriel advances certain elements attached to Goldberry. Her statement, "We could almost call Goldberry 'Galadriel Lite'" (142), while humorous, is perhaps not entirely inappropriate.
9. I would include as a sort of "sub-set" here the allegorical dream visions of the Middle Ages, most notably *Pearl*. An excellent discussion of, specifically, the relation of the "pearl-maiden" and Dante's Beatrice to Galadriel can be found in Sarah Downey's recent "Cordial Dislike: Reinventing the Celestial Ladies of *Pearl* and *Purgatorio* in Tolkien's Galadriel" *Mythlore 29:* 3–4 (Spring/Summer 2011): 101–117. However, the dream vision, as a narrative genre, is distinct from romance and saga, the primary forms informing *The Lord of the Rings*, and so I have omitted it here.
10. *The Story of the Volsungs and Niblungs,* trans. William Morris and Erik Magnusson (London: George Prior, 1980), 3, 69.
11. On a slight tangent, the image, no doubt a quite conscious echo on Tolkien's part, suggests that elements of Éowyn's character are informed by the Norse Valkyrie, female warrior demi-gods in service of Odin. While Brynhild, following her marriage to Gunther, becomes fully humanized, in her initial appearance she is (as we see) armed, and associated with a mountainous castle surrounded by a supernatural light. That the narrative pattern of Brynhild's life, from unabashed warrior and disappointed lover, to wife within a context reflecting more conventional gender norms, underscores the pattern of Éowyn's life (with, of course, significant thematic and dramatic alterations on Tolkien's part) is obvious. An excellent, detailed discussion of Tolkien's use of the Valkyrie figure can be found in Leslie Donovan, "The Valkyrie Reflex in *The Lord of the Rings*." *Tolkien the Medievalist*, ed. Jane Chance, 106–32 (New York: Routledge, 2003).
12. *Sir Gawain and the Green Knight, Pearl, Sir Orfeo,* trans. J.R.R. Tolkien (New York: Ballantine, 1980), 4, 48.

13. "Sir Launfal," *Middle English Verse Romances*, ed. Donald B. Sands (New York: Holt Rinehart and Winston, 1966), 5, 210, ll.235–46.
14. Ibid., 5, 212, ll. 292-7.
15. "Kilhwch and Olwen," *The Mabinogion*, trans. Lady Charlotte Guest (Chicago: John Jones Cardiff, 1977), 6, 233.
16. "The Exile of the Sons of Usnech," *Ancient Irish Tales*, ed. Tom Peete and Clark Harris Slover (Totowa, NJ: Barnes and Noble, 1981), 7, 240.
17. *Letters*, 2, 25.
18. *Letters*, 2, 26.
19. J.R.R. Tolkien, "English and Welsh," *The Monsters and the Critics and Other Essays*, ed. Christopher Tolkien (Boston: Houghton Mifflin, 1983), 8, 162.
20. Jason Fisher's excellent "Tolkien and Source Criticism: Remarking and Remaking" *Tolkien and the Study of His Sources*, ed. Jason Fisher (Jefferson, NC: McFarland, 2011) gives an excellent analysis of the various layers of possible "source" detection in Tolkien's work. Of the works cited here, the only which I would contend as a likely conscious source is the least significant, that concerning Brynhild. While Tolkien knew *Sir Gawain and the Green Knight* intimately, that does not mean he had the passage I cite in mind while writing any of the passages cited in *The Lord of the Rings*. Of the remaining works, it is unlikely that he did not know them, as he was thoroughly familiar with the respective "pools" of material from which they are drawn, but he never specifically discusses any of them. But again, my purpose here is to illustrate a technique that proliferates throughout these "pools," not to isolate individual sources. In an interesting passage, Fisher discusses the play on "fair" and "foul" between Frodo and Aragorn, and raises the question: did Tolkien borrow it from *MacBeth*? *Cymbeline*? Spenser's *Faerie Queene*? Pointedly, Fisher interjects, "...if he borrowed it at all" (38). This, I would take it, does not mean that Tolkien invented the play, but that he may have met it in a number of sources long before writing the Bree chapters. Like plot motifs in the Cauldron of Story, the varied examples of the play may well have merged in Tolkien's mind in such a way that the attempt to link it to any one of them is not particularly meaningful.
21. The translations of traditional material used in the latter part of this essay were chosen, not as the most up to date and accurate, but as those which were most common during the earlier twentieth century. The lines from *Sir Gawain and the Green Knight* are an exception, being appropriately (in the present context) drawn from Tolkien's translation.

Works Consulted

Basso, Ann McCauley. "Fair Lady Goldberry, Daughter of the River." *Mythlore* 27: 1–2, (Fall/Winter 2008): 137–146.
Downey, Sarah. "Cordial Dislike: Reinventing the Celestial Ladies of *Pearl* and *Purgatorio* in Tolkien's Galadriel." *Mythlore 29:* 3-4 (Spring/Summer 2011): 101–117.
"The Exile of the Sons of Usnech." *Ancient Irish Tales*, ed. Tom Peete and Clark Harris Slover. Totowa, NJ: Barnes and Noble, 1981.
Fisher, Jason. "Tolkien and Source Criticism: Remarking and Remaking." *Tolkien and the Study of His Sources*, ed. Jason Fisher, 29–44. Jefferson, NC: McFarland, 2011.
"Kilhwch and Olwen." *The Mabinogion,* trans. Lady Charlotte Guest. Chicago: John Jones Cardiff, 1977.
Sir Gawain and the Green Knight, Pearl, Sir Orfeo, trans. J.R.R. Tolkien. New York: Ballantine, 1980.
"Sir Launfal." *Middle English Verse Romances*, ed. Donald B. Sands. New York: Holt Rinehart and Winston, 1966.

The Story of the Volsungs and Niblungs, trans. William Morris and Erik Magnusson. London: George Prior, 1980.

Taylor, Taryne Jade. "Investigating the Role and Origin of Goldberry in Tolkien's Mythology." *Mythlore* 27: 1–2 (Fall/Winter 2008): 147–156.

Tolkien, J.R.R. "English and Welsh." *The Monsters and the Critics and Other Essays,* ed. Christopher Tolkien. Boston: Houghton Mifflin, 1983.

_____. "Lay of Leithian." *The Lays of Beleriand,* ed. Christopher Tolkien. Boston: Houghton Mifflin, 1985.

Extending the Reach of the Invisible Hand
A Gift Looks for Gain in the Gifting Economy of Middle-earth

JENNIFER CULVER

The gifting economy of the medieval period resembled a cycle bonding the gift and the giver, a ritual action both cementing the hierarchy within a singular society and also linking one society with another. Above all other interactions, gift giving represented the "foremost expression of rank and status" and accompanied all kinds of interactions.[1] Gift giving accompanied treaty signings and the finalizing of contracts, with some gifts only seeming voluntary when, in fact, it was an understood expectation.[2] Scholars have noted that the gifting economies of the Germanic cultures were some of the most clearly defined of the period,[3] as even noted in the literature of the period and region. From farther north, the "Hávamál" from the *Poetic Edda* contains many verses advising the listener about gifting practices, including stanza 145:

> 'Tis better unasked than offered overmuch;
> for ay doth a gift look for gain;
> 'tis better unasked than offered overmuch;
> thus did Odin write ere the earth began,
> when up he rose in after time [Hollander trans.].

For a gifting economy to function successfully, the implicit understanding of the giving of a gift must be fully appreciated by all. Gift giving, according to Walter Burkert, "recognizes not just an adversary, but a partner of equal status, whose thoughts and interests can be represented through empathy," meaning that the transaction must be understood by all sides to be fully realized.[4] What is given must also be something that is considered useful and of value.[5] In many ways, giving a gift represents giving of oneself to another, and the gift must represent not only the bond but also the value of the relationship. Unlike commerce, which assigns values to specific items that one can purchase freely, a gift contains an inherent worth that represents the newly formed bond between individuals.[6] The gift itself could have very little monetary value, sometimes being only a stone to commemorate the occasion and words spoken. Not gifting at an expected occasion, be it a parting, celebration, etc. could be grounds not only for offense but warfare.[7] Because a gifting society required gifts to remain in circulation, generosity, or the ability to be "open-handed" was prized. With the extension of the open hand, a lord broadened his reach.

Beowulf clearly reflects the idea that one measure of a good lord was being generous with gifts. Both Scild and Hrothgar in the early sections of the poem are noted for their generosity, with the poet reminding the reader that generosity during peacetime begets loyalty in times of conflict. One analogy used to describe Shild's generosity would be a body analogy, the analogy of extending the "reach" of a lord. "Reach" here indicates influence, authority, and presence. While Tolkien may not have used this analogy extensively throughout *The Lord of the Rings*, Gimli did note at Caradhras that the "arm" of the enemy has grown long if he can manipulate the weather in the North, and Gandalf agrees (*FR*, II, iii, 302). While looking at how reach is extended or forged through gifting in Middle-earth, one can see both expected and unexpected results. The process of gifting can be broken down into the giver, the receiver, and the importance of reciprocity.

The Process of Gifting

Presentation of a gift must be public.[8] In *Beowulf*, for example, Hrothgar boasts that Heorot will become a place of gifting, and he remains true to his word. Part of the glory of the hall resides in the fact that it is a place for the official, public exchange of gifts.[9] In fact, one of the kennings for Heorot in the poem is *gifheal* (gift hall) in line 838.[10] The rest of the folk must witness the exchange for the gift giving to carry its full symbolic weight, as the gift giving process is to confirm the status of each. The common place for gift giving in an Anglo-Saxon hall was in *symbel*, a ritualized event of drinking, toasting, making boasts and giving gifts. It is the ritual feast that confirms and strengthens the bonds of society while reaffirming the structure inherent within. It is in *symbel* where the gift stool mentioned in "The Wanderer" is produced and the lord's generosity was seen by his folk. Galadriel's presentation of parting gifts in *Fellowship* has many similar features to this *symbel* setting. Without a public to witness the exchange, misrepresentations can be made, seen in both Bilbo's and Gollum's accounts regarding how each acquired the ring.

Even in a place where structured practices and expectations of gifting might be forgotten, such as the road to Mordor, examples exist, demonstrating the embedded mindset of the gifting culture in Middle-earth. Upon Gollum's capture by Sam and Frodo in "The Taming of Sméagol," Frodo tells Gollum that in exchange for mercy Gollum must guide them because "one good turn deserves another," which is reminiscent of our "Havamal" stanza (*TT*, IV, I, 222). Later in their journey, despite a relationship first initiated as one of captor/hostage, Faramir soon befriends Frodo and Sam and gives them walking staves made in Gondor as parting gifts. Here, the gift changes the relationship between the two groups, abolishes a boundary, and eases tensions, which, as Burkert notes, accompanies the practice of gift giving.[11] In both accounts, it is clear that offering gifts, either intangible in the form of mercy or tangible in the form of walking staves, appears as a self-referential act meant to extend the hand of the giver to another, thus increasing the "body" of community.

The gifting from Galadriel and Faramir introduces the circular nature of gifting. Because he is gifting as a representative of Gondor, Faramir does not specifically expect a gift in turn. Galadriel knows that she may not see the members of the Fellowship again; her intent is to further cement the bonds within the Fellowship and within the races of Middle-earth the Fellowship represents. In these cases, Galadriel and Faramir gift blindly, trusting that the "body" of Middle-earth as a whole or Gondor respectively will be rewarded because of their generosity. In this fashion, the act of gifting shows the recipients they are attached to the "body" of Gondor and Lórien, meaning that the reach of both lands would extend over the members of the Fellowship, including protection, whenever possible. According to Hyde, a gift represents "the preferred interior commerce at those times when the psyche is in need of integration."[12] A gift passing out of direct sight, as these are, runs less risk for manipulation. This is because the gift is no longer in control of just one giver and one receiver; the "body" of the community bears the responsibility for maintaining the reciprocal and balanced state.[13] This represents both sides of the exchange, which also then strengthens the bond of the Fellowship and makes them one "body" for a time.

The Wild Man understands gifting symbolism, too, noted in the exchange of offers and services with Théoden and Éomer in "The Ride of the Rohirrim," astutely observing that dead men can "give them no gifts" (*RK*, V, v, 107). For even an archetypal outsider whose "home is the forest, the wilderness outside the boundaries set by civilization"[14] to understand the importance in the exchange of promises and gifts illustrates the pervasiveness of the gifting economy in Middle-earth. In this passage, the Wild Man demonstrates his knowledge of a gifting economy because he emphasizes the reciprocal nature of gifting. Because of the gravity of the times, the Wild Man chooses not to enter completely into reciprocal relationship as the Rohirrim may not live long enough to return any gift. Even should the Rohirrim survive, they may not be able to return a gift equal in weight to the assistance so desperately needed. Additionally, the Wild Man may wish to remain "wild," and a more concrete reciprocal gift could be perceived as a desire for more connection with the race of man. Giving a gift is not enough. For the bond to be complete, the gift must be accepted and reciprocated in some way.

The Giver

A lord's open-handedness was a measure of his worth and the more generous the gifts, the more prosperous the lord was seen to be. To give a gift means the giver is presenting a part of himself if not a part of his soul.[15] To withhold a gift threatens the life of the community,[16] as seen in Tolkien's poem "The Hoard." Gifts upon departure or arrival of guests on the part of lord or host are motivated by establishing a tie upon the guests between him and his people[17] and many guests would arrive carrying gifts to reciprocate. Honor and rivalry and reputation are at stake, even subtly, in this process,[18] as it is a reflection of the "luck" of the lord or king.

What the giver presents is equally as important, as the object itself can have much significance.[19] Gifts could be tangible or intangible, such as the obligation of hospitality or wise words. Tangible gifts such as a weapon or boar-crested helmet, for example, would have their own qualities and power,[20] for the boar is an animal that was vicious to hunt and obtain meat from, as mentioned in the *Nibelungenlied* and *Sir Gawain and the Green Knight*, possibly creating a form of sympathetic magic to have the wearer be able to call on the strength of the creature in times of need[21] or to give the warriors the aggressiveness and teanacity of the boar.[22] A gift is a product representing both people and their relationships to each other.[23]

In Lórien, Celeborn and Galadriel are known as great gift givers. The departing gifts to the Fellowship served many purposes. Done in a ritual setting, as noted with the traditional use of the cup of parting, these gifts, unlike the cloaks earlier, had specific intent. Not only were the gifts chosen by Galadriel, through her foresight, to help each person on his journey, but the gifts also served to bind them to Lórien, to serve as a token to remind them of Lothlorien once they left (*FR*, II, viii, 391). Galadriel presents the first gift to Aragorn and acknowledges him as the leader, a formal distinction important now after the recent fall of Gandalf. By doing this, she makes the hierarchy within the Fellowship concrete. She also gifts Aragorn a jewel from Arwen, citing her lineage as Arwen's grandmother and placing their hopes in his task, as well as her acknowledgment of their intended union. Members of the Fellowship note that Aragorn now appears "kingly" when he did not before (*FR*,

II, viii, 391). Each successive gift marked a noted ability or aspect of the recipient, especially the changed heart of Gimli towards elves in her generous gifts of three golden hairs from her head, which she foretells will mark gold flowing from his hands should their task succeed (*FR*, II, viii, 393). Another significant gift, as it is an object deeply connected to history, is the phial containing the light of Eärendil's star given to Frodo. With her grace and her gifts, Galadriel has extended her reach beyond the borders of her forest.

Galadriel superbly demonstrates how women had their own role to play as gift-giver. Galadriel has many similarities to Wealththeow in *Beowulf*. Like Wealththeow, Galadriel rules with composure and grace and references to her also allude to radiance and light.[24] Her gifting at this departure represents historically what only a woman's gift and presence can do in that it "unifies conflicting motives and desires among the Company." Although the members of the Company will later be separated from each other, their intensely powerful personal experiences of Galadriel and Lothlórien, culminating in the combined cup-bearing and gift-giving ceremony, "establish a commonality that continues to join the individuals to each other and to their larger purpose."[25] Arwen also fulfills this role by sewing a banner for Aragorn, which both reminds him of his lineage and inspires those who see it as they enter into battle.[26] In each case, not just anyone could have given such gifts and had the significance of the action remain intact.

Hospitality, the obligation to invite, also reflects the generosity and reputation of the leader. Opening up doors and being inviting was considered a form of gift. In the cold Northern lands travelers in the winter would stake their lives on the hospitality of a lord. While the "Hávamál" has lines detailing the importance of hospitality, "Grimnismál," also within the *Poetic Edda*, deals with this issue most directly, as the god Odin appears in a hall disguised to test the hospitality of a lord and instead of welcome finds himself hanging between two fires. *Beowulf* also jokes about the lack of hospitality Grendel found on his last visit to Heorot.[27] Gandalf observes not much more of a welcome when he seeks Théoden and reproaches him, saying, "The courtesy of your hall has somewhat lessened of late" (*TT*, III, vi, 118).

This tradition continues in the later Middle Ages seen in a treatise from 1476 in Germany that a mayor was to "receive all who visit his house kindly and not entertain them too meagerly."[28] This openness and generosity appears best in the one place in Middle-earth where the folk were left untouched from the evils of the world the longest: the Shire. Tolkien states in his prologue "Concerning Hobbits" that hobbits gave presents eagerly and, as a whole, were a very generous and hospitable race (Prologue, 11). Bilbo is said to be "free with his money" (*FR*, I, i, 31), which makes him a good hobbit in the eyes of the Gaffer.

Bilbo's birthday party presents a prime scene for exploring gifting traditions and expectations among hobbits, as the hobbit having the birthday gave presents to others in attendance at his/her party. Tolkien reports to the reader that in Hobbiton and Bywater birthdays occurred daily, meaning "every hobbit in those parts had a fair chance of at least one present at least once a week" (*FR*, I, i, 35). To clarify the practice in a letter, Tolkien writes that the receiving of gifts, "was an ancient ritual connected with *kinship*."[29] Giving, Tolkien notes in the same letter, was not limited to kinship and reflected a form of "thanksgiving, and taken as a recognition of services, benefits, and friendship shown,"[30] The oldest custom, which was not noted in the text because Tolkien felt the information was not as relevant to the plot of the party, was the reception of guests.[31] Looking at Bilbo's party from the standpoint of reflection of custom, the reader notes that the long-standing gifting practices remain firmly entrenched in the hobbits of the Shire.

Equally generous, Elrond opens Rivendell to many and equips the Fellowship with all they need before the perilous journey, despite the possible dire consequences. This is another example of the circular gifting mentioned above, as Elrond also trusts in the "body" of the community instead of expecting a direct reciprocal gift. Elrond's tokens represent his friendship as well as the backing of Rivendell, and, as Hyde states, such gifts come with "transformation, friendship, and love."[32] The transformation in this case appears in the creation of the Fellowship, a new "body" comprised of once disparate races and backgrounds united by cause and gift.

Bjork notes that the words coinciding with the material exchange are equally important in the gifting process.[33] Many times throughout *Beowulf* words are equated as objects and shown in specific places that the word is not differentiated from the deed.[34] As noted in the cases from Middle-earth above, each time a gift was meant to have more import, the giver accompanied the presentation with weighty words fit for the occasion. Bilbo's parting gifts in "Many Partings" also came with well-placed words, especially in the form of advice to Merry and Pippin (*RK*, VI, vi, 265). Throughout the story, words of advice contain as much benefit, especially to the hobbits, as an item such as a length of rope.

The Gifted

As important as it was for a lord to give, the significance of reciprocation cannot be forgotten or understated, as it was not merely expected but a "spiritual" obligation,[35] or, according to Mauss, an "*Angebinde.*" These objects, then, are infused with the power from the ritual aspect of gifting as well as the soul of the giver and can create a "magical or religious hold" over the recipient until the gift is reciprocated in some way.[36] This can create complications, because receiving gifts, as giving them, appears an obligation among people during this time period. Refusing a gift, whether it be a hospitality or a material object, could be the equivalent of rejecting or refusing to recognize the bonds of a community.[37] Bilbo acknowledges this state of indebtedness when he presents Frodo with Sting and his mithril coat, saying all he asks for in return is to take care and bring back news, tales and songs for him to record. Examining things in retrospect, Treebeard finds hints of problems with Saruman early on for reasons involving reciprocity, saying:

> I told him many things that he would never have found out by himself; but he never repaid me in like kind [*TT*, III, iv, 76].

Treebeard acknowledges here one of the truths of Middle-earth: knowledge is power. Treebeard's knowledge of history and the workings of this are comprehensive, as seen in the songs of the Ents that categorize as much as describe.[38] Saruman takes in this knowledge while giving nothing in return and there is no lack of irony later when his disregard for living things is a large part of the cause for Ents to flood Isengard.[39] When Éowyn gives Merry an heirloom horn of Rohan which when blown will bring his friends to him and produce fear in his enemies, he takes the horn, "for it could not be refused" (*RK*, VI, vi, 256).

In all the records of gifting, particularly in Germany, there are very rare mentions of a refusal of a gift. What if the recipient cannot reciprocate from a lavish gift? This is a quite practical question, as this instance would have happened quite often. Mere land-owners could not compete with kings in wealth and gifts, and a king or lord would know this when presenting them with expensive objects. The returned gift in these cases would not be an object in and of itself, but fealty. Whether a formal slavery period of indentured servitude, entry into a comitatus, subordinate role within a tribe, or feudal understanding, a degree of a bond of loyalty in return for accepting the gift has been established.[40] Hostages were also viewed in this way, seen in the Eddic "Voluspa" with the trading of Aesir and Vanir, forging peace. Often some kind of animate object would be given to symbolize the pledge (*wadium* for the Germanic tribes, later seen in the English word for wage) in the form of a kind of sympathetic magic, being usually something of little or no value such as sticks.[41] These trivial items represent the pledge or oath both parties made regarding the exchange, and oath-making was considered a very serious business.[42] In Bree, Strider makes an interesting twist on this very situation. In exchange for information and much-needed advice for the hobbits, Strider compels Frodo to agree to take him with them, as he is not trusted yet (*FR*, I, x, 184). Other touching examples of fealty are seen throughout *The Lord of the Rings*, including Pippin's offer to join the service of Gondor in repayment for Boromir's sacrifice, Merry's similar offer to Theoden, and Gollum's oath to serve Frodo. Even Aragorn's coronation, asking Frodo to bear the crown and Gandalf to place it on his head, demonstrates much reciprocity and shows to all what kind of king Aragorn plans to be, as well as how far his reach extends, as contemporary residents of the Shire never before acknowledged Gondor's reach into their lands, or even of themselves as members of a larger "body" of Middle-earth.

Fealty can be seen as the gift of the literal body from thegn to lord. The poem "The Wanderer" reflects the rite as:

> In his mind it seems to him that he lord
> he calls and kisses, and onto his knee he lays
> his hands and head, as at times before
> in days of old he enjoyed the treasure-seats [Pollington trans.].[43]

As the body is being used in a physical sense to reflect the gift of the body in service, the entrance into the war-band ritual would make the new person a kinsman,[44] so the lord's reach is enhanced through the gift of the physical body. A more literal example from literature is seen in the tale of Nornagest, *Nornagests þáttr*, in which at the moment when fealty is given, Nornagest is able to literally gift his new lord with his life, as a spell has been placed over him that his life would end when a certain candle completely burns down. Nornagest's trust is well placed, and he lives a long life span, finally deciding, with his lord, to let the candle burn. Aragorn's decision to end his life reflects this tale, as he decides his own time to leave, saying he must sleep and return the gift (Appendix A, 343).

Another type of gifting of the literal body would include the gift of the peace bride. Seen mainly in Anglo-Saxon literature, such as *Beowulf* or "The Wife's Lament," a woman could be gifted to another tribe in hopes of creating amicability. At times, this process succeeds, as with Wealhtheow. In other situations, as in the Finn Fragment and as projected by Beowulf with Hrothgar's daughter, the presence of the woman in a hostile tribe is not enough to forge lasting peace. It is unknown how much emotion, if any existed between man and woman before the wedding. "The Wife's Lament" implies genuine love between the two, placing his family in the blame for attempting to ruin the relationship by sending him away and exiling her to a cave. In Middle-earth, there is no doubt that the union of Aragorn and Arwen will forge a union, that of elves and men as in the days of Beren and Lúthien. Aragorn refers to Arwen as a "treasure" in Lórien (*FR*, II, viii, 391) and in the story "Here Follows a Part of the Tale of Aragorn and Arwen" (Appendix A, 339, 340). With Arwen's marriage to Aragorn, she also freely relinquishes her immortality to remain with him (Appendix A, 342).

The same could be said of Éowyn. According to Éomer, with this marriage the Mark and Gondor "are bound with a new bond" (*RK*, VI, vi, 255). According to Hyde, the woman given or promised in marriage "takes on typical functions of the gift. She too establishes a bond (between clans or families), and as part of an ongoing system of kinship, she, like any gift, becomes "an agent of the community's cohesion and stability."[45] Like Arwen, Éowyn freely chooses to marry. Once all of the effects of the shadow have passed and she is healed, Éowyn finds love and purpose in her new role in Gondor. Rohan's "gift" of Éowyn to Gondor will be a concrete sign for all in Gondor to see, a sign of Rohan's commitment and affection.

The Darker Side of Gifting

Another side of gifting requires discussion. The peril of the gifting economy, as noted by Bjork, is fragility of the structure.[46] Lee agrees, noting the irony in the early reference to giving gifts with the expectations of loyalty because Beowulf's experience shows "the fragility in practice of the ideal" considering how many did not come in his hour of need.[47] Even the meaning of the word "gift" in Germanic languages belies a darker, more dangerous component in the role of the gift, and that is the spread of a gift creating destruction like a poison.[48] Examples of a "fatal" gift would be the cursed Rhine gold from the *Völsunga saga* or Hagen's cup, which causes mortality for the hero who drinks from it. Groebner refers to this aspect of the gift as its "evil twin"[49] while arguing also that the motivation of gifting, even not cursed gifts, can be suspect in other ways.

According to Groebner, a gift could "contain a threat" when powerful men gave not only from their own supply but from others' goods. Groebner also cites Castiglione's caution from *The Book of the Courtier*: Not all those who give many gifts are generous.[50] As the Middle Ages wore on, "official" gifts were kept secret and oaths were made to hide the exact amount officials spent wining and dining guests and others.[51] These gifts given in a political sense were recorded in a secret code, possibly because the implication accompanying accepting and giving gifts could be seen from the outside as affecting powerful placements and decisions. Gifting could also be seen as threatening as when a dignitary arrives full force in a town or village expecting gifts and a grand reception.

Sauron asks for a gift in the guise of friendship from the dwarves when he sends a messenger to find information about a "thief" and the Ring, as disclosed by Glóin at The Council of Elrond (*FR*, II, ii, 254). The Ring is called a "trifle" and the dwarves are bribed with the possible reward of the return of the three old dwarven rings and ownership of Moria. The threat here is not so subtle, however, as Glóin was told to refuse would mean that "things will not seem so well" (*FR*, II, ii, 254). Later, the Messenger states that he will only return three times for an answer before some form of retribution will take place.

Physical bodies are also given as gifts, both in the form of hostage exchanges and in the form of sacrifice. Gollum certainly means to "gift" Shelob with Frodo and Sam, hoping to receive the Ring in return. In some ways, Gandalf and Aragorn are willing to gift themselves to the greater cause at the Black Gate if it gives Frodo the time he needs to finish this task, to "keep his Eye from his true peril." (RK, V, ix, 156).

The contents of a gift itself could mean harm to the physical body as well. In both *Egils saga* and *Völsunga saga* men are gifted with drink that is meant to do them harm. Egil traces runes over the horn and it shatters, revealing the ill intent of the contents. Sigurd, however, drinks deep from what is given to him, thus forgetting his love Brynhild and his oaths to her. *Völsunga saga* also contains the gift of the weregild treasure that includes the cursed ring. The treasure proceeds to destroy the family, even turning one son into the dragon Fafnir. While Biblo's gift of the Ring to Frodo was not done in malice, the gift did have an impact on Frodo, physically, mentally, and spiritually. This will be discussed more below.

Unresolved Issues

With this look at Middle-earth as a gifting economy, there are still some unresolved issues when looking through this lens. One centers around the question of a gift being received by one for which it was not intended. An example here is Éowyn. Éowyn's fealty and service deserves mention. Éowyn accepts arms and a man-like obligation to lead her people from her king and expresses throughout the text a desire to fulfill this martial oath and fight, yet had been directed to stay out of the fray. By changing her appearance, she can place herself in a situation to receive gifts that would accompany the ideas of fealty and service in battle.

The encounter with the dwarves was certainly not Sauron's only sinister use of gifting. One question asked in my classroom when we discuss *The Lord of the Rings* deals with why the nine kings accepted Sauron's gift of rings in the first place, especially when they had nothing to reciprocate. Wouldn't a king, of all people, understand the indebtedness incurred from such an action? A true understanding of gifting culture brings light to the dilemma of the kings, illustrating how Sauron uses their adherence to societal and cultural norms against them and forces them to accept the gift and all that entails. This serves as a distinct and sharp contrast to the gifting seen by Galadriel.

Finally, the issue of the One Ring lingers. With all the passing of ownership, the Ring is rarely offered voluntarily, much less as a gift. Bilbo only leaves the Ring to Frodo reluctantly and with much "encouragement" from Gandalf. As noted, keeping items out of circulation, hoarding them, if you will, was very frowned upon. Sam can return the Ring to Frodo because he has had the Ring a short time and nothing will rise in importance to Sam over his duty to Frodo. It is true, also, that Frodo offers the Ring to Gandalf and Galadriel (and lets Tom Bombadil handle it), but the reader can argue that Frodo's time as a Ringbearer has been very brief and the Ring has not yet taken hold of his soul as it did Bilbo and Gollum (and others) before him. Instead, Frodo continues to reflect the ideas of a gifting economy until the Ring has taken a stronger hold of him, as he later will refuse to let Sam help carry the burden. This underscores the reach of the Ring on the wearer.

Tolkien brilliantly crafted a world in which both the positive and negative sides of a gifting economy were observed, leaving the reader yet another measuring tool to evaluate the actions and words of characters.

Notes

1. Walter Burkert, *The Creation of the Sacred: Tracks of Biology in Early Religions* (Cambridge: Harvard University Press, 1996), 130.
2. Marcel Mauss, *The Gift: The Form and Reason for Exchange in Archaic Societies* (New York: W.W. Norton, 2000), 3. Burkert also notes that gifts accompanied the signing of treaties since the Bronze Age.
3. Ibid., 61.
4. Burkert, *The Creation of the Sacred*, 132. Burkert believes that gift giving from human to human parallels gifts given from gods to men and vice versa.
5. Mauss, *The Gift*, 5.
6. Lewis Hyde, *The Gift: Imagination and the Erotic Life of Property* (New York: Vintage, 1983), 61.
7. Mauss, *The Gift*, 5.
8. Valentin Groebner, *Liquid Assets, Dangerous Gifts: Presents and Politics at the End of the Middle Ages* (Philadelphia: University of Pennsylvania Press, 2000), 12.
9. Alvin Lee, *Gold-Hall and Earth-Dragon: Beowulf as Metaphor* (Toronto: University of Toronto Press, 1998), 153. Lee notes that Hrothgar's promise of giving gifts in Heorot provides a form of "verbal power" to the building of the hall, as the promise of great things to happen in such a place would aid in its construction.
10. Ibid., 155. Lee also notes other kennings for the hall in the poem associated with treasure and the generosity accompanying giving gifts.
11. Burkert, *The Creation of the Sacred*, 154. According to Burkert, gifts are given often to overcome anxiety and fears of instability.
12. Hyde, *The Gift*, 58.
13. Ibid., 16.
14. Verlyn Flieger, "Tolkien's Wild Men: from Medieval to Modern," *Tolkien the Medievalist*, ed. Jane Chance (New York: Routledge, 2003), 95.
15. Mauss, *The Gift*, 12.
16. Vilhelm Gronbech, *Culture of the Teutons* (Oxford: Oxford University Press, 1931), 2.58
17. Ibid., 28.
18. Ibid., 37.
19. Mauss, *The Gift*, 3.
20. Stephen Glosecki, *Shamanism and Old English Poetry* (New York: Garland, 1989), 53.

21. Ibid.
22. Ibid., 54.
23. Groebner, *Liquid Assets*, 8.
24. Leslie Donovan, "The Valkyrie Reflex in *The Lord of the Rings*," *Tolkien the Medievalist*, ed. Jane Chance (New York: Routledge, 2003), 112.
25. Ibid., 116.
26. Ibid., 127.
27. Lee notes in his list of kennings for Heorot descriptors noting the hall as a place specifically to accommodate and welcome guests.
28. Groebner, *Liquid Assets*, 21.
29. *Letters*, 291.
30. Ibid.
31. Ibid., 290.
32. Hyde, *The Gift*, 68.
33. Robert E. Bjork, "Speech as Gift in Beowulf," *Speculum* 69 (1994), 996.
34. Ibid.
35. Mauss, *The Gift*, 7.
36. Ibid., 12.
37. Ibid., 13.
38. Jane Chance, *Tolkien's Art: A Mythology for England* (Lexington: University Press of Kentucky, 2001), 59.
39. Ibid., 60.
40. Mauss, *The Gift*, 42.
41. Ibid., 48.
42. Ibid., 62.
43. Stephen Pollington, *The Mead Hall* (Norfolk: Anglo-Saxon, 2003), 247.
44. Ibid., 259.
45. Hyde, *The Gift*, 99.
46. Bjork, "Speech as Gift," 995.
47. Lee, *Gold-Hall*, 32.
48. Mauss, *The Gift*, 63.
49. Groebner, *Liquid Assets*, 11.
50. Ibid., 14. Burkert would agree, citing more recent manipulative gifting situations with figures such as local mafia or marauding soldiers.
51. Ibid., 21.

Works Consulted

Bjork, Robert E. "Speech as Gift in Beowulf." *Speculum* 69 (1994): 993–1022.
Burkert, Walter. *Creation of the Sacred: Tracks of Biology in Early Religions*. Cambridge: Harvard University Press, 1996.
Chance, Jane. *The Lord of the Rings: The Mythology of Power*. Lexington: University Press of Kentucky, 2001.
_____. *Tolkien's Art: A Mythology for England*. Lexington: University Press of Kentucky, 2001.
Chickering, Howell D., trans. *Beowulf*. New York: Doubleday, 1977.
Donovan, Leslie. "The Valkyrie Reflex in *The Lord of the Rings*." *Tolkien the Medievalist*, ed. Jane Chance, 106–132. New York: Routledge, 2003.
Flieger, Verlyn. "Tolkien's Wild Men: From Medieval to Modern." *Tolkien the Medievalist*, ed. Jane Chance, 97–104. New York: Routledge, 2003.
Garbowski, Christopher. "Eucatastrophe and the Gift of Iluvatar in Middle-earth." *Mallorn* 35 (1997): 25–32.

Glosecki, Stephen O. *Shamanism and Old English Poetry*. New York: Garland, 1989.
_____. "Wolf Dancers and Whispering Beasts: Shamanic Motifs from Sutton Hoo." *Mankind Quarterly* (2001): 305-319.
Griffiths, Bill. *Aspects of Anglo-Saxon Magic*. Norfolk: Anglo-Saxon, 2002.
Groebner, Valentin. *Liquid Assets, Dangerous Gifts: Presents and Politics at the End of the Middle Ages*. Philadelphia: University of Pennsylvania Press, 2000.
Gronbech, Vilhelm. *Culture of the Teutons*. Oxford: Oxford University Press, 1931.
Hollander, Lee, trans. *The Poetic Edda*. Austin: University of Texas Press, 1994.
Hyde, Lewis. *The Gift: Imagination and the Erotic Life of Property*. New York: Vintage, 1983.
Lee, Alvin. *Gold-Hall and Earth-Dragon: Beowulf as Metaphor*. Toronto: University of Toronto Press, 1998.
Mauss, Marcel. *The Gift: The Form and Reason for Exchange in Archaic Societies*. New York: W.W. Norton, 2000.
Rubin, Gayle. "The Traffic in Women." *Literary Theory: An Anthology*, ed. Julie Rivkin and Michael Ryan, 770-794, 2d ed. Malden, MA: Blackwell, 2004.
Tolkien, J.R.R. "Ofermod." *The Tolkien Reader*. New York: Ballantine, 1966.
Williamson, Craig, ed. and trans. *Beowulf and Other Old English Poems*. Philadelphia: University of Pennsylvania Press, 2011.

Tolkien's Whimsical Mode
Physicalities in The Hobbit

Christopher Vaccaro

Tolkien's ability to create memorable scenes through a thoughtful and controlled employment of stylistic effects is today widely recognized. Michael Drout, for example, offers evidence of Tolkien's deliberate use of an archaic prose style in order to amplify themes initially encountered in source-texts such as Shakespeare's *King Lear*.[1] Such conclusions are true of *The Lord of the Rings* and to a great degree *The Hobbit* though that text was composed and written initially from a series of "Winter Reads" to Tolkien's children sometime around 1930 with different objectives and source-texts in mind, at least at its beginning.[2] In both instances, Tolkien's stylistic choices serve his purposes. Such choices affect not only the syntax and diction of the prose but set certain parameters upon character speech acts and the descriptions and employments of the physical bodies in the text, the latter being the subject of this analysis. A "high" and epic style will often restrain bodies from displaying clumsy, crude or embarrassing behaviors, keeping descriptions abstract, symbolic and typological while a "low" style will allow or even encourage carnivalesque and farcical moments. Ocassionally, an accomplished author can weave these "high" and "low" styles together in a text. Tolkien's earliest stylistic objectives in writing *The Hobbit* delivered a physicality designed to amuse and captivate readers, but over the course of writing, Tolkien's shifting style draws from both "high" and "low" sources of his own and of others and constructs a number of "physicalities" along the way.[3]

One thing that is immediately clear is that a consistent style does not run through *The Hobbit*. Though he does not pay much attention to physicalities in his own analysis, Tom Shippey notes numerous examples in the text of both modern and ancient/medieval behaviors and speech acts.[4] Tolkien himself reminds Milton Waldman of this inconsistency in his 1951 letter:

The generally different tone and style of *The Hobbit* is due ... to it being taken by me as a matter from the great cycle susceptible of treatment as a "fairy-story," for children.... For in effect this is a study of simple ordinary man, neither artistic nor noble and heroic ... against a high setting–and in fact ... the tone and style change with the Hobbit's development, passing from fairy-tale to the noble and high and relapsing with the return.[5]

And, in his 1959 response to Walter Allen, he writes of his dissatisfaction with his initial use of a style he would later not wish to sustain:

I think that *The Hobbit* can be seen to begin in what might be called a more "whimsy" mode, and in places even more facetious, and move steadily to a more serious or significant, and more consistent and historical... But I regret much of it all the same.[6]

Though Tolkien does not fully articulate in the letter what this "whimsy" mode means, he did refer to *The Hobbit* in a letter from 1937 as "this rabble of Eddaic-named dwarves out of *Voluspa*, newfangled hobbits and gollums (invented in an idle hour) and Anglo-Saxon runes,"[7] suggesting that this mode can most accurately be described as a weave of both the pre-modern northern European sagas/epics and the fairy-tales adapted for children; however, the latter was predominant for much of the first third of the narrative.

Significant examples underscore the fact that bodies do matter in Middle-earth. In both styles, Tolkien uses physicality to create a high level of verisimilitude, situating character and reader within the environmental setting, to confirm what Tolkien called in his 1939 lecture "On Fairy Stories" an "inner consistency of reality."[8] Bilbo and the dwarves are described as shivering and wet (*Hobbit*, 102) when they made their way atop the Misty Mountains. Much later, the dwarves emerged from their barrels in extreme physical discomfort (247), while Bilbo suffered a cold for three days afterwards (252). Heat and panic cause characters equal discomfort. Sweat dripped down Bombur's nose as the dwarves escaped the goblin lair (113), and when Bilbo sneaked closer to Smaug's lair, he was sweating (270), and his legs slowed his forward movement with their shaking (271) after he grasped the great cup. Hunger too takes it toll on the body. Before being caught in the trees by the goblins, Bilbo appeared to be starving (142). He declared, "my legs ache, and my stomach is wagging like an empty sack" (144). In Mirkwood, the entire company suffered significantly from hunger and thirst (201–02). Most significant is Bilbo's understanding (coming to him while barrel-riding) of the contrast between this life and the one he had previously lived: "And he knew now only too well what it was to be really hungry, not merely politely interested in the dainties of a well-filled larder" (238). Similarly, readers are twice reminded of the protagonist's shoeless condition, first when Bilbo complained moments before the wargs and goblins attack (144), and again while fleeing Smaug's breath (283). If Tolkien's ability to set a scene through landscapes and onomastics were not enough, his use of bodies reminds the reader of the length of days gone without food, the chill of water, the sharpness of rocks, and the heat belched from a dragon's belly.

Tolkien's appreciation of a "high" style developed from his professional and personal interest in and imitation of the languages and literatures of early medieval North-Western Europe. From the courses Tolkien taught at Oxford between 1926–1932, we can arrange a list of "high" source-texts available when he likely composed *The Hobbit*.[9] The list reveals the great number of classes devoted to Scandinavian eddas and sagas and to Anglo-Saxon heroic and elegiac poetry. The "high" style in *The Hobbit* through which bodies are constituted is characterized by the replacement of specific bodily descriptions with similes and metaphors often conveying a character's virtues or a greater mythical importance. Without being allegorical, such material can be highly symbolic while its seriousness restricts laughter and inspires awe, respect, and pathos.[10]

In his letter to the editor of the *Observer* (1938), Tolkien once again reiterates that source material sprang from "epic, mythology, and fairy-story," and admits openly that *Beowulf* was one of his most valued sources.[11] The Anglo-Saxon poem certainly does not shy away from descriptions of bodies, particularly if such descriptions convey the brutality of the monster, Grendel:

> The monster was not minded to put it off, but quickly seized a sleeping warrior as a first start, rent him undisturbed, bit his sinews, drank the blood from his veins, swallowed bite after bite, and soon he had eaten up all of the dead man, (even) his feet and hands.[12]

Despite this attention to violent details, *Beowulf* also possesses an awareness of the transience of the body, of its uselessness in the hereafter. When the hero suggests to his men that they discard his body if he fails to destroy the monster, he states: "He will bear off the bloody corpse, will set his mind upon devouring it. The lonely one will feast unpityingly, and stain his swamp-lair; — no longer wilt thou need to care about my body's sustenance."[13] Also common with this epic style is a tendency to prioritize physical ambiguity and attention to speech acts and symbolic gestures over detailed bodily descriptions; we will see this in the analysis to follow.

As he wrote and revised *The Hobbit*, Tolkien's passion for his history of the elves, *The Silmarillion*, became more prominent in his writing. This material serves as another historical "source" from which he would draw inspiration. He writes in a letter:

> The Silmarillion and all that has refused to be suppressed... Its shadow was deep on the later parts of *The Hobbit*.[14]

Paul Thomas argues that the last six chapters of *The Hobbit* clearly reflect *The Silmarillion*'s influence. Though he too fails to consider bodies as indicators of stylistic shifts, Thomas notes that chapters fourteen to nineteen possess a more serious style, elevated language, fewer direct addresses from the narrator and offer, "utterances more appropriate to a heroic tale than to a children's story."[15] Tolkien did mention (*Observer* January 1938) that *The Hobbit* was, "not consciously based on any other book — save one, and that is unpublished; the 'Silmarillion,' a history of the Elves, to which frequent allusion is made."[16] Physicality in Tolkien's historical/mythological verse material is quite different from what readers encounter at *The Hobbit*'s beginning. In *The Lay of Leithian*, begun in 1925 and abandoned in 1931, Tolkien elevates the diction and the degree of structure, rhythm, and rhyme. Descriptions of physicality conform to this more "noble" style as we see in the well-known description of the elven princess, Lúthien, whose body is described through similes of nature imagery: "Her arms like ivory were gleaming/Her long hair like a cloud was streaming"[17] and is bound by symbolic images of a light diminished[18]:

> A! lissom limbs and shadowy hair
> and chaplet of white snowdrops there;
> O! starry diadem and white
> pale hands beneath the pale moonlight!
> She left his arms and slipped away
> just at the breaking of the day [ll. 752–757].

Alongside such emblematic descriptions as Williamson speaks of in this collection, male heroes are also described in the most elevated language such as when metaphor veils the physical descriptions of Lúthien's mortal lover, the great hero, Beren: "Then Beren waking swiftly sought/his sword and bow, and sped like wind that cuts with knives the branches thinned/of autumn trees."[19]

The "low" style with which Tolkien begins *The Hobbit* is similar to Andrew Lang's colorful collection of adapted fairy-tales such as "Snowdrop," other tales of the Brothers Grimm, E. H. Knatchbull-Hugessen's 1869 "Pusscat Mew," and to E. A. Wyke-Smith's 1928 *The Marvellous Land of the Snergs*. Tolkien's familiarity with such texts began at a very early age and was renewed when he began reading children stories (his own and those of others) to his children. The style of these texts is characterized by physical comedy, playful and even childish similes, colorful descriptions, and gruesome violence muted through lyric and onomatopoeia. The stories develop and employ corporeality in similar ways and fit closely with what Tolkien constructs early in *The Hobbit*. One only has to consider folk-tales from the Grimm brothers' well-recognized collection to recall its descriptions of comedic and violent physicality. Tolkien himself acknowledged that Bilbo's comic story contained characters out of the Grimm's fairy-tales.[20] One such example is in the tale of "Snowdrop" adapted by Andrew Lang in which fairly comical dwarves receive and protect the beautiful Snowdrop from the wicked queen. Not much description of the dwarves is provided. What is given is a repetition of a qualifier reinforcing their diminutive size. Snowdrop finds a "little house" in the forest with "seven little beds." At their return, the dwarves light their "seven little lamps" and ask one after the other who it was who touched his "little chair," "little loaf," "little plate," "little fork," "little knife," and "little tumbler."[21] The diminutive aspect to the scene insures that the style remains light and playful.

Shifting Physicalities in The Hobbit

A close survey of the physical descriptions in *The Hobbit* offers insights into the sources and styles from which Tolkien drew at each instance. The physical description of hobbits is clearly composed to be endearing and more in line with books Tolkien read to his children. The hobbit's body itself is a site of comfort and affection in close proximity to the earth. Douglas Anderson, John Rateliff and others have succeeded in tracing the similarities between Tolkien's hobbits and Wyke-Smith's *The Marvellous Land of the Snergs*. Wyke-Smith also provides fairly whimsical descriptions of those creatures after which hobbits were likely modeled:

> The Snergs are a race of people only slightly taller than the average table but broad in the shoulders and of great strength. Probably they are some some offshoot of the pixies who once inhabited the hills and forests of England, and who finally disappeared about the reign of Henry VIII.[22]

Additionally, other texts are recognized as having an influence on Tolkien's depiction of hobbit physicality. Marjorie Burns convincingly argues for the inclusion of Dickson McCunn from John Buchan's *Huntingtower* and of William Morris himself in his own *Icelandic Journals*.[23]

We know that Tolkien's mental picture of Gandalf was inspired by a postcard image of Josef Madlener's portrait *Der Berggeist*. In that portrait, an old white-bearded figure dressed in a large red cloak and broad hat sits under some trees and welcomes a fawn in his open hands. The rest is Tolkien's invention: "He had a tall pointed blue hat, a long grey cloak, a silver scarf over which his long white beard hung down below his waist, and immense black boots" (32). The description of Gandalf appears more noble than comical; laughing at the wizard is not encouraged. However, it is interesting that originally Tolkien had in mind Gandalf as "a little old man" up through early drafts of *The Lord of the Rings*.[24]

The playful physical description of Dwalin, the first dwarf to arrive at Bilbo's home, belies the epic level of the source material from which he comes: "It was a dwarf with a blue beard tucked into a golden belt, and very bright eyes under his dark-green hood" (36). Originally, Tolkien borrowed the name

"Dwalin" from the famous "Dvalin" of Eddaic poetry, which does not offer much physical description.[25] Characteristically, Tolkien borrowed from the much older material and supplied imaginative colors to the dwarves' beards. Even more so than hobbits, the physicality of dwarves encourages a music-hall and slap-stick comedy. The arrival of the dwarves at Bag-End sets the tone as Bilbo "pulled open the door with a jerk, and they all fell in, one on top of the other" (40). As the dwarves and Gandalf rest from their temporary escape from the goblins of the Misty Mountains, the dwarf Dori recounts to Gandalf the near tragic but perfectly comical misadventures inside the goblin caves in order to explain his misplacement of their hobbit burglar (139). Later, after having been captured by the spiders of Mirkwood, the dwarf Fili emerges–marionette-like from the spider webbing, "jerking his stiff arms and legs as he danced on the spider string under his armpits" (213). Even Beorn has to chuckle when he sees the dwarves, "nodding and bending and bowing and waving their hoods before their knees (in proper dwarf-fashion), till he stopped frowning and burst into a chuckling laugh: they looked so comical" (172). The fumbling, jerking, and bowing of dwarven bodies is quintessential Tolkienian low-brow physical comedy.

The trolls in the chapter "Roast Mutton" (the food reference already aptly describes the nature of the threat) are big, brawny, sloppy, and rather clumsy adversaries. Along with his expert use of dialect, Tolkien relies on their bodies for comedic effect. It is amusing to spy on their fairly endearing eating habits as they sit "licking the gravy off their fingers," and wipe their lips after taking big bites of meat. The scene in general provides little to frighten readers; in fact, it is one of the most sensually comforting scenes in the text until the narrator reminds us, as he must, that they are trolls (70). It is not long before the trolls reveal their proclivity toward violence and they quickly fall into fighting one another, as they must have done numerous times in the past (77). That Bert, Tom, and William represent pure physicality is clear when they threaten to squash into jelly the dwarves and Bilbo with the weight of their own bodies (78).[26]

Following this scene, the introduction of Rivendell has a noticeable influence on *The Hobbit*'s stylistic direction. Though it does not raise the descriptions to the level found in *The Lord of the Rings*, the chapter "A Short Rest" introduces a significant shift in style so that the physicality of Elrond is withdrawn behind a veil of heroic similes: "He was as noble and as fair in face as an elf-lord, as strong as a warrior, as wise as a wizard, as venerable as a king of dwarves, and as kind as summer" (94).

This description changed slightly over the course of Tolkien's revisions. Initially he used the very playful simile "as kind as Christmas" but replaced that with the more mature phrase "as kind as summer."[27] William Green makes the argument that *The Hobbit* discovers its prevailing tone and style at this point:

It is here that the tone solidifies, taking on muted resonances of *Beowulf,* Norse sagas, and the Bible ... after Rivendell it is stylistically sound and heroic in tone. The "children's book" fatuities of the early chapters vanish like mist, leaving only a few odd wisps behind.²⁸

While Tolkien's familiarity with epic sources becomes more influential at this point, it is largely due to the inclusion of the name Elrond borrowed from his own mythology in the earliest versions of *The Silmarillion*. This initially arbitrary naming of the character brought with it the physical descriptions of the more serious work. The sentence describing Elrond's house links a joy of the physical pleasures of eating, sleeping, and working to the more mature activity of story-telling.

Tolkien continues to borrow from his own works when describing the physicality of Gollum. In Tolkien's *Tales and Songs of Bimble Bay* there appears a well-composed poem of thirty-two lines titled "Glip" in which, as Douglas Anderson points out, one finds "Gollum's antecedent"²⁹:

> Glip is his name, as blind as a mole
> In his two round eyes
> While day light lasts; but when night falls
> With a pale gleam they shine
> Like green jelly, and out he crawls
> All long and wet with slime.

"Glip" is composed in a playful yet complicated folk ballad form of alternating tetrameter and trimeter. While this style does not appear in *The Hobbit*, the description of Glip must have come to mind as Tolkien wrote the Gollum scene: "He was Gollum — as dark as darkness, except for two big round pale eyes in his thin face" (118). The gleaming eyes of Glip are Gollum's most characteristic physical feature aside from his gurgling. Such an emphasis on eyes is seen throughout Tolkien's texts as is evidenced by Sauron's synecdochic reduction to "The Great Eye" in *The Lord of the Rings* but also in *The Lay of Leithian* such as when Sauron (named Thû) looks upon the captured Beren and King Felagund: "Then his flaming eyes he on them bent, and darkness black fell round them all."³⁰ More applicable to the Gollum scene in *The Hobbit* might be some sixty lines later in *The Lay of Leithian* when Thû sends wolf-demons to feast on the captured elves accompanying Beren and King Felagund: "From time to time in the eyeless dark two eyes would grow, and they would hark To frightful cries.³¹ The description of Gollum's pale gleaming eyes also has a potential source in *Beowulf*'s Grendel, who enters Heorot enraged: "out of his eyes there started a weird light, most like a flame" ("him of ēagum stōd/ligge gelīcost/leoht unfæger").³²

As *The Hobbit* continues, so does its well-recognized preoccupation with food. Its immoderate consumption becomes a noticeable comic subtext circulating around the dwarf Bombur whose fat body becomes a spectacle within the text.³³ A series of instances serve to illustrate the stylistic tenor, which remains fairly consistent. The first five appear as authorial commentary and clearly poke fun at Bombur's obesity. This happens as the fat and heavy dwarf falls on top of Thorin at Bag End (40–41), as he complains about carrying Bilbo through the goblin tunnels (113), as he catches up with the others to meet Beorn (174), as he becomes a sleeping heavy burden in Mirkwood (198), and as he stands guard at the Lonely Mountain (327). Three other comments come directly from characters. Both Gandalf (166) and Thorin (196) point out the inconveniences caused by Bombur's overweight condition, as does Bombur himself (261). Tolkien's use of the overweight body for comedic effect is not limited to his early stylistic mode though its employment diminishes considerably with his use of the "high" style.³⁴

The goblin scenes are the most physically violent in *The Hobbit*, and while Richard Hughes saw the intensity of violence as a "snag,"³⁵ Tolkien had little concern over the impact of gruesome imagery and willful malevolence: "the presence (even if only on the borders) of the terrible is, I believe, what gives this imagined world its verisimilitude."³⁶ In fact, he attributed something powerful and unexplainable to their presence in a fairy story.³⁷ The most gruesome physical violence in the text is couched in song. When the goblins of the Misty Mountains chain the dwarves with Bilbo at the rear and strike them with whips, assonance, alliteration, and end rhyme disguise the severity of the goblin's activity (107). Children listening to the story as Tolkien's did would develop an understanding of the existence of evil; the adult imagination would recognize the scene's implicit physical violence. Unlike the hill trolls, the goblins represent less the farce of violence and more its horrific actualization. Though simplistic and even silly, the goblin songs sufficiently convey the degree of the threat.

If their first song briefly describes physical punishments, the second goblin song sustains the horror and elevates it. This is the scene in which the wargs and goblins threaten in song to burn the company alive:

> Bake and toast 'em, fry and roast 'em!
> Till beards blaze, and eyes glaze;
> Till hair smells and skins crack,
> Fat melts, and bones black [see 151–52].

Again, alliteration and assonance dull the edge of the violence. The magnitude of the physical violence threatened in this song goes beyond the parameters found in Tolkien's prose. Compare this scene to the two most graphic scenes in *The Lord of the Rings* where Grishnakh threatens to "untie every string" in Merry and Pippin's bodies (*TT*, III, iii, 59), or when Wormtongue cuts Saruman's throat in the vicinity of Bag End (*RK*, VI, ix, 300). In Jacob and Wilhelm's *Von dem Machandelboom* "The Juniper Tree" referred to by Tolkien in his essay "On Fairy Stories," the violence is surprisingly shocking and is summarized through a song sung by the bird/spirit of a slain boy:

> My mother, she killed me,
> My father, he ate me,
> My sister Marlene
> Collected all my bones
> Tied them up in a silk cloth,
> Laid them under the juniper.
> Tweet, tweet, what a beautiful bird I am![38]

This summary sung by the bird/spirit of the boy dismembered by his stepmother and served to his own unsuspecting father occurs eight times in this version the Grimm brothers acquired from Philipp Otto Runge. While disturbing in its violence, the description of cannibalism and murder of children, fairly common to the fairy-tale genre, is offset, as it is in *The Hobbit*'s goblin scene, by the lyric quality and comic scene.

In "Puss-cat Mew" likewise composed for a children's audience, Knatchbull-Hugessen offers similar descriptions. One such scene occurs as Joe Brown is deposited in a room by the ogres:

> A stout farmer, in boots and breeches, quite dead, hung by the chin from one hook, and from his appearance was evidently nearly fit for dressing. A priest hung next, with his throat cut from ear to ear, who did not seem to be dead long; and these two were the sole occupants of the Ogre's larder.[39]

Another scene occurs with the death of the ogre Grindbones: "Joes hesitated no longer, but ... plunged his steel dagger into the monster's throat, and had just time to sever his head from his body before the latter disappeared for ever, swallowed up by the fatal quicksand of the Fairy Green."[40] In each case, a children's story retains scenes of gruesome violence. In *The Hobbit*, Tolkien's goblins introduce such a comedic yet violent tone into the narrative.[41]

Beorn "is in a way the least invented character in the book"[42] and his physicality inserts that something "larger and more heroic" Tolkien refers to in his letter to Christopher Bretherton.[43] Beorn's name is an Old English word for "man" and also for "bear," and his body is very similar in physicality to the characters Beowulf and Böthvarr Bjarki from the Norse *Saga of Hrólfr Kraki* who sends his bear spirit to fight in his stead. Bjarki and Beowulf are translated as Little Bear and Bear respectively, and Beorn is bear-like as a human and capable of morphing into a bear seemingly at will (167). As a shape-changer, he is physically linked to the Norse sagas particularly *The Volsunga Saga* where Sigmund and Sinfjotli take on the skins of wolves.[44]

Following the story-telling episode with Beorn, Bilbo and the dwarves follow the path into Mirkwood and encounter the spider lair and the elven community ruled by King Thranduil. While not as serious and sorrowful in tone as the elven episodes in *The Lord of the Rings*, the episode with the elves of Mirkwood is more mature than that of Rivendell. However, Tolkien does describe the King of the Elves in a fashion similar to his description of Elrond[45]:

In a great hall with pillars hewn out of the living stone sat the Elven King on a chair of carven wood. On his head was a crown of berries and red leaves, for the autumn was come again. In the spring, he wore a crown of woodland flowers. In his hand he held a carven staff of oak [223].

As with Elrond, symbolic description overtakes the physicality of Thranduil; however, there is less repetition and no endearing similes comparing the king to summer. The crown connotes nobility and strength, the staff, knowledge and authority, and the berries and leaves suggest a strong connection to the earth.

The next significant character is Bard. By the time of the second phase of composition, his character walks confidently out from a "high" and noble literary mode as "grim-voiced and grim-faced" (307) as Faramir and as heroic as Aragorn:

> A dispossessed heir, he lives to achieve unexpected victory over the surpassingly strong hereditary foe who had destroyed his homeland, re-establishes the kingship, and founds a dynasty that renews alliances with non-human neighbors and helps bring renewed prosperity to the region. In short, he is a precursor of Strider (Aragorn), who through his own efforts and the great deeds of others claims his ancestor's throne and re-establishes his kingdom... However, the primary external influence for Bard's sudden emergence ... probably lies not in fairy tales but (as so often the case in the Smaug chapters) in *Beowulf*.[16]

Typically, medieval epic and romance places greater emphasis on a hero's virtues and great deeds than on his physical description; this is true of Beowulf. Emerging from the mer after slaying Grendel's mother, Beowulf reaches the surface in a scene reminiscent of Bard's step forward after slaying the dragon:

> Then came to the land the sea-men's chief, sturdily swimming, and reveled in his lake-booty, the mighty burden that he had with him. Then went the trusty band of followers towards him; they thanked God, rejoiced about their lord, that they could see him safe and sound.[47]

A detailed description of Beowulf is secondary to the display of his virtues, of his success, courage and strength. Tolkien seems to borrow from this scene of reemergence and amplifies its degree of physicality:

> And in the midst of their talk a tall figure stepped from the shadows. He was drenched with water, his black hair hung wet over his face and shoulders; a fierce light was in his eyes [213].[48]

The level of physical description in Bard's reemergence scene compares to the most realistic and detailed scenes elsewhere in Tolkien's writing. The syntax is clear and unencumbered by archaisms and yet serious and heroic in tone.

Much has been written concerning Tolkien's appreciation of dragons particularly of those found in *Beowulf* and *The Volsunga Saga*. In *The Hobbit*, it is very apparent to readers that the dragon's introduction scene in *Beowulf* was the inspiration for Smaug. The most interesting point of comparison is the description of the dragon's dead body under the water. *Beowulf*'s dragon receives a brief statement that signifies the end of the threat and the deliberately improper burial of the monster: "Also they shoved the dragon, that reptile, over the cliff-wall, — let the waves take the treasure-warder, the flood enfathom him."[49] Tolkien's amplification of Smaug's physicality gives attention to the decay of the dragon's corpse and does so in the manner of the great epics:

> He would never again return to his golden bed, but was stretched cold [as stone, twisted][50] upon the floor of the shallows. There for ages his huge bones could be seen in calm weather amid the ruined piles of the old town. But few dared to cross the cursed spot, and none dared to dive into the shivering water or recover the precious stones that fell from his rotting carcase [313].

Stylistically, physicalities have here fully matured to the level of *The Lord of the Rings*. The late alteration from "stretched cold upon the floor" to "stretched cold as stone, twisted upon the floor" foreshadows Tolkien's employment of writhing/wraithed bodies that will come to occupy his imagination.[51]

This maturation is most obvious in the physical development of previously encountered characters reappearing later in the narrative. Dain's army is described for the first time in chapter seventeen "The Clouds Burst," but they are related to the dwarves of Bilbo's company: "Their beards were forked and plaited and thrust into their belts. Their caps were of iron and they were shod with iron, and their faces were grim" (336). Dain's dwarves hardly have any physical resemblance to the imaginatively colorful beards and fumbling comedic bodies of Thorin's company, and Thorin himself is seen differently as he is moments away from leaving his broken body behind: "There indeed lay Thorin Oakenshield, wounded with many wounds, and his rent armour and notched axe were cast upon the floor" (348). Likewise, Beorn's heroic physicality during the battle of five armies shifts even further into the epic style as his description emphasizes his ferocity and strength in battle: "The roar of his voice was like drums and guns; and he tossed wolves and goblins from his path like straws and feathers" (349). Reminiscent of a Norse beserker, Beorn surpasses his own earlier ferocity and size. In some ways, Beorn's imperviousness and larger than life form and voice recalls that of Huan, wolf-hound of Valinor who grew large and fierce, mostly invulnerable, and very capable of slaying wolves: "he loved them best; /he loved to find their throats and wrest/their snarling lives and evil breath."[52] Huan's physical form would certainly be a possible source for Beorn's physicality towards *The Hobbit*'s end.

Lastly, there is Bilbo. Our first glimpse of Bilbo is of a rather typical hobbit whose well-brushed toes match his lifestyle (31). For the most part, Bilbo's physicality is tied to invisibility and to a comedy of smallness in the text. When Dori drops Bilbo in the goblin tunnels and leaves him behind, it seems mere accident. Before the wolves arrive carrying goblins from the mountains, the dwarves and Gandalf scamper up the tall trees, but Bilbo is left down below much like a rabbit (146). Beorn actually comments that the "little bunny" is getting fat (181). And when the eagles arrive, Bilbo is again nearly left behind (153).[53]

The disappearance of one's physical form is an important theme in *The Lord of the Rings*. In *The Hobbit*, Bilbo's forgotten presence, his comically small body, his concealments and vanishings hint at the theme's nascence. A useful vocational skill at first, his stealth and new invisibility are transformed over the course of Tolkien's thought into the One Ring's ability to wraith, twist, and stretch thin the bodies of those carrying it. In *The Lord of the Rings*, Tolkien uses the image of the wraithed and disappearing body as a catalyst for suspense and terror; in *The Hobbit*, there is a slow shift from the comedy of smallness to actual concern over Bilbo's enfeeblement. As the eagles drop the company upon their eyries, Bilbo exhibits a foreboding sign of his potential disappearance as Gandalf speaks to the eagles regarding the need for food:

> "We are deeply obliged to you. But in the meantime, we are famished with hunger."
> "I am nearly dead of it," said Bilbo in a weak little voice that nobody heard [159].

By the time Bilbo reaches the halls of Thranduil his body has all but disappeared. He is left "a thin and wobbly" (226) shadow of his former self until, when talking to Thorin, Bilbo is merely, a "little voice at his key-hole" (227). A shift appears in which the familiar comical imagery is replaced by more serious hints at physical enfeeblement.

In *Tolkien's Art*, Jane Chance explained the psychological binary of Bilbo's character in a way that opens a space for the interpretation of Bilbo's bodies. Bilbo is simultaneously a Baggins and a Took; he enjoys physical comforts and routine and yet is ready to break from that routine and risk physical perils. He is at once a grocer and a burglar, and in fact the text follows the development of the grocer hobbit as he becomes a bourgeois burglar of sorts.[54] Chance describes this distinction as both physical and spiritual:

> It is almost as if the Baggins side represents the temptations of the body as the Took side represents the desire for fulfillment of the soul. The desire is expressed through the image of the burglar, which the Took side of Bilbo is asked to become.[55]

This distinction is insightful, and I would like to take its implications further. The Baggins' side of Bilbo *does* represent bodily temptations and the Took, a physical renunciation. Yet, Bilbo, in effect, has three bodies: the "low" style constitutes the Baggins body: comfortable, well-fed, sorrowfully untested, and comical; while the "high" style constructs a complex corporeal binary: the first is that of a Took: lean and hungry, familiar with renunciation, tested to its physical limits, and proficient at wielding a weapon despite being practically "immune to the paraphernalia of heroism"[56]; the other belongs to Bilbo's shadow body the emaciated, pale, addicted body of Gollum. Bilbo's Took side evinces mental and spiritual discipline over the body and an agency over its environment. The Baggins body belongs more to the early narrative style.

Conclusion

The stylistic milieu in which *The Hobbit* was written can be understood through a close examination of those texts from which Tolkien found his inspiration. Initially, texts such as Wyke-Smith's *The Marvellous Land of the Snergs*, Knatchbull-Hugessen's "Puss-cat Mew," and MacDonald's *The Princess and the Goblin* along with Grimm's tales adapted for children by Andrew Lang filled the ladle of Tolkien's "Cauldron of Story," but slowly at first these gave way to the Norse and Anglo-Saxon epics and to Tolkien's own early historical/mythical compositions making up what we now call his Legendarium. As this shift in influence occurred, the narrator's voice, the characters' speech acts, and Tolkien's own prosody shifted. What has gone left unexamined in most of the scholarship and what this essay hopes to address is how such a shift affected also the bodies in the text. Physicalities in *The Hobbit* conform to style as more serious similes replace the childish and facetious ones; "high" and noble images stand in for playful ones. Redactions, amplifications, and extensions in the various drafts of *The Hobbit* give insight into Tolkien's shifting attitude towards physical descriptions and point to the greater influence of texts such as *The Lay of Leithian* upon bodies in the text.

Notes

1. "It becomes clear that Tolkien's deliberate stylistic construct is in fact remarkably rich and successful not only in his own terms but also in terms of the stylistic canons of Modernist Literature in which, supposedly, form follows function." Michael Drout, "Tolkien's Prose Style and its Literary and Rhetorical Effects," *Tolkien Studies* 1, ed. Douglas Anderson, Michael D.C. Drout, and Verlyn Flieger (Morgantown: West Virginia Press, 2004), 154–55.

2. According to interviews and letters, 1926 is the earliest date Tolkien may have begun *The Hobbit* and the summer of 1930 is recognized as the *terminus ad quem* of the story's commencement.

3. I take "source" to mean any text from which Tolkien drew inspiration, the textual context surrounding the moment of composition and so include his own earliest mythopoeic corpus in this analysis. As with any criticism involving sources, I attempt to keep in mind the concerns expressed by Michael Drout and Hilary Wynne ("Tom Shippey's *J.R.R. Tolkien: Author of the Century* and a Look Back at Tolkien Criticism Since 1982," 2000) and reiterated by Jason Fisher over the "deeply embedded assumption that once a source has been identified, the meaning of Tolkien's text has been discovered." Jason Fisher, "Tolkien and Source Criticism: Remarking and Remaking," *Tolkien and the Study of His*

Sources: Critical Essays, ed. Jason Fisher (Jefferson, NC: McFarland, 2011), 39. This essay seeks to compare similar styles and perhaps to point out possible influential images and phrasings within those sources already identified.
    4. Tom Shippey, *The Road to Middle-earth*, (Boston: Houghton Mifflin, 2003).
    5. *Letters*, 159.
    6. Ibid., 298.
    7. Letter to G. E. Selby, 14 Dec. 1937, in *The Return of the Shadow*, ed. Christopher Tolkien (Boston: Houghton Mifflin, 1988), 7.
    8. "On Fairy Stories," *Essays Presented to Charles Williams* (Grand Rapids: William B. Eerdmans, 1968), 67.
    9. Tolkien taught the following courses arranged by year and avoiding repetition: Germanic Philology, Beowulf, The Fight at Finnesburg, Judith, Exodus, Gothic, Anglo-Saxon Reader, Old English Philology, Old Icelandic Texts, Volsunga Saga, King Horn, Eldar Edda, Deor's Lament, Battle of Maldon, Brunanburh, Legends of the Goths, the Germanic Verb, Old Norse, Common Germanic Consonant Changes, Baldrs Draumar, Old English Textual Criticism, Guðrunarkviða en forna, Atlakviða, Bandamanna Saga, Hænsaþoris Saga, Havard's Saga Halta, Germanic Numerals, Waldere, The Ruinic Poem, Elene, The Wanderer, The Sea-farer, The Dream of the Rood, The Riddles, Gothic Traditions, Scaldic Poetry, The Language of the Vespasian Psalter Glosses, Old English Prosody, and the Voluspa. Compiled from Christina Scull and Wayne Hammond, *The Tolkien Companion and Guide: Chronology* (Boston: Houghton Mifflin, 2006).
    10. Tolkien's attitudes towards the body stem from his religious views, and his pull away from low-mimetic physicality is a result of his understanding of the Fall of humanity.
    11. *Letters*, 31.
    12. John Clark Hall, trans., "Beowulf," *The Tolkien Fan's Medieval Reader*, ed. Turgon (Cold Spring Harbor, NY: Cold Spring Press, 2004), 26.
       Nē þæt se āglæca yldan þōhte,
       ac hē gefēng hraðe forman sīðe
       slæpendne rinc, slāt unwearnum,
       bāt bānlocan, blōd ēdrum dranc,
       synsnædum swealh; sona hæfde
       unlyfigendes eal gefeormod,
       fēt ond folma
[Klaeber, *Beowulf*, ed. R.D. Fulk, Robert E. Bjork, and John D. Niles, 4th ed. (Toronto: University of Toronto Press, 2008), ll. 739–745a].
    13. Turgon, 22.
       byreð blodig wæl byrgean þenceð
       eteð angenga unmurnlice
       mearcað morhopu- no ðu ymb mines ne þearft
       lices feorme leng sorgian [Klaeber, *Beowulf*, 17, ll. 448–451].
    14. Letter to Stanley Unwin, 24 Feb. 1950, *Letters*, 136.
    15. Paul Edmund Thomas, "Some of Tolkien's Narrators," *Tolkien's Legendarium: Essays on* The History of Middle-earth, ed. Verlyn Flieger and Carl F. Hostetter (Westport, CT: Greenwood Press, 2000), 179.
    16. *Letters*, 31.
    17. J.R.R. Tolkien, *The Lays of Beleriand*, ed. Christopher Tolkien (Boston: Houghton Mifflin, 1985), ll. 527–528.
    18. Verlyn Flieger fits Lúthien's description into a hierarchy of light and points out the subtle change: "None the less, she is light dimmed and diminished, as far removed from its source in the Trees as she is physically removed from Valinor." *Splintered Light* (Kent, OH: Kent University State Press), 131.

19. *Lays of Beleriand*, 272–275.
20. Letter to Stanley Unwin, Dec. 1937, *Letters*, 26.
21. Andrew Lang, ed., *The Red Fairy Book* (New York: Dover, 1966), 331–332.
22. E.A. Wyke-Smith, *The Marvellous Land of the Snergs* (Mineola, NY: Dover, 2006), 7.
23. Douglas Anderson, ed., *Tales Before Tolkien* (2003). John D. Rateliff's *The History of the Hobbit* (2007). Marjorie Burns, "Tracking the Elusive Hobbit (In its Pre-Shire Den)" (2007) and *Perilous Realms* (2005).
24. *Hobbit*, 36, fn. 13.
25. Rateliff 42, fn. 9.
26. Tolkien may have adapted this scene from the Grimm's tale "Der gelernte Jäger" (The Expert Huntsman). *Hobbit*, 72.
27. Rateliff, 115.
28. William Green, *The Hobbit: A Journey into Maturity* (Toronto: Maxwell Macmillan, 1995), 61.
29. "Glip," *Hobbit*, 119. Anderson suggests a composition date around 1928.
30. *The Lays of Beleriand* (ll. 2168–69), 230.
31. *The Lays of Belerieand* (ll. 2232–2237), 231–232.
32. Ll. 726b-727. Turgon, "Beowulf," 26; Klaeber, 26. Will N. Rogers II and Michael R. Underwood argue for the influence of Sir Henry Rider Haggard's character Gagool in his 1885 novel *King Solomon's Mines* in "Gagool and Gollum: Exemplars of Degeneration in *King Solomon's Mines* and *The Hobbit*," *J.R.R. Tolkien and His Literary Resonances: Views of Middle-earth*, ed. George Clark and Daniel Timmons (Westport, CT: Greenwood Press, 2000) and William Green makes a similar comparison in "King Thorin's Mines: *The Hobbit* as Victorian Adventure Novel," *Extrapolation* 42.1 (2001): 53–64.
33. In fact, Tolkien's comedy may accidentally have stumbled into the final stage of what had become by the Victorian period a fat-phobic tradition in which overweight characters were depicted as burdens to their families and friends and unable to share in the communal work-load. See Joyce L. Huff's "'A 'Horror of Corpulence': Interrogating Bantingism and Mid-Nineteenth-Century Fat-Phobia," *Bodies out of Bonds: Fatness and Transgression*, ed. Jana Evans Braziel and Kathleen LeBesco (Berkeley: University of California Press, 2000).
34. The facetious style of *The Hobbit* appears occasionally in other texts, and there we also find the fat body as a primary source of the humor. In *The Lord of the Rings*, Tolkien inserts the story of Will Whitfoot for comedic effect (*FR*, I, ix, 168). See also Fatty Bolger of *The Lord of the Rings* and Fatty Dorkins of *Mr. Bliss* (fn Rateliff, 63). Also, in a draft of his letter to Mr. A.C. Nunn when expounding the history of family governance among the Shirefolk, Tolkien refers to the "well-known case" of Lalia the Great "or less courteously the Fat" (*Letters*, 295).
35. "[M]any parents ... may be afraid that certain parts of [*The Hobbit*] would be too terrifying for bedside reading" from Richard Hughes' letter to Stanley Unwin, 1937. In his review in *Books for Pre-Adults* (*New Statesman and Nation*, 4 December 1937), Hughes argues that "a child has a natural capacity for terror which is next to impossible to curtail" (946).
36. *Letters*, 24.
37. Christina Scull and Wayne G. Hammond remind us that Tolkien felt unharmed "by the beauty and the horror of tales such as "The Juniper Tree." *Tolkien Companion and Guide*, 815.
38. *The Grimm's German Folk Tales*, trans. Francis P. Magoun Jr. (Carbondale: Southern Illinois University Press, 1969), 172.
39. Anderson, *Tales Before Tolkien*, 54.
40. Ibid., 85.

41. The physicality of goblins in *The Hobbit* was also influenced by George MacDonald's 1872 book *The Princess and the Goblin* though Tolkien seems to have given their soft feet to his character Gollum. MacDonald writes that goblins were, "not ordinarily ugly, but either absolutely hideous, or ludicrously grotesque both in face and form" (Puffin Books, 1996, 4) and "dwarfed and misshapen" (5). The original illustrations by Arthur Hughes depict goblins as bearded like dwarves with pointed ears and malicious grins.
42. Shippey, *Road*, 80.
43. *Letters*, 346.
44. We need look no further than Felagund's disguising of his troop in *The Lay of Leithian* for other instances of shape-changing Tolkien was writing around the time he wrote *The Hobbit* (ll. 2009–2013).
45. Plot notes and a different type of paper suggest this point in the narrative corresponds with one of the two year-long breaks in composition. Rateliff, *History*, 379.
46. Ibid., 557.
47. Turgon, *Tolkien's Fans*, 39.
48. The third phase of composition begins at "with water" with no change to Bard's description. Rateliff, *History*, 638.
49. Turgon, *Tolkien's Fans*, 60.
Dracan ēc scufun,
wyrm ofer weall-clif, lēton wēg niman,
Flōd fædmian frætwa hyrde [ll. 3131b–3133, Klaeber, *Beowulf*, 106].
50. Added during a later phase. Rateliff, 641.
51. The *Oxford English Dictionary* offers *wriðan* [to twist, contort, wring, and wreathe] as the etymological source of the term "writhe" and connections can be made between *wriðan* and "wraith" though this term is listed as having obscure origins. *OED Online OED Online*, s.v. "writhe, v.¹" *The Oxford English Dictionary*, 2d ed. (Oxford University Press, 1989), accessed April 28, 2011, http://www.oed.com.ezproxy.uvm.edu/view/Entry/230764?. It is of course well known also that Tolkien contributed to the W section of the *OED* himself.
52. *Lays of Beleriand*, ll. 2284–2286.
53. As Douglas Anderson reminds readers, Tolkien likely offers a more comic version of Chaucer's eagle scenes in "The House of Fame." Anderson, *Tales*, 156–57.
54. See Shippey's *Road* for more on this subject.
55. Jane Chance, *Tolkien's Art: A Mythology for England* (Lexington: University of Kentucky Press, 2001), 42.
56. Shippey, *Road*, 84.

Works Consulted

Anderson, Douglas, ed. *Tales Before Tolkien*. New York: Ballantine, 2003.
Chance, Jane. *Tolkien's Art: A Mythology for England*. Lexington: University of Kentucky Press, 2001.
Drout, Michael. "Tolkien's Prose Style and its Literary and Rhetorical Effects." *Tolkien Studies* 1 (2004): 137–162.
_____, and Hilary Wynne. "Tom Shippey's *J.R.R. Tolkien: Author of the Century* and a Look Back at Tolkien Criticism Since 1982." *Envoi* 9.2 (Fall 2000): 101–67.
Fisher, Jason. "Tolkien and Source Criticism: Remarking and Remaking." *Tolkien and the Study of His Sources: Critical Essays*, ed. Jason Fisher, 29–44. Jefferson, NC: McFarland, 2011.
Green, William. "King Thorin's Mines: *The Hobbit* as Victorian Adventure Novel." *Extrapolation* 42.1 (2001): 53–64.

Grimm, Jacob, and Wilhelm Grimm. *The Grimm's German Folk Tales*, trans. Francis P. Magoun Jr. Carbondale: Southern Illinois University Press, 1969.

Klaeber, Frederick. *Beowulf and the Fight at Finnsburg*, eds. R.D. Fulk, Robert E. Bjork, and John D. Niles, 4th ed. Toronto: University of Toronto Press, 2008.

Rateliff, John D. *The History of the Hobbit*. Boston: Houghton Mifflin, 2007.

Rogers, Will N., II, and Michael R. Underwood. "Gagool and Gollum: Exemplars of Degeneration in *King Solomon's Mines* and *The Hobbit*." *J.R.R. Tolkien and His Literary Resonances: Views of Middle-earth*, ed. George Clark and Daniel Timmons, 121–131. Westport, CT: Greenwood Press, 2000.

Scull, Christina, and Wayne Hammond. *The J.R.R. Tolkien Companion and Guide: Reader's Guide*. Boston: Houghton Mifflin, 2006.

Shippey, Tom. *The Road to Middle-earth*. Boston: Houghton Mifflin, 2003.

Thomas, Paul Edmund. "Some of Tolkien's Narrators." *Tolkien's Legendarium: Essays on The History of Middle-earth*, ed. Verlyn Flieger and Carl F. Hostetter, 161–181. Westport, CT: Greenwood Press, 2000.

Tolkien, J.R.R. "On Fairy Stories." *Essays Presented to Charles Williams*. Grand Rapids: William B. Eerdmans, 1968.

_____. *The Return of the Shadow*, ed. Christopher Tolkien. Boston: Houghton Mifflin, 1988.

Turgon, ed. *The Tolkien Fan's Medieval Reader*. Cold Spring Harbor, NY: Cold Spring Press, 2004.

About the Contributors

Jennifer **Culver** is a doctoral student at the University of Texas at Dallas with a concentrarion in the history of ideas. She participated in the 2004 NEH Tolkien Institute and has presented papers concerning Tolkien, including "Teaching Tolkien: Using Tolkien's Work as a Bridge to Literature" at the International Medieval Congress at Kalamazoo and "Threads of Tolkien: Using *The Lord of the Rings* to Help Students Connect to Literature" at the National Council of Teachers of English Annual Conference. She received a master of arts in literature from the University of North Texas 2007.

Matthew **Dickerson** is a full professor at Middlebury College in Vermont. He is the author of several books including *A Hobbit Journey: Discovering the Enchantment of J.R.R. Tolkien's Middle-earth* (2012), *Ents, Elves, and Eriador: The Environmental Vision of J.R.R. Tolkien* (with Jonathan Evans, 2006), and *From Homer to Harry Potter: A Handbook of Myth and Fantasy* (2006). He resides in the Champlain Valley.

Verlyn **Flieger** is a professor emerita in the Department of English at the University of Maryland, where for 36 years she taught courses in Tolkien, medieval literature, and comparative mythology. She is the author of four books on Tolkien including *Green Suns and Faërie* (2012), a collection of her essays; editor or co-editor of four more; and with Douglas A. Anderson and Michael D.C. Drout she edits *Tolkien Studies*, an annual journal. Professor Flieger also writes fiction.

Yvette **Kisor** is an associate professor of literature at Ramapo College of New Jersey. She has published a number of articles, including "Using the History of Middle-earth Series with Tolkien's Fiction" (forthcoming); "Poor Sméagol: Gollum as Exile in *The Lord of the Rings*" (forthcoming); "Making the Connection on Page and Screen in Tolkien's and Jackson's *The Lord of the Rings*" (2011); and "Totemic Reflexes in Tolkien's Middle-earth" (2010). She contributed six entries to *The J.R.R. Tolkien Encyclopedia* (2006).

Jolanta N. **Komornicka** is a doctoral candidate in history at Boston University. Her fields include court culture and aristocratic identity in late medieval Poland and judicial torture in Europe after Lateran IV. Her doctoral research focuses on the bureaucracy of torture in France during the Hundred Years War. She is the author of "The Jews in the Medieval Polish Economy: Some Thoughts on the Historiography of the Twentieth Century" (2009).

Gergely **Nagy** is a junior assistant professor at the Institute of English and American Studies, University of Szeged, Hungary, where he teaches courses on Old and Middle

English literature, orality and literature, and Tolkien. Nagy's publications include "The 'Lost' Subject of Middle-earth: Elements and Motifs of the Constitution of the Subject in the Figure of Gollum in *The Lord of the Rings*" (2006), and "Fictitious Fairy Tales: Writing a Fictitious Character in *The Lord of the Rings*" (2011), along with entries in *The J.R.R. Tolkien Encyclopedia*.

Robin Anne **Reid** received a doctorate from the University of Washington in 1992. She teaches creative writing, critical theory, and new media. Her major area of scholarship is science fiction, fantasy, and fandom. Her publications include *The Encyclopedia of Women in Science Fiction and Fantasy* (2008), *Ray Bradbury: A Critical Companion* (2000) and *Arthur C. Clarke: A Critical Companion* (1997), and the articles "Mythology and History: A Stylistic Analysis of *The Lord of the Rings*" (2009) and "'Tree and flower, leaf and grass': The Grammar of Middle-earth in *The Lord of the Rings*" (2007).

Anna **Smol** is an associate professor in the Department of English at Mount Saint Vincent University in Halifax, Nova Scotia, where she teaches courses on medical literature and on Tolkien. Her articles on Tolkien include "The Child, the Primitive, and the Medieval: The Making of Medieval Heroes in the Nineteenth and Early Twentieth Centuries" (2008), and "Male Friendship in *The Lord of the Rings*: Medievalism, the First World War, and Contemporary Rewritings" (2008). She contributed three entries to *The J.R.R. Tolkien Encyclopedia* (2007). She is the president of the Canadian Society of Medievalists.

Christopher **Vaccaro** is a senior lecturer at the University of Vermont, where he teaches courses on Tolkien, Old English language and literature, British literature, and sex and gender identity studies. He is the organizer of the annual Tolkien at UVM conference. Since receiving a Ph.D. in 2003 from the CUNY Graduate School, he has published entries for *The J.R.R. Tolkien Encyclopedia* (2007) as well as "'Inbryrded Breostsefa': Compunction in l. 841a of Cynewulf's *Elene*" (2005) and "'And One White Tree': The Cosmological Cross and the *Arbor Vitae* in J.R.R. Tolkien's *The Lord of the Rings* and *The Silmarillion*" (2004).

James T. **Williamson** is a senior lecturer at the University of Vermont, where he also completed a master's in English literature, writing a thesis on *Phantastes: A Faerie Romance* by Tolkien's nineteenth century predecessor George MacDonald. He has recently completed a critical history of fantasy from the eighteenth century to the 1960s, tentatively titled *From Antiquarianism to the Ballantine Adult Fantasy Series: The Construction of Modern Fantasy*. He lives in Burlington, Vermont.

Index

Ainulindalë 78, 138
Ainur 65, 73, 78, 84–85, 88, 120; Maiar 75, 132n37, 136, 154n7; Valar 65–67, 80n8, 121
Aquinas, Thomas 84–86, 93
Aragorn 50, 69, 108, 143
arda 1, 32n4, 74, 132
Arwen 102–04, 106–07, 111–15, 141–44, 161, 164
Augustine 2, 84, 87, 93
Aulë 73, 85–86, 132n32

Bard 179
Bilbo 69, 171; disappearing physicality 181–82
Boethius 84
Boromir 76, 140
Butler, Judith 3
Bynum, Caroline Walker 7

Catholic Church 2–3
Chance, Jane 3, 30, 53, 60, 116, 128, 181
Christ 3, 56
corpulence 184n33

Derrida, Jacques 119
Drout, Michael D.C. 100, 170
dwarves 86, 132n32, 171, 174–75, 180

Eä 65, 80, 84
Elrond 30, 32, 162, 175–76
Éowyn 102–103, 105–10, 112–15, 117n5, 144–46, 154n11, 164–66; healing 69
Eru see Ilúvatar

Faramir 76, 159
Fëa 1, 64, 68–70, 72, 76–78, 88
food 3, 73, 90, 92, 93, 175–76, 181
Foucault, Michel 3, 7
Freud, Sigmund 43–44, 147
Frodo 12–18, 19n5, 22, 24, 26–31, 33n14, 35n44, 37n68, 39–42, 44–45, 47–57, 70
Fussell, Paul 42, 46, 54–55

Galadriel 76, 102–07, 112–15, 125, 137–44, 146, 158–61
Gandalf 20; angelic being 75; transformation 25–27, 31, 35n35, 37n68, 68

Garth, John 40, 44–45, 52, 56, 58n2
gender 2–3, 54, 98–100, 116n1
Gimli 158
Glorfindel 15, 28–30, 36n48, 36n50, 51, 68
Goldberry 102–06, 111–15, 136–41, 146, 149–52, 154n7, 154n8
Gollum 3–4, 3n20, 12, 16, 48, 55, 60n53, 70, 128, 176; see also Sméagol
Grima Wormtongue 53, 177

heterosexuality 55, 107–08
The Hobbit 72, 170–82
hobbits 48, 72–73, 162, 174
homosexuality 3, 109
hröa 1, 64, 68–70, 72, 76–77, 79, 80n8, 92; see also Fëa

Ilúvatar 6, 65–67, 73–74, 78–79, 119
Istari 75

Kristeva, Julia 47–48, 57, 60n53

Lacan, Jacques 4
The Lord of the Rings 40, 58n3, 66–67, 75, 99, 147, 152–53, 170; drafts 28, 31n2, 33n12, 34n29, 36n47

Melkor see Morgoth
Merry 23, 92, 163
Middle-earth 64, 73, 119, 159, 164
Morgoth 4, 79, 84, 84–89, 91, 93, 122–23, 132n32

Nazgûl see Ringwraiths

orcs 60, 83–93
Owen, Wilfred 47, 49, 56
Oxford English Dictionary 32n5

queer 4, 5, 54, 60n57, 98–100, 107–08, 110–11, 116, 118n22

race 80, 88, 91
Ringwraiths 14–15, 20, 22–28, 31, 32n10, 33n14, 34n26, 34n27, 34n28, 35n33, 128

189

Rohy, Valerie 4, 8*n*23
Rosie Cotton 146, 153
Russell, Bertrand 64–65

Samwise Gamgee 30–31, 46–50, 53–55, 57, 138, 140, 167
Saruman 3, 13, 69, 132*n*37
Sauron 4, 20–21, 24, 30, 36*n*48, 43, 120–30, 176
Sassoon, Siegfried 49
Sedgwick, Eve Kosofsky 3, 107
Shelob 3, 52, 101–03, 105–07, 112–15; Kristevan reading 60*n*53
Shippey, Tom 22, 34*n*25, 34*n*27, 34*n*28, 35, 37*n*68, 44, 50, 58*n*2, 128, 170
signification 5, 125–26, 128
The Silmarillion 43, 66, 70, 78–79, 80*n*3, 84, 87, 89, 91, 93, 123, 151, 172–73

Smaug 180
Sméagol 48, 69–70; *see also* Gollum
Strider *see* Aragorn

Théoden 66, 76
Tolkien, J.R.R. 64, 87, 99; Catholicism 67, 73, 76–79; letters 13, 18, 34*n*30, 52, 70, 74, 80*n*10, 84, 91–92, 109, 136, 162, 170–72, 178, 184*n*34; teaching 172; World War I writer 40, 54, 56, 58*n*2

violence 177–78

wizards 1, 35*n*41, 75; *see also* Istari
Wormtongue 53, 177